Unwanted Claims

Unwanted Claims

The Politics of Participation in the U.S. Welfare System

Joe Soss

Ann Arbor

THE UNIVERSITY OF MICHIGAN PRESS

To Kira

Copyright © by the University of Michigan 2000
All rights reserved
Published in the United States of America by
The University of Michigan Press
Manufactured in the United States of America
♾ Printed on acid-free paper

2003   2002   2001   2000   4   3   2   1

*A CIP catalog record for this book is available
from the British Library.*

Library of Congress Cataloging-in-Publication Data

Soss, Joe, 1967–
    Unwanted claims : the politics of participation in the U.S.
welfare system / Joe Soss.
        p.   cm.
    Includes bibliographical references and index.
    ISBN 0-472-11168-X
    1. Public welfare—United States.   2. Welfare recipients—
United States—Interviews.   I. Title.
HV91 .S637   2000
362.5′0973—dc21   00-008551

Contents

Acknowledgments   vii

1. Whose Welfare Politics?   1

2. Research Design and Methodology   17

3. Functions and Dilemmas of Welfare Claiming   26

4. Welfare Claiming as Survival Politics   60

5. Evaluating the Application Encounter   90

6. Welfare Participation and the Client's Dilemma of Action   124

7. Policy Design, Political Learning, and Political Action   157

8. Conclusion   186

Appendixes   205

Notes   215

Bibliography   223

Index   241

Acknowledgments

This book is a product of many conversations. It began with a particularly good one, a late-night exchange of ideas that left me with far too much to think about. Other conversations soon followed, and I now find that I have accumulated a large number of intellectual and emotional debts. Perhaps the greatest of these debts is the one I owe to the women and men who welcomed me into their homes and allowed me to talk with them about their lives. Interview-based research inevitably depends on the trust and kindness of people who are willing to share their stories. I will always be grateful to the people who gave their time to make this study possible. Thank you all for your patience with my ignorance, your encouragement, and both the challenges and pleasures of our conversations. You taught me more than I can express in these pages, and I can only hope that my efforts have not betrayed any of the trust you extended me.

The field research for this project would not have been possible without the assistance I received from many people working in local organizations. I am especially indebted to the staff and residents of the shelter for homeless families where I worked for over a year. My gratitude also goes to the staff and membership of the local chapter of the MS Society, the staff and parents at Head Start centers, and many other activist and service organizations in the community. The University of Wisconsin-Madison provided generous support for this research through a 1995–96 WARF Dissertation Fellowship. I am also grateful to two journals for permission to reprint published work. Material from an earlier version of chapter 5, "Welfare Application Encounters: Subordination, Satisfaction, and the Puzzle of Client Evaluations," *Administration & Society* 31 (1): 50–94, © 1999 Sage Publications, is reprinted here by permission of Sage Publications, Inc. Chapters 6 and 7 include revised material from "Lessons of Welfare: Policy Design, Political Learning, and Political Action," *American Political Science Review* 93(2): 363–80, © 1999 American Political Science Association, reprinted here by permission of the American Political Science Association.

Because this book began as my Ph.D. dissertation, its central ideas were worked out in long conversations with graduate students and faculty in the department of political science at the University of Wisconsin-Madison. I owe a special debt to the members of my dissertation committee, Gina Sapiro, Bert

Kritzer, and David Canon, who offered unflagging support. I could not have hoped for a more challenging and enthusiastic group of collaborators or have found three scholars more worthy of emulation. In the early stages of this project, I benefited immensely from discussions with Murray Edelman and Marion Smiley. While working on the dissertation, I was also the fortunate recipient of advice and assistance from Ken Meier. My efforts to turn the dissertation into a book have been aided immeasurably by conversations with Frances Fox Piven, Joel Handler, Paula Pettavino, Nathan Dietz, Lael Keiser, and Sandy Schram. Sandy, in particular, has been a tireless reader and a seemingly endless source of insight and inspiration. My gratitude also goes to Erin O'Brien for providing first-rate research assistance and asking thought-provoking questions.

For their many wonderful ideas, for their encouragement, and for trying to keep me within shouting distance of sanity, I would particularly like to thank Brian Kroeger, Dutch Toenjes, Sam Nelson, Mark Cassell, Amy Hanauer, Julie White, Tracy Wahl, John Meyer, Carolyn Benson, Dana Ansel, Jutta Joachim, Andy Murphy, Mike Barletta, Greg Streich, Beverlee Garb, Peter Hoeffel, Mark Kessenich, Holly Monka, Patrick Gallagher, and friends in D.C. and New York City. I owe a special thanks to the entire Sparkman family, especially Jerry, for many years of conversation, love, and support. I am also deeply grateful to Bill and Kathy Dahlk for welcoming me into their loving family and for all the encouragement they have given me.

My parents, Susan and Jerry Becker and Sheldon and Terri Soss, cannot be thanked enough for all they have brought to my life and for their encouragement throughout the long process of completing this project. No one could ask for more caring and supportive parents. My sisters Kim and Renee, my brother Jason, and my brother-in-law Ed have also provided me with the best kinds of support and friendship.

Finally, this book is dedicated to my wife, Kira Dahlk, for filling my days with her intelligence, love, and laughter. Thank you for the countless ideas you have contributed to this project, for helping me keep it in perspective, and for the patience and encouragement you have provided as I have worked to complete it.

CHAPTER 1

Whose Welfare Politics?

When most people think of welfare politics, the everyday activities of recipients do not come immediately to mind. There are, of course, those rare and turbulent times when clients of the welfare system rise up to make collective demands, but these disruptive moments are the exception, not the norm (Piven and Cloward 1977). More often, welfare politics seems to be the province of lawmakers and advocates (Heclo 1994). We recognize the politics of welfare when public officials unveil their new plans to fight poverty or end dependence on the dole. We see it when candidates in the heat of a campaign profess their tough love for the "underclass" or their outrage at desperate need in an affluent society. In these moments, welfare politics becomes a captivating drama and a flashpoint for anxieties over the nation's social and political order. Clients, however, do not have to wait for televised speeches or new policy agendas to experience welfare politics. When the dust settles from these sensational events, the quieter politics of everyday life in the welfare system remains.

The purpose of this book is to investigate the political dimensions of welfare participation. Welfare institutions have become key sites of political action for a surprisingly large number of people in the United States. In midterm election years, for example, the number of Americans who make claims on the welfare system is typically greater than the number who vote (Nelson 1980, 1984).[1] For poor people, who tend to be disadvantaged and infrequent participants in more traditional channels of political action (Verba, Schlozman, and Brady 1995), welfare programs serve as particularly critical avenues for demands on government. The welfare system is where the poor make their most pressing claims, negotiate the policy decisions that affect them most directly, and come face to face with the state's capacity to punish or protect.

Despite these facts, the welfare system has rarely been recognized as a political institution that allows citizens to mobilize government personnel and resources. When welfare institutions are designed, little thought is directed toward the political functions they serve for citizens. When they are evaluated, almost no attention is given to the criteria that are usually applied to political institutions in a democracy (Schneider and Ingram 1997). Welfare institutions have the potential to empower or marginalize their clients; they can contribute to a more capable and engaged citizenry or reinforce political inequalities and quiescence (Smith and Ingram 1993). Yet as public officials periodically return to the task of "reforming" welfare, it is the potential for welfare programs to influence client work effort and personal behavior that is hotly debated and examined in exquisite detail. Few stop to ask whether newly designed policies will help or harm the quality of political life for clients.

Like public officials, scholars have also tended to ignore the political dimensions of welfare participation. Lost in the spaces that separate disciplines, welfare claims have been the unwanted orphan of political analysis (Nelson 1980, 1984). In the field of political behavior, none of the major studies of political action have addressed demands on the welfare system (Barnes and Kaase 1979; Campbell et al. 1960; Lane 1959; Milbrath and Goel 1982; Rosenstone and Hansen 1993; Verba and Nie 1972; Verba, Schlozman, and Brady 1995). In the field of public policy, research has almost always focused on the social and economic dimensions of welfare usage, not its political functions or consequences (Bane and Ellwood 1994; Blank 1997; Ellwood 1988). Even in research on street-level bureaucracy, where one can find an explicitly political analysis of welfare administration, only cursory attention has been given to the activities of the client as a political actor (Lipsky 1980).

The failure to recognize the welfare system as an arena of mass politics can be traced to a variety of factors. With its heavy connotations of need, dependence, and passivity, welfare receipt has hardly seemed like an active form of citizen participation (Fraser and Gordon 1993, 1994). Welfare claims are not aimed directly at political elites. They seldom produce significant changes in government policy or allow citizens to register the breadth of their preferences regarding the policy process. Indeed, by making welfare claims, citizens may even become the degraded and regulated targets of public policy (Abramovitz 1988; Piven and Cloward 1993). To participants and observers alike, welfare receipt seems mundane and unfortunate, hard to square with noble images of democratic self-governance and participation in public life.

As the welfare state has grown to affect more and more aspects of citizens' lives, however, it has become a critical channel for demands on government and a powerful instrument for social control (Esping-Andersen 1990; Hasenfeld, Rafferty, and Zald 1987; Piven and Cloward 1993; Verba 1978). The "classically democratic components" of political life have been joined by new dimensions of political action that focus on the state's attempts to extract and distribute resources (Nelson 1984, 224). In the process, citizenship has grown to include an expanded repertoire of political roles (Culpitt 1992; Marshall 1964, 1972). Citizens now relate to government not just as voters and constituents but also as applicants and clients (Goodsell 1981; Lipsky 1980).

The chapters that follow present a comparative case study of the politics of participation in the U.S. welfare system based on in-depth interviews with clients in two welfare programs. In this chapter, I begin by framing the study of welfare participation in terms suggested by participatory-democratic theory. I then explore the political significance of welfare participation from standpoints offered by theories of social citizenship and social control. I conclude by combining these theories to formulate an analysis that focuses on the U.S. welfare system's two-tier structure. Chapter 2 outlines this project's approaches to research design, data collection, and data analysis.

The empirical chapters of this book can be loosely organized in three sections. Chapters 3 and 4 investigate the political functions, uses, and tactics of welfare claiming. Chapters 5 and 6 explore citizens' political lives within welfare institutions, first as applicants and then as clients. Finally, in chapter 7, I investigate the ways in which citizens' experiences of welfare participation affect their broader orientations toward government and political action.

However anemic the U.S. welfare system may seem in comparative perspective (Noble 1997), it serves important political functions for its clients. Welfare claims allow citizens to combat the debilitating and isolating effects of poverty. In doing so, such claims permit clients to construct for themselves the basic preconditions of political involvement. By making welfare claims, citizens can escape immediate and substantial threats to autonomy, such as domestic abuse, institutionalization, and homelessness. They also can enhance their abilities to fulfill social obligations and participate in social networks—to care for family members, assist neighbors, contribute to kin networks, and become involved in their communities. By exploring these aspects of welfare claiming, chapter 3 demonstrates that the much-maligned welfare system bolsters the security and engagement of citizens who would be far more vulnerable and marginal if it did not exist.

Chapter 4 takes up a question of political process. How do eligible individuals convert their objective needs into demands on government? Surprising as it may seem, large numbers of people who are eligible for welfare benefits fail to claim them each year (Blank and Ruggles 1993). Analyzing the pursuit of welfare benefits as a form of survival politics (Hardy-Fanta 1993), I outline a variety of barriers to articulating welfare demands that can help to explain this fact and suggest that individuals' abilities to overcome these barriers are likely to depend on the resources and support they can derive from social networks and local organizations. Recent work on civil society and democracy has emphasized that attachments to networks and organizations enable citizens to be more effective in gaining desired responses from government (Edwards and Foley 1998; Putnam 1995; Putnam, Leonardi, and Nanetti 1993). Evidence from the welfare context is consistent with this view: networks and organizations supply potential applicants with critical information and assistance needed to recognize their eligibility and convert it into tangible benefits.

The culmination of the welfare-claiming process, for those who make it, is also the first experience of welfare participation: the application encounter.

Three questions about this encounter serve as the focal point for chapter 5. First, how do clients evaluate their application experiences? Second, how do differences in program design affect these evaluations? Third, how do applicants' first impressions lay the groundwork for the political relationships they will experience as clients? The evidence presented in this chapter suggests that institutional designs teach applicants lessons about the nature of the client role and the terms of authority that will guide their welfare relationships. The analysis in this chapter also helps to resolve a long-standing paradox from the literature on client evaluations. While research based on direct observation suggests that the "degradation of clients is endemic" (Rosenbloom and O'Leary 1997, 125), survey research suggests that clients are in fact quite satisfied with the treatment they receive (Goodsell 1985; Nelson 1981). Through a political analysis of the application encounter, it is possible to make sense of this puzzling mixture of subordination and satisfaction.

As welfare clients, citizens confront dilemmas of political action that resemble those found in other domains of political life. Claimants must decide whether to engage or retreat from decision-making processes, whether to voice grievances and protest injustices or remain silent. Chapter 6 explores these dilemmas of political action, paying particular attention to how they are shaped by institutional design. Through participation experiences, clients develop program-specific sets of beliefs about agency responsiveness and about what is likely to happen if they challenge administrators, assert their interests, or even express their needs. These beliefs, in turn, have important effects on clients' decisions about whether to speak up on their own behalf or silently accept decisions they find objectionable.

Chapter 7 provides the final piece in this political analysis, exploring the effects of welfare participation on citizens' broader political orientations. The evidence presented in this chapter suggests that the political consequences of welfare participation run deeper than one might expect. Welfare institutions provide many citizens with their most direct and significant experience of government. As a result, encounters with welfare institutions frequently provide the basis for citizens' perceptions of government as a whole. The lessons clients learn in welfare programs shape their beliefs about whether they can expect government institutions to be responsive and whether they can expect political action beyond the welfare system to be effective. Consequently, welfare institutions' designs have significant consequences for broader patterns of political action and quiescence.

The empirical evidence for this comparative case study comes primarily from in-depth interviews with fifty welfare recipients: twenty-five from a public assistance program (Aid to Families with Dependent Children, or AFDC) and twenty-five from a social insurance program (Social Security Disability Insurance, or SSDI). These interviews were conducted from August 1994 to

August 1995 in a midsized Midwestern city. During this same period, I also conducted ethnographic fieldwork, principally at a shelter serving homeless families in AFDC but also in disability support groups serving people in SSDI. To directly observe clients and administrators in welfare relationships, I engaged in participant observation at welfare agencies, accompanying individuals as they applied for benefits or returned for case reviews. Finally, I also draw on a fourth source of evidence: survey data collected for the National Elections Study in 1992 (Miller, Kinder, and Rosenstone 1993). These data, along with the field observations, are used primarily as a basis for evaluating inferences made from the interviews.

The remainder of this first chapter presents the theoretical basis for the larger study. Can citizens' welfare activities be viewed and studied as a form of political action? In the section that follows, I show how these activities can be reconciled with traditional conceptions of political participation and how participatory theory can be used as a basis for studying program usage. Next, I draw on theories of social citizenship and social control to form expectations regarding the political uses and consequences of welfare participation. Building on these theories, I develop a comparative strategy for research on citizen participation in the two channels of the U.S. welfare system.

Welfare as Political Action

At times during the twentieth century, at least some Americans have recognized welfare participation as an important practice of citizenship and even as a political act. During the New Deal era, for example, the Roosevelt administration and social-movement activists portrayed the diversity of emerging social welfare programs as important sites for citizen participation (Gordon 1994). In the 1960s, with the rise of the National Welfare Rights Organization (NWRO), activists again argued for a fundamental right to claim and receive welfare. This time, however, they flooded welfare agencies with the claims of poor people in a strategic effort to register demands, win public resources, disrupt the political order, and (it was hoped) pressure policymakers into establishing a national income guarantee (Davis 1993; Piven and Cloward 1977; Reich 1964; Rosenblatt 1982; Sparer 1970; West 1981).

For a variety of reasons, a political view of welfare claiming has also been a recurrent theme in African American activism. From their inception, groups such as the National Urban League and National Association for the Advancement of Colored People struggled for equal access to welfare resources—not only against policymakers who could define the limits of social provision (Brown 1999; Quadagno 1994) but also against administrators who controlled access to benefits in public bureaucracies and hence could dissuade or discriminate against black claimants (Hamilton and Hamilton 1997). Just as voting rights proved meaningless if they could not be exercised at the ballot box and civil rights rang hollow if they could not be invoked at the courthouse, black people found that social rights to welfare brought no tangible benefits if their claims were turned away at the welfare agency (Amott 1990). The consistent experience of discrimination across these various dimensions of citizenship served to underscore, for many African Americans, the political nature of welfare claims.

> [F]or blacks welfare was . . . indistinguishable from equal rights. . . . The intersection of discrimination and poverty in the black experience meant that welfare claims seemed not so different from the right to vote or to ride the public transportation system. We see here a necessary connection between political and social citizenship: Without some minimum level of security, well-being, and dignity, people cannot function as citizens. And vice versa: To work for welfare was to work against inequality and against discrimination. (Gordon 1994, 141–42)

A political conception of welfare demand-making has also had its academic proponents. Frances Fox Piven and Richard A. Cloward (1977, 1993), the scholar-activists who invented the NWRO's crisis strategy, published several important works arguing that welfare demands can serve as an effective political act for the poor. In the early 1980s, Barbara Nelson (1980, 1984) identified welfare claiming as the "least studied form of individual political behavior" and called for researchers to study it as a form of political action. Others, especially feminist theorists, have echoed this call. Asserting that "turning to the state for redress of apparently private grievances constitutes political participation" (Jones 1990, 802), feminist scholars have identified welfare claiming as a "fundamental type of citizenship participation" (Gordon 1994, 247) and suggested that it is the "dominant form of political participation" among poor women (Jones 1990, 788).

Unfortunately, such calls to inquiry have drawn little attention from those who research political action. The reason for this lack of response is that welfare claims have not fit comfortably into the conception of politics that has prevailed in the field. Studies of political action have traditionally focused on the citizenship activities that are emphasized in theories of representative democracy. The focal point of politics, in this theoretical tradition, lies in the work of elite representatives in government. The majority of citizens are in a sense only indirect participants. They engage in political action primarily when they try to choose or sway the elected officials who participate more directly in the governing process (Hardy-Fanta 1993; Pateman 1970).

Accordingly, research on political action has traditionally identified the elected institutions of government as the center of the political system and asked how citizens fulfill their role as a source of "input" for the elite decision makers who participate directly in the creation of public policy (Conway 1985; Milbrath and Goel 1982; Verba and Nie 1972; Verba, Schlozman, and Brady 1995). Political action, in this view, includes "acts that aim at influencing the government, either by affecting the choice of government personnel or by affecting the choices made by government personnel" (Verba and Nie 1972, 2; Conway 1985, 1991). In strict terms, this definition might be seen as including citizens' demands on all government personnel, including those who implement public policy. But in practice, researchers have studied citizens' efforts to choose and influence their elected representatives while dismissing their direct claims on the administration of public policy as essentially "apolitical" (Milbrath and Goel 1982, 9; Verba and Nie 1972, 3).

In addition to being viewed as administrative matters, welfare claims have also struck observers as less than political for a second reason. Political action traditionally has been understood as a public activity in which citizens advance their interests and preferences regarding "public issues" (Mills 1959, 8; Verba 1978, 4). By contrast, welfare claims have been perceived as "important mainly for the applicant, not for society as a whole" (Nelson 1980, 177). Viewed as an expression of familial need and other "personal troubles of milieu," welfare claims have appeared to fall outside the public sphere in which citizens engage matters of general societal concern (Mills 1959, 8; Fraser 1987, 1989). Thus, as Nancy Fraser has argued, these claims have been viewed as "private-domestic or personal-familial matters in contradistinction to political matters" (1989, 298–99).

The simplest way to respond to these prevailing views is to concentrate first on the distinction between politics and administration, bracketing for the moment the question of whether personal needs constitute a suitable basis for "political" demands. Scholars outside the field of political behavior rejected this distinction long ago and embraced a more political view of demands that are made through government courts and bureaucracies (Goodsell 1981; Lipsky 1980; Zemans 1983).[2] Because policy implementation unavoidably entails discretion in decisions regarding rules and resources, it is always a "continuation of policy-making by other means" (Lineberry 1977, 71). In the distributive politics of "who gets what, when, how," what citizens get certainly depends on policy design (Lasswell 1936), but it also depends on the extent to which they demand their entitlements through participation in the policy-implementation process (Zemans 1983, 694). A conception of politics that excludes these demands is not only too restrictive, it is also biased against the disadvantaged. Groups that are unable to wield influence with policymakers will, almost by definition, have the greatest need to make demands at the implementation stage (Cornelius 1978).[3]

Fortunately, recent scholarship on political action offers greater hope for incorporating citizens' demands on bureaucracies. *Voice and Equality* (Verba, Schlozman, and Brady 1995), the most recent major study of citizen participation, suggests an expanded definition of political action that includes efforts to influence either the formation or the implementation of government policies. With this change in hand, welfare demands can easily be integrated into a conventional, government-centered definition of political action. Welfare claims are made on institutions that implement government policy, they are directed at government personnel, they are sanctioned by law, and their intent and effect is to influence the allocation of public resources.[4]

There is, however, an alternative approach to the problem of integrating welfare claims into the study of political action. Instead of building incrementally on the prevailing view, one can begin with a conception of politics that recognizes welfare claims without suggesting that citizens' actions are political if and only if they are aimed at government. A more complete definition of political action would include not only citizens' attempts to influence government—as voters, constituents, litigants, and clients—but also their extra-governmental efforts in social movements, disruptive protests, and informal community actions. Such a definition would allow researchers to integrate the governmental and nongovernmental aspects of citizens' political lives within a single frame of analysis.

Looking beyond the constraints imposed by theories of representative democracy, a broader conception of political action can be found in participatory-democratic theory (Barber 1984; Berry, Portnoy, and Thomson 1993; Mansbridge 1980, 1999; Pateman 1970) and in feminist theories of politics (Hardy-Fanta 1993; Jones 1988, 1990; Morgen and Bookman 1988). Participatory-democratic theory positions citizens as direct participants in the process of self-government who engage and learn from the political process based on firsthand experience.

> The basic idea [of participatory democracy] is simple: people can and should govern themselves. They do not need specially bred or anointed rulers, nor a special caste or class to run their affairs. Everyone has the capacity for autonomy, even quite ordinary people—the uneducated, the poor, housewives, laborers, peasants, the outsiders and castoffs of society. Each is capable not merely of self-control, of privately taking charge of his own life, but also of self-government, of sharing in the deliberate shaping of their common life. Exercising this capacity is prerequisite both to the freedom and full development of each, and to the freedom and justness of the community. (Pitkin and Shumer 1982, 43)

Because participatory theory locates the principle of self-government in the relationships that make up political communities, it suggests a more integrated view of formal and informal politics that draws connections between demands on government and political processes embedded in daily life (Abrahams 1992; Hardy-Fanta 1993). Political action, in this view, can include any individual or group attempt to negotiate, alter, or entrench patterns of social values and resources (for discussion, see Abrahams 1992).[5] From this vantage point, the political status of welfare demands does not depend on the government arenas that happen to serve as their locale. Welfare demands may be recognized as political action because they involve citizens taking direct action to claim (that is, to negotiate and alter patterns of) community resources.

Participatory theory also offers a second advantage in conceptualizing citizens' welfare activities as political action. Unlike theorists of representative democracy, participatory theorists identify the personal experience of economic needs and relations as critical facets of political life (Dahl 1985; Gould 1988; Greenberg 1986; Pateman 1970; Witte 1980). Far from being apolitical, these "bread and butter issues" are the "essence of lower class politics and resistance" (Scott 1985, 295; Singerman 1995); they make up the heart of what might be termed "survival politics" (Hardy-Fanta 1993, 45–46). As Hanna Pitkin explains, to deem needs-based claims beneath the status of politics

> means simply the exclusion of the exploited by their exploiters, who can afford not to discuss economics, and to devote themselves to "higher things," because they live off of the work of others. . . . The concept of justice is precisely about the connections between . . . private claim and public policy. . . . It is no use banishing the body, economic concerns, or the social question [of poverty] from public life; we do not rid ourselves of their power in that way, but only impoverish public life. (1981, 336, 343, 346)

Participatory theory not only facilitates recognition of welfare participation as a form of political action, it also suggests a set of empirical questions for political analysis. The questions I ask about welfare participation in this study are drawn directly from four themes found in participatory-democratic theory. First, political action is, among other things, an instrumental and expressive activity (Conway 1985, 2–3). Applied in the welfare context, this idea suggests the importance of asking why individuals decide to advance welfare claims, how they are able to accomplish this task, and what they believe their actions convey to others. Similar questions must be asked about citizens' client activities. What factors make welfare recipients more or less likely to make demands, raise grievances, or remain silent in their relationships with government bureaucracies?

Second, participatory theory also suggests that political action is an educative experience that leaves its imprint on what citizens know and believe. (Bachrach 1967; Benello and Roussopoulos 1971; Cook and Morgan 1971; Pateman 1970). The experience of participation is expected to teach individuals about politics, to provide them with new skills, and to change their orientations toward political involvement. (Finkel 1985, 1987; Leighley 1991; Mansbridge 1980, 1999). Thus, if welfare participation is viewed as political action, one must ask what lessons it holds for citizens. How do the participation experiences citizens find in the welfare system influence what they know and believe about politics, government, and themselves? How do these experiences affect citizens' orientations toward demand-making, both within and beyond the welfare agency?

Third, participatory theory encourages us to investigate the links between formal political demands and the social relationships of everyday life (Hardy-Fanta 1993). For years, feminist scholars have argued for a view of political life that attends to the ways in which social roles encumber, motivate, and shape individuals (Benhabib 1987; Dietz 1984; England 1993; Gilligan 1982; Held 1990; Jones 1990). This position has proved to be a good match with participatory theories that identify politics as a community process and draw connections between political institutions and social relationships (Hardy-Fanta 1993; Mansbridge 1980). Applied in the welfare context, these theories suggest the need to ask how welfare claims emerge from and transform individuals' roles in relation to others. How do citizens' formal welfare claims relate to the informal claims that others make on them? How does welfare participation affect the levels of status, security, and control that individuals possess in relation to those who make up their community?

Fourth and finally, participatory theory directs us to ask how institutional arrangements may leave distinctive imprints on citizens' political beliefs and actions. As Pateman (1970, 42, 29) explains, "the theory of participatory democracy is built round the central assertion that individuals and their institutions cannot be considered in isolation from one another. . . . [P]olitical action depends largely on the sort of institutions within which the individual has, politically, to act." Institutional designs vary considerably across the welfare system (Gordon 1994, chap. 10). How do these institutional differences shape citizens' political experiences? Do these differences influence patterns of client demand-making in welfare programs? Do institutional design differences affect what clients come to believe about the way government works? Do they affect the likelihood that clients will pursue a wider range of ways to participate in political life?

By pursuing these four themes, it is possible to develop a political analysis of citizens' welfare activities and to integrate them into the study of political action. Doing so, I would argue, is an essential step toward a less distorted image of the political lives of disadvantaged groups. Researchers have produced a great deal of evidence demonstrating that the poor are disengaged from and do not participate in major aspects of American politics (Delli Carpini and Keeter 1996; Rosenstone and Hansen 1993; Verba, Schlozman, and Brady 1995). This evidence of marginality tells an important half of the political story, but it should not be allowed to completely overshadow the activities that make up the remainder of political life in poor communities.[6] Today in the United States, welfare participation is one of the most critical of these activities.

Poverty, Social Citizenship, and Social Control

What role does welfare participation play within the broader political life of the citizen? From the individual's standpoint, what are the political functions and consequences of welfare claiming? As the chapters that follow will show, there are many answers to these questions, but all of them have roots in the problem of poverty. Welfare systems distribute resources and citizens claim them in an effort to combat poverty. And as theorists of democracy and citizenship have frequently pointed out, the problems of poverty are not only social and economic but also political (Gaffaney 1999; King and Waldron 1988, 425–26).

Poverty generated by markets can produce at least two kinds of problems for democratic politics. First, the drain of persistent poverty can debilitate and marginalize citizens (King and Waldron 1988, 428). Extreme poverty can undercut capacities needed for political involvement and force a retreat from broader matters of public concern. Formal guarantees of civil and political rights can become meaningless if poverty is allowed to undermine the security, capacity, status, or will needed to exercise them. Second, while marginality may be the more common threat, poverty can also give rise to more direct strains on the political system. If left unmet, the urgent demands of those in need can touch off disruptive forms of political participation: uprisings and revolts that threaten the stability of the political order. Even in less volatile times, as Hannah Arendt noted, civic politics and careful deliberation are not easily maintained amid a "clamouring for bread and constant demands for 'action now, not words'" (King and Waldron 1988, 428; Pitkin 1981).

Two theoretical traditions have emerged to explain how welfare systems might function to ameliorate these threats and, more broadly, enable democratic polities to coexist with capitalist economies. The first is the theory of social citizenship advanced by T. H. Marshall (1964); the second is the theory of social control developed by Piven and Cloward (1993). Taken together, these two theories mark out a range of expectations regarding the political functions and consequences of welfare participation for the individual.

In "Citizenship and Social Class," Marshall suggests that citizenship is a status that evolves over time toward "a fuller measure of equality, an enrichment of the stuff of which the status is made and an increase in the number of those on whom the status is bestowed" (1964, 84). Generalizing from British history, Marshall argues that citizens first acquire civil rights, including those of speech, property, contract, personal liberty, faith, and justice. To these rights, citizens later add political rights to self-government, "to participate in the exercise of political power" (72). Finally, individuals acquire the social rights of citizenship, which are expressed through and protected by the state's welfare institutions; they extend from the "right to a modicum of economic welfare and security to the right to a share in the full social heritage and to live the life of a civilized being according to the standards prevailing in the society" (72).

By dulling the sharpest edges of poverty and inequality, Marshall suggests that the welfare state serves to protect the long-term stability of a capitalist and democratic society. Social rights, in this view, represent more than a public bulwark against economic destitution. They are more fundamentally an expression of "liberal themes of rights and equal respect; communitarian norms of solidarity and shared responsibility; and republican ideals of participation in public life" (Fraser and Gordon 1993, 45–46). Social rights can be expected to bolster the poor's political status and capacities in two respects. First, these rights guarantee access to essential resources that might otherwise be denied by the market—not only income but also housing, employment, health care, and education. By acting on their social rights to claim these resources, the disadvantaged can secure the skills, status, and well-being they need to participate actively in their communities, to exercise their civil and political rights, and to fulfill their duties as citizens.

Second, social citizenship theory suggests that the act of exercising social rights might itself make individuals feel "more rather than less deserving, more rather than less a citizen" (Gordon 1994, 247). By participating in welfare institutions that are shared by all, the poor can affirm, to themselves and others, that they are equal citizens who deserve equal respect and full civil and political rights (Fraser and Gordon 1993, 45–46). To realize this benefit of welfare participation, however, the entire citizenry must share access to welfare institutions that are structured in an "equal and just manner so as to express the solidarity of a national community" (Heclo 1995, 671). Full rights of social citizenship can only be realized by "provision for need that is given universally, that is provided without supplication or stigma, and that avoids as far as possible the invidious operation of official discretion" (King and Waldron 1988, 422).[7]

In both of these respects, Marshall's work highlights the potential for welfare participation to draw individuals into a more equal, inclusive, and active polity. By exercising their social rights, the disadvantaged can win resources

that protect them against poverty's debilitating and marginalizing consequences. Through this activity, the poor can also gain an experience of participation that reinforces, for themselves and others, their full and equal status as
citizens. Thus, the great promise of social citizenship theory is that, through
welfare participation, citizens will acquire the social, psychological, and material resources they need to be more capable and engaged, more secure and assertive. They will become more effective and active political agents in their
communities and in relation to government.

Marshall's account contains, however, an important note of caution that
concerns the question of institutional design. The quality of citizens' social
rights depends not only on the fact of welfare provision but equally on the institutional form of provision. While welfare systems have great potential to
strengthen poor people's attachments to the polity, this potential may be squan-
dered if welfare is provided in divisive or degrading ways that undermine recipients' equal respect and dignity.

Social control theory, by contrast, offers a more highly developed account
of how welfare institutions may function to reinforce the marginality of poor
people. In *Regulating the Poor* (1993), Piven and Cloward argue that the welfare system's primary function is not to provide relief per se but rather to maintain the legitimacy of political institutions and the viability of economic institutions. While Marshall views the extension of social provision as part of an
evolution of consensual norms surrounding citizenship, Piven and Cloward's
account places greater emphasis on conflict, disruption, and dissension. In their
view, expansions of welfare benefits and institutions occur chiefly in response
to pressure from below, generally in the form of civil unrest. The extension of
aid serves to mollify the poor and restore political legitimacy both by providing material relief and by conveying symbolic reassurances.

After restoring political legitimacy, however, the provision of welfare begins to pose problems for the economic order. To the extent that fears of destitution and starvation normally force the poor to serve as a compliant source of
labor, welfare policies that protect against these fates increase the likelihood
that workers might forgo or protest the worst forms of employment. This tension between the political and economic functions of the relief system gives rise
to a perennial catch-22 in welfare provision: aid must be high enough to convey a genuine attempt to help the poor but must also maintain incentives for the
unemployed to seek and accept whatever jobs are available in the market
(Schram 1995, 126).

The solution to this problem, according to Piven and Cloward, lies in the
design of welfare institutions. Instead of providing universal programs that
serve all citizens, the welfare system offers separate programs that segregate
the "undeserving" poor (those deemed capable of working) from more "deserving" beneficiaries (those considered unable to work). Once segregated in

this manner, the undeserving poor are provided with welfare in a form that is "so degrading and punitive as to instill in the laboring masses a fear of the fate that awaits them should they relax into beggary and pauperism. To demean and punish those who do not work is to exalt by contrast even the meanest labor at the meanest wages" (Piven and Cloward 1993, 396).[8]

The key points in this analysis extend well beyond the question of work effort. First, social control theory suggests that poverty is not only debilitating but also coercive. Someone who is poor is less than free to resist the terms set by those who might offer the means of subsistence, whether an employer, a party boss, a religious organization, a spouse, or anyone else. Thus, by claiming welfare, poor people mobilize public resources in a way that enhances their power as actors in the market, the polity, civil society, and domestic relations. Applied as part of a gender analysis of domestic relations, for example, this theory suggests that women who are dependent on male breadwinners are less than free to leave or assert their interests; the opportunity to claim welfare benefits can open new possibilities for voice or exit (Abramovitz 1988; Gordon 1994).

Second, social control theory suggests that welfare systems function to promote cohesion and order in the broader society by isolating, punishing, and degrading individuals who are cast as failures in relation to key societal values. Such values might include the work ethic and self-sufficiency, two-parent familial norms, or the variety of role expectations surrounding categories of gender, class, race, and ethnicity (Schram 1995, 124–30). In all of these areas, social control theory argues that "welfare policy . . . is an affirmation of majoritarian values through the creation of deviants. The poor are held hostage to make sure that the rest of us behave" (Handler 1995, 8–9). Far from realizing the social-citizenship ideal of promoting solidarity and inclusion, the welfare system in this account serves to isolate and marginalize the poor.

> By segregating the poor into different programs, U.S. welfare policy reinforces the separation of the poor from working- and middle-class Americans, and also creates divisions among the poor. Moreover, once separated by the programs, the poor are also more likely to be denigrated by the treatment accorded them. Benefits are less likely to be a matter of right and more likely to be discretionary, subject to the successful hurdling of bureaucratic inquisitions and runarounds and continuing bureaucratic surveillance, all of which shapes the understandings of both the people who endure this treatment and the people who in a sense are the public audience for it. Finally, and very important, recipients receive benefits that keep them very poor, ensuring their marginalization in an affluent and materialistic society. (Piven 1995, xiv)

Thus, like social citizenship theory, social control theory suggests that important political consequences emerge from both the fact and the form of welfare provision. Benefits won through welfare claiming can be empowering for disadvantaged citizens, as long as the benefits are sufficient to relieve the coercive threat of destitution. But the form of welfare provision, in this view, is expected to reinforce the marginality of the poor. Instead of being affirmed as equal citizens, recipients are segregated and vilified as dependent and deviant "others," made into a pariah class that the broader political community shuns and scorns. At the same time, welfare participation itself takes place under such harsh conditions that it can be expected to take a toll on recipients. As a result, the experience of welfare participation can erode the security and assertiveness of clients, both within and beyond the welfare agency (Piven and Cloward 1997a, 200).

Dual Welfare Provision and Policy Design
for Democracy

Thus, theories of social citizenship and social control offer good reasons to suspect that welfare participation can have either positive or negative political consequences for citizens. In this regard, scholars have tended to emphasize the striking differences between program designs in the two tiers of the U.S. welfare system (Gordon 1994; Nelson 1984, 1990; Tussing 1974, 1975). The public assistance programs found in the system's inferior tier are typically associated with the "undeserving" poor. These programs offer lower benefits on a means-tested basis, are administered primarily at the state and local levels, and place clients in discretionary casework relationships. These programs are disproportionately likely to be the site of welfare participation for people of color, women, and people who have lived in poverty (M. Katz 1989; Pearce 1990; Trattner 1989).[9] The social insurance programs in the superior tier offer higher benefits that do not vary across the states. They are administered at the federal level and are not subject to means testing. They are typically associated with more "deserving" groups such as the disabled and elderly of all classes who have proven work histories.

Because the two tiers of the welfare system offer markedly different benefits and treatment, critics have suggested that they function to sustain a hierarchy of dual social citizenship (Fraser 1987; Gordon 1994, chap. 10; Nelson 1990; Sapiro 1990). In this view, social insurance recipients are treated as something akin to social citizens—they are "rights-bearing beneficiaries and purchasing consumers of services"—while public assistance recipients are treated as dependent objects of social control (Fraser 1987, 113). Integrating theories of social citizenship and social control, the concept of dual social citizenship suggests that while social insurance programs allow individuals to act as more effective political agents, public assistance programs reinforce the marginality of the poor.

This study investigates this claim through a comparative case study of participation in one social insurance program, SSDI, and one public assistance program, AFDC. From the perspective of participatory theory, the two-tier welfare system represents more than a hierarchy of provision: it is also as an unequal framework of institutional settings for political participation. Institutional differences across the system matter not only because of disparities in what clients receive but also because they may position clients differently as political actors and teach them different lessons about themselves, their government, and the value of political involvement.

By investigating the political consequences of this institutional variation, this study provides empirical evidence bearing on a fundamental political question: how might the welfare system be designed to support a more engaged citizenry and a more participatory democracy? A considerable amount of interest in this question has recently been generated as scholars have advanced alternative visions of how welfare policies might be used to improve the quality of democratic citizenship (compare, for example, the "new paternalism" of Mead [1992, 1997b] with the work on "policy design for democracy" by Schneider and Ingram [1997]). To date, however, theoretical arguments have not been joined by or subjected to much empirical research.

This book offers a political analysis of the welfare system, its functions, and its consequences from the bottom-up perspective of the client (Schram 1995). For too long, welfare politics has been understood solely as the domain of elite representatives, voters, and advocates. The citizens who make the most direct claims on the welfare system have been viewed only as its passive beneficiaries or victims. As the chapters that follow will show, welfare participation is a complex and contradictory form of political action. It can subject citizens to harsh forms of social discipline, but it can also be an unusually effective way for them to win tangible, immediate, and helpful actions from government. It rarely gives clients power over others, but it can enhance their power to accomplish goals and serve as capable members of the polity. To be sure, welfare claiming can be a limited form of political action, and many clients would not choose it if they could avoid it. But however limited and unwanted these claims may be, they have come to occupy a central place in modern politics.

CHAPTER 2

Research Design and Methodology

In the chapters that follow, I analyze the political dimensions of welfare participation, drawing on interviews and experiences with clients in two welfare programs. The types of evidence used in this study have been outlined in the preceding chapter. Here, I present a more detailed account of my approaches to research design, case selection, informant sampling, data collection, and data analysis.

Research Design and Case Selection

The research design for this project can be classified as a multiple case study (Yin 1989, chap. 2). Following theories of dual welfare provision, which emphasize institutional variation across the two tiers of the welfare system (Gordon 1994; Nelson 1984), this study investigates welfare participation in two programs: one from the social insurance tier (Social Security Disability Insurance, or SSDI) and one from the public assistance tier (Aid to Families with Dependent Children, or AFDC). Unlike a single case study of welfare participation, a comparative approach makes it possible to identify patterns of similarity and difference across the two tiers of the system. Using each program as a backdrop for the other, general characteristics of welfare participation can be distinguished from characteristics that are unique to a given program. AFDC and SSDI were selected as the two cases based on several factors, each of which relates to a key independent variable in the analysis (Geddes 1990; Gary King, Keohane, and Verba 1994; Ragin 1987).[1]

First, and most importantly, the AFDC and SSDI programs exemplify the policy design differences that distinguish the two tiers of the welfare system. As a result, they offer citizens very different institutional settings for welfare participation. The AFDC program includes means testing, mandatory child support enforcement, casework relationships, regular case reviews, and a variety of other features that combine to create a policy design that differs markedly from the one found in SSDI. As a result, a comparison of these two programs can shed light on how institutional variation shapes clients' participation experiences and patterns of political learning.

17

Second, AFDC and SSDI are both cash-transfer programs that offer citizens direct income assistance as well as access to additional benefits such as health coverage. This aspect of the research design serves two purposes. In the chapters on welfare claiming, it allows for some generalization across the two programs regarding the functions served by these types of benefits and the processes that give rise to successful welfare demands. In the chapters on welfare participation and its consequences, this feature of the design makes it possible to rule out benefit provision as an explanation for outcomes that differ across the two programs. For example, because AFDC and SSDI clients both depend on welfare benefits, this fact cannot explain why clients in one program feel more secure or assertive than clients in the other program.

Third, the demographic characteristics of recipients in AFDC and SSDI differ considerably but overlap enough to allow for comparisons of similar subgroups. The diversity of these two program populations serves as an advantage in attempting to draw general conclusions about the welfare-claiming process—that is, it provides protection against idiosyncratic explanations built around the characteristic experiences of a single group. Differences between these two populations, however, create problems in identifying how institutional designs affect clients' participation experiences, beliefs, and actions. The analytic problem, of course, is how to distinguish the effects of policy design from effects that arise out of preexisting differences between the two groups of clients. To address this problem, it was necessary to pick programs that offered some similar subgroups of clients.[2]

All of the social insurance programs in the United States provide institutional designs and program populations that differ from AFDC, but SSDI is the one most likely to have some recipients that share characteristics with AFDC clients. Unlike recipients of Social Security Old-Age Insurance, for example, SSDI clients vary widely in age (U.S. House of Representatives 1998). In addition, like AFDC clients, people with disabilities are more likely than the general population to be women, to be people of color, to be poor, and to have lower levels of formal education (Albrecht 1992, 15; Howards, Brehm, and Nagi 1980). As a result, the SSDI program provides an optimal companion to AFDC as a case for this study. SSDI serves a program population that differs from but overlaps with the AFDC population, shares AFDC's status as a cash-transfer program, and differs significantly in its institutional design.

As the preceding discussion suggests, the purpose of this study is not to produce an analysis of the AFDC program or the SSDI program per se. Rather, these cases have been chosen because they allow for comparisons and contrasts that can be expected to shed light on more general political questions regarding welfare participation and institutional design.[3] This point is especially important because the federal government abolished the AFDC program in 1996, replacing it with a block-grant program named Temporary Assistance for Needy Families (TANF). Although this change in policy has major social and politi-

cal implications (Mink 1998), it is less important in an analytic sense for the issues explored in this book. The political functions of welfare claiming and the
political consequences of institutional variation (investigated here through a
comparison of AFDC and SSDI) will remain important so long as welfare institutions are designed for and engaged by citizens.

Selection of Methods

This study is based on four approaches to data collection. In-depth interviews
with clients serve as the primary source of evidence, augmented by participant
observation at agencies administering each program, ethnographic fieldwork
with the two program populations, and survey data collected for the 1992
National Elections Study (NES) (Miller, Kinder, and Rosenstone 1993). Each
method offers a different standpoint for observation and a different type of evidence within the project. As a result, reliance on these four different approaches
helps to compensate for the biases and limitations of each individual method
and makes it possible to assess the validity of observations and explanations
based on different sources of evidence (commonly called triangulation; see
Gary King, Keohane, and Verba 1994; Miles and Huberman 1984, 234–35). As
expected, different sources of evidence occasionally pointed toward different
conclusions. More frequently, however, conclusions based on the interview
data were supported by evidence obtained through the other three methods.

Statistical analyses of survey data from the 1992 NES play a limited role
in the study. Survey data are difficult to obtain for most of the questions pursued here. In 1992, however, the NES included questions regarding welfare
program usage, creating an opportunity to analyze the relationship between
welfare participation and broader forms of political belief and action. In chapter 7, these survey data are used to corroborate conclusions based on the interviews. The large, national sample available in the NES data set allows for control over a larger number of differences between the program populations and
for stronger generalizations to the national population. For variable descriptions, see appendix B.

Participant observation at the agencies offered opportunities to witness
and be a part of interactions I could only hear about in interviews with clients.
When interview informants recount their own experiences, their stories are
shaped by what they perceived at the time of the events, what they can remember during the interview, and what they are willing to share with the in-
terviewer. Direct observation offers some compensation for these weaknesses
(Adler and Adler 1987; Jorgensen 1989; Liebow 1967, 1993). Moreover, no
matter how often I listened to descriptions of welfare encounters, it was something different to go with clients and experience these encounters firsthand—
to wait for long periods on cold plastic chairs; to meet with overworked and

frustrated administrators; to see if, how, and when a client would raise the question or complaint she had told me about on the way to the agency. Although I do not quote directly from my field notes on these experiences, evidence obtained through direct participation and observation offered an invaluable check on my interpretations of evidence from the interviews.

Ethnographic fieldwork for this project was conducted principally in a shelter for homeless families serving AFDC recipients but also took place in disability support groups serving SSDI recipients. This method was intended to serve three purposes. First, I hoped it would provide access to clients who might be more difficult to locate or who might differ from those who would agree to a formal interview. Second, it provided direct contact with the politics of welfare participation in everyday life. It allowed me to see the functions of welfare claiming for clients, to talk with eligible people as they decided whether to claim benefits, and to interact with clients during the periods in which they dealt with problems in their welfare relationships. As a result, I was able to directly observe (and in some cases, be involved in) experiences I could only capture retrospectively in the interviews. Third, the ethnographic work allowed for insight into how clients talk about welfare programs among themselves in an informal setting rather than in a formal interview with a researcher. These conversations raised issues I never would have thought to ask about and provided valuable insight into the meanings of unfamiliar practices and vocabularies (Lofland and Lofland 1995; Spradley 1979).

In-depth interviews were chosen as the primary method of data collection in this project for several reasons. First, because this method maximizes the depth of one-on-one interaction, I hoped that it would produce familiarity and trust that, in turn, would enhance the validity of the findings (Berg 1998, chap. 4; Kirk and Miller 1986). Second, this relatively open-ended approach allowed clients to emphasize the aspects of their experiences that they perceived to be most important and to describe them in their own words (Spradley 1979). In addition to ensuring that informants were not limited by my preconceptions about what issues would be important, this approach also offered greater opportunity to explore the ambivalence that often accompanied recipients' beliefs and opinions (Chong 1993; Hochschild 1981). Finally, the flexibility of semistructured interviews also provided opportunities to probe initial answers, rephrase complicated questions, and explore the assumptions and reasoning that supported recipients' views.

Informant Selection: Access and Sampling

I entered the field to begin research for this project in August 1994. As expected, gaining access to informants was a slow process (Spradley 1979, 45–54). I spent approximately four months working through local organizations and social networks before I began to feel that interviews with clients would be comfortable and productive. I attended Head Start meetings and disability support groups. I met clients through my work at the shelter and through people in my neighborhood. During this initial period I tried to establish some familiarity with the community and some rapport with people who later became informants. This early period of the fieldwork also included conversations with clients and people in community organizations who suggested ways to revise my schedule of interview questions.

The individual clients I interviewed were identified through purposive rather than probability sampling. I began by selecting a small group of clients who seemed like they would be especially informative and easy to interview (what Fetterman calls "judgmental sampling" [1989, 43]). I then pursued a stop-and-start "snowball" strategy aimed at locating a diverse sample of clients. Clients with connections to local organizations were the easiest to find and became the first people I interviewed. Not wanting to bias the sample toward more engaged clients, I stopped interviewing until I could locate clients who did not have organizational ties. I continued to meet informants through other people I had interviewed, through neighbors and friends, and through residents at the shelter for homeless families.[4]

Since the vast majority of AFDC clients were women, I did not try to locate men for that half of the sample. By contrast, I worked intentionally to include racial diversity among my AFDC informants. Because of social and residential segregation, I had to resist the tendency for social networks to produce a racially uniform sample. The final group of twenty-five AFDC informants included women who considered themselves to be African American (52 percent), white (28 percent), Latina (12 percent), and Native American (4 percent).[5] All of the AFDC clients I interviewed were women. Their education levels varied considerably, falling into the following categories: no high school education (4 percent), some high school (44 percent), high school graduate (32 percent), some college (16 percent), and college graduate (4 percent). Their ages ranged from eighteen to forty-eight, with a mean age of about twenty-seven and a standard deviation of about seven.

I expected experiences applying to SSDI to vary according to the type of health condition that an applicant used to claim benefits. Consequently, I tried to avoid relying on informants who shared similar disability histories. The final group of twenty-five clients was made up of men and women who claimed benefits on the basis of physical (44 percent), mental (20 percent), and neurological (36 percent) conditions. The SSDI clients included ten men (40 percent) and fifteen women (60 percent). As expected, this half of the sample had higher levels of formal education, breaking down along the following lines: some high school education (8 percent), high school graduate (32 percent), some college (16 percent), and college graduate (44 percent). In addition, the SSDI informants were predominantly white (84 percent) but included a small number of African Americans (12 percent) and one Native American (4 percent). Their ages ranged from twenty-nine to sixty-five, with a mean age of about forty-four and a standard deviation of about nine.

The program samples differ considerably along lines of sex, race, education, and age (see appendix A for a summary) but include enough overlap to allow for comparisons of similar subgroups. As described earlier, these comparisons were needed to control for background characteristics and isolate effects associated with program participation. The sample includes eight people in each program (32 percent) who had high school diplomas but no college experience. Similarly, the eight AFDC clients (32 percent) who were between thirty and thirty-nine years old could be compared with the nine SSDI clients in this same age group (36 percent). The seven white AFDC clients (28 percent) allowed for comparisons with the larger group of white SSDI clients (84 percent). Finally, gender differences were controlled by comparing the fifteen women in SSDI to the twenty-five women in AFDC.

Data Collection

Although some interviews were conducted at workplaces, day care centers, and a local diner, the vast majority took place in clients' homes. The duration of the interviews ranged from forty-five minutes to two and a half hours. However, it was common for home visits to last considerably longer, with casual conversation both before and after the interview. In a number of cases, I spent close to the whole day with clients before conducting the interview. The informal time together helped to build up some rapport (Spradley 1979, 78–83) and provided clues about which interview topics might be important or sensitive and some context for understanding the stories people told after the interviews began. When clients made important comments outside the interview, I either asked them to repeat themselves on tape or asked permission to take handwritten notes and then later added the comments to the transcripts.

All of the people who participated in this study were promised confidentiality in any public materials based on their interviews and were invited to choose their own pseudonym. They were also assured that neither the researcher nor this project was connected to a government welfare agency or program. Informants were explicitly told that choosing not to be interviewed would not adversely affect them in any way. I also asked them if they would feel more comfortable with a tape recording or with handwritten notes. Forty-nine of the fifty interviews were taped using a microcassette recorder. One client (a woman in SSDI) objected to the use of a tape recorder, but she was comfortable with note taking. None of the other clients expressed concerns about being taped. Although there were several cases in which I noted that clients seemed anxious at first, most informants appeared surprisingly relaxed and comfortable with the interviews.

I conducted most of the ethnographic fieldwork for this project while serving as a volunteer staff member at a shelter for homeless families. I worked two six-hour shifts each week for one year. According to shelter records, roughly 80 percent of the resident families received AFDC during that time. Because residents could only stay at the shelter for a maximum of two weeks, this work allowed for informal conversations with a large number of AFDC clients over the course of the year. On many nights, I stayed up late with residents talking about their experiences in AFDC and asking about issues that had been raised in my interviews. At the end of each shift, I returned home to type up field notes on the events of the night. These notes were based on memory and occasional reminders to myself scribbled on scraps of paper during my shift. The file of field notes also served as a journal of my field experience. It became a junk shop full of discoveries and half-baked ideas as well as an outlet for my personal reactions to experiences in interviews and at the shelter.

As part of my shelter work, I also attended biweekly support group meetings in which residents discussed personal problems among themselves. Although the groups were ostensibly set up to discuss alcohol and drug problems, most discussions focused on other issues. As a frequent source of difficulties for women at the shelter, the AFDC program was a common topic of conversation. The support groups offered what might loosely be called a natural focus group (Krueger 1994; Morgan 1997). I could not depend on residents to discuss AFDC; nor could I control the flow of conversation (I never said anything in the meetings). But when conversation did turn to AFDC, residents were very frank in retelling their own experiences and advising one another on how to deal with the agency.

Although it was more sporadic and limited, I conducted similar fieldwork on the SSDI side of the study by attending disability support group meetings. At first, this approach was intended as a way to learn about disability-related issues in the community and to meet prospective informants. However, I continued to attend on an irregular basis because the meetings allowed some insight into the local disability community and occasionally involved discussions of SSDI. This fieldwork was not as extensive as the work at the shelter but offered similar opportunities to listen to casual conversations among clients.[6]

Participant observation at welfare agencies was conducted at irregular intervals. Over the course of the year, I spent a number of days in the waiting rooms of these offices. On these visits, I discussed welfare-related issues with people waiting nearby and sometimes with administrators. In other cases, I accompanied clients to the agency offices and followed along as they dealt with administrators. In most cases, these clients were women I had met at the shelter. However, on a couple of occasions, I went along with clients I had previously interviewed. To guard against a distorted view of conditions and interactions at welfare agencies, I attempted to visit a number of different agencies, to go with a number of different clients, and to do so on different days of the week and at different times of day. I suspect, however, that the total number of visits was insufficient to cover the range of variation that might arise from these factors.

Data Analysis

After the interviews, I used a word processor to transcribe each tape in its entirety and verbatim. I then printed out full-length copies of each transcript, creating a hard copy that I used throughout the analysis and writing stages to check the context of individual quotations. I began by analyzing the fifty separate transcripts as coherent wholes. On the first pass, I labeled noteworthy points in the text and assigned passages to very general categories that eventually became the topics for each of the five empirical chapters. I then extracted quotations from the larger transcripts (up to twenty lines), and printed them on index cards. Because the cards defined the data set for each chapter, I tried to err on the side of inclusion. In addition to the excerpts, each card also contained demographic information about the informant. Although a spreadsheet was used on a few occasions, the vast majority of the data analysis was done by sorting the cards into piles and keeping written lists of the results.

Three major strategies were used to analyze the transcripts. The first, which can be seen primarily in the first three chapters, emphasizes induction with the goal of creating general typologies. Building up from an "open" coding approach, I first labeled the cards with descriptive themes (Strauss 1987, 59–68) and then grouped seemingly related cards into clusters (Miles and Huberman 1984, 218–21). The final stage of data reduction involved what Miles and Huberman call "factoring" because it resembles the statistical technique of factor analysis (1984, 223–25). At this stage, I combined the thematic clusters into the smallest number of underlying dimensions that could remain internally coherent and distinctive from one another. In the analysis presented in chapter 3, for example, I conclude that the many functions and dilemmas of welfare claiming can be organized along three dimensions: power and dependence, identity and obligation, and economic well-being.

The second strategy, often termed "pattern matching" (Yin 1989, 109–13), places greater emphasis on hypothesis testing. Using theory-based expectations as a template, I analyzed the evidence from clients' accounts to see if it matched the patterns I expected to find. Typically, this process involved sorting cards to see if the patterns matched my expectation that there would be differences across the two programs. To rule out rival hypotheses, I then checked to see (a) if additional, unexpected patterns could also be found and (b) if the hypothesized differences across programs disappeared after isolating subgroups of clients with similar demographics.

The third analytic strategy involved "explanation building" (Yin 1989, 113–15): in this case, stipulating and investigating a set of causal links connecting policy designs to clients' political beliefs and actions. Based on a pattern-matching analysis for each "link," I tried to establish a logical chain of evidence that moved from (1) policy designs to (2) welfare participation experiences to (3) beliefs about the nature of welfare relationships to (4) clients' willingness to voice grievances in welfare programs. Finally, through (5) clients' tendencies to identify welfare agencies with government as a whole, the chain ends with (6) differences in levels of political efficacy and (7) differences in rates of political action.

The research design and methods used in this project allow for what might be termed a bottom-up analysis of the U.S. welfare system (Schram 1995). In the chapters that follow, I investigate how this system is perceived by and affects the people for whom it serves as a primary site of politics. Like any approach to research, this bottom-up perspective comes with blind spots as well as strengths. As I hope to show, however, a qualitative, client-centered research strategy offers real advantages for exploring the functions and consequences of welfare participation as a political activity. In the first two empirical chapters, I pursue an interpretive approach to qualitative social science, attempting to understand the applicant's reasons for engaging in welfare claiming and the activities that make up this practice. In the final three empirical chapters, I blend positivist and interpretivist goals, seeking to make inferences about causal relationships and to explain the processes and mechanisms that underlie these relationships (see Lin 1998).

CHAPTER 3

Functions and Dilemmas of Welfare Claiming

Like registered voters, people who are eligible for welfare benefits make up a pool of individuals with the potential to make themselves heard by government. To receive tangible resources distributed through welfare policies, members of this pool must be willing and able to advance their claims in welfare bureaucracies. The political significance of this fact was demonstrated in dramatic fashion by the welfare rights movement of the 1960s. As part of a "crisis strategy" designed to seize resources for the poor and force policymakers to pass stronger antipoverty measures, activists mobilized the reserve pool of eligible claimants and flooded welfare agencies with their demands (Piven and Cloward 1975, 89–106). In doing so, activists demonstrated that the conversion of welfare eligibility into claims on government depends on a number of factors: the skills and resources available to potential applicants, social and administrative efforts to dissuade or encourage applicants, and, in all cases, individuals' decisions about whether to act on their eligibility.

This chapter explores the subjective considerations that shape decisions to claim welfare benefits and, in so doing, illuminates the political significance of this act for claimants. Like other forms of political action, welfare claiming has both instrumental and expressive dimensions (Edelman 1964, chap. 1). That is, to understand why eligible people do or do not claim benefits, one must know, first, what these demands on government accomplish and, second, what they mean for individuals in particular social settings. The instrumental and expressive dimensions of welfare claiming have received little attention in traditional welfare research, which has tended to focus instead on the social and economic correlates of program usage (Bane and Ellwood 1994; Gottschalk, McLanahan, and Sandefur 1994; Handler and Hasenfeld 1997, 42–53). As a result, little is known about the subjective considerations (the reasons) that motivate individuals to pursue or forgo their entitlement. Existing research provides a detailed portrait of the characteristics of claimants and their environments but offers almost no insight into how decisions about whether to claim benefits are made (Nelson 1980, 178).

People who are eligible for welfare benefits confront a dilemma of action. To gain access to welfare resources, they must enter a relationship with government that, to varying degrees, may appear repellent. However, if they forgo their welfare entitlement, they run the risk of being unable to meet basic needs and of being forced to depend on alternative relationships that may carry their own objectionable terms. By studying the ways in which individuals perceive and resolve this dilemma, it is possible to gain insight into two important political questions.

First, given the clear material incentives for claiming welfare benefits, why do so many eligible people fail to make it to the agency doorway (Nelson 1980)? There is a well-known puzzle in political action research that is often termed the paradox of participation or the problem of rational abstention. Because the personal costs of participation are generally so much larger and more immediate than the personal benefits, it seems difficult to explain why "rational" citizens engage in political action at all (Downs 1957; Ferejohn and Fiorina 1974; Jackman 1993; Riker and Ordeshook 1968; Rosenstone and Hansen 1993). This paradox is turned on its head in the welfare context. Claims on welfare agencies allow citizens to gain benefits that are direct and tangible, yet eligible people frequently do not step forward. In the AFDC program, for example, about 72 percent of the spells in which individuals are eligible for benefits do not produce demands (Blank and Ruggles 1993, 37). As Robert Moffitt notes, this failure to claim individualized benefits violates "perhaps the most basic assumption of the economic theory of consumer demand . . . that more is better than less" (1983, 1023). From a political standpoint, the significance of this seemingly irrational pattern is deepened by the fact that it varies across the two tiers of the welfare system: eligible people fail to claim benefits far more frequently in public assistance programs than in social insurance programs (van Oorschot 1991).

The applicant's dilemma of action also holds clues to a second important question. As a mode of political action, what are the functions and uses of welfare claiming for the individual? Given that so many eligibility spells do not produce demands, one must ask what attraction welfare claiming holds for those who press their claims. In most research on welfare usage, the answer to this question is treated as no mystery at all. Cash benefits are understood essentially as ends in themselves, sought, presumably, as a financial support that supplies individuals with basic material goods.[1] By contrast, to treat welfare claiming as a form of political action is to ask how this act may serve as a means to achieve broader ends. Students of electoral behavior, for example, do not assume that the act of voting is an end in itself. Rather, they ask what individuals are trying to prevent or achieve when they cast their ballots, what the act of voting symbolizes to those who do it, and how voters imagine (rightly or wrongly) that their actions might benefit them or some group they care about. To understand why citizens make demands on welfare bureaucracies, one must ask similar questions about the instrumental and expressive functions of welfare claiming.

The analysis that follows presents welfare claiming as a purposive activity pursued by socially encumbered individuals who confront a limited range of options. On one side, this analysis suggests that welfare participation is not simply the free choice of an unencumbered individual, as is often suggested by economic models of welfare usage (Hutchens 1981; Moffitt 1983) and by conservative critics of welfare provision (Gilder 1981; Mead 1992; Murray 1984). Individualistic images of detached moral agents who maximize utility across "net income-leisure constraints" (Hutchens 1981, 219) distort and oversimplify clients' decision-making processes, obscuring some of the most important social, symbolic, and political aspects of welfare claiming. Welfare-claiming decisions cannot be adequately understood without confronting the factors that, in the applicant's eyes, compel a claim for benefits. Applicants arrive at the agency, in part, because they feel driven to do so by vulnerability, deprivation, obligation, and a shrinking range of options. In every interview except two, the clients I interviewed echoed Kisha, an AFDC recipient who recalled, "It was the only thing. It was the only thing. I had no other choice."[2]

On the other side, however, welfare claiming is equally distorted by those who emphasize structural constraints to such a degree that they blot out individual agency. In this view, welfare applicants appear to be little more than the passive and innocent losers of an economic game of musical chairs (Rank 1994). Buffeted by forces beyond their control, they are presumed to be "nonvoluntary; . . . their participation in the welfare system is hardly voluntary if they have no income alternatives" (Lipsky 1980, 54). The fact that so many eligible people do not file applications for benefits should suggest that there is something incomplete about these deterministic images of welfare claiming. Indeed, the women and men I interviewed believed that they confronted and made important decisions. They described the alternatives available to them when they initially applied; they explained why they had avoided or delayed making claims in the past and why they eventually decided to turn to government. Likewise, the eligible people I met at the shelter and at disability support groups frequently described confronting a difficult choice. By ignoring these decisions, deterministic images of welfare claiming forestall inquiry into the reasons why citizens act on their program eligibility. Determinism obscures welfare claiming's instrumental functions, its role within clients' efforts to fulfill immediate obligations and achieve long-term goals.

My goal in this chapter is not to determine the ultimate causes of welfare usage or the degree to which the individual or society is responsible for welfare participation. Rather, my goal reflects a more interpretive approach to social science. Assuming that actions make some kind of sense to the actors involved, I try to develop a more coherent understanding of the circumstances and beliefs that lead sensible people to claim or forgo welfare benefits (see Becker 1998, 24–28). The paths that applicants follow to the agency doorway inevitably include distinctive elements that reflect the unique features of their lives. The considerations that make applicants hesitate or push forward along these paths, however, share quite a bit in common.

To develop a general framework for understanding claiming decisions, this chapter organizes the applicant's dilemmas into three broad categories: (1) power and dependence, (2) identity and obligation, and (3) economic security. Each of these dimensions identifies important functions of welfare claiming for the individual, each suggests reasons why eligible people may resist or accept making a claim on government, and each points toward factors that may help to explain why rates of welfare claiming are higher in social insurance programs than in public assistance programs.

The empirical analysis that follows also provides an opportunity to flesh out insights drawn from theories of social citizenship and social control. As described in chapter 1, social citizenship theory suggests the potential for welfare provision to bolster the status and autonomy of citizens and to enhance their abilities to fulfill their obligations as community members (Marshall 1964). Social control theory suggests that welfare benefits may function to protect citizens from coercion in social and economic relations; but welfare institutions may pose a countervailing threat of social control and degradation (Abramovitz 1988; Piven and Cloward 1993). Through an analysis of clients' welfare-claiming decisions, it is possible to assess how demands on each tier of the U.S. welfare system reflect and fulfill these potentials. Although outsiders may be more likely to see welfare claiming simply as a financial plea for help, applicants' accounts reveal an underlying foundation of social and political motives: the struggle to escape vulnerability and achieve autonomy,[3] to maintain respectability and fulfill obligations to others, and to meet immediate needs while holding onto long-term aspirations.

Power and Dependence

Like other state institutions, the welfare system can protect citizens against people or circumstances that might threaten their autonomy, but the system equally can infringe on this autonomy and subjugate the individual. Of these two possibilities, the second often seems to receive more attention in American politics. On the right, critics cast the welfare state as a threat to individual liberty (Murray 1984) and portray welfare participation as the ultimate form of dependence (Mead 1992). Liberals tend to offer a pale echo of these concerns, worrying that there is something "intrinsically authoritarian or, to use a less loaded but rather horrible word, paternalistic" about welfare policy decisions (Marshall 1972, 20) On the left, observers have emphasized the welfare system's disciplinary potential and street-level bureaucrats' discretionary power over clients (Abramovitz 1988; Handler 1992; Hasenfeld 1987; Lipsky 1980; Piven and Cloward 1993).

In deciding whether to file a welfare application, people who are eligible for welfare benefits tend to be acutely aware that program participation will carry them into an unusually direct and personal relationship with government. The nature of power in client relationships serves as a major consideration shaping individuals' decisions about whether to claim benefits. But while concerns about client autonomy affect claiming decisions in both tiers of the welfare system, there are important differences between the SSDI and AFDC programs. While SSDI claimants tend to report a vague sense of anxiety about getting tangled up with government, people who apply to AFDC elaborate much more specific concerns about the scope and degree of agency power. In addition, SSDI applicants who are more familiar with the program tend to be slightly less concerned about the state's potential to infringe on their autonomy. By contrast, program familiarity tends to fuel anxiety among AFDC claimants.

Unlike SSDI, the AFDC program's design requires clients to enter individual casework relationships. Although these relationships can offer an important source of personalized assistance, they have also historically served as mechanisms for surveillance and discipline aimed at the economic, parental, and sexual behaviors of clients (Abramovitz 1988; Gordon 1994). Many applicants know about this feature of the program through their own childhood experiences or through stories told in their neighborhood. Josephine, for example, feared for her privacy when she applied to AFDC because "they used to send surprise workers out to check up. When I was younger, they used to do that to my aunt." Nancy initially resisted acting on her eligibility for similar reasons: "My family was on welfare as a child, and I remember running to hide the telephone and the iron because the welfare lady was coming. So I grew up knowing that poor people didn't get treated right."

In addition to fearing that they will be scrutinized by the watchful eye of the agency, AFDC applicants also tend to worry that welfare personnel and regulations will strip them of their ability to direct their own lives. Waiting in line to get application forms, for example, Sandra got a warning about social control in welfare programs from the woman standing next to her:

> "It's like you apply for AFDC and you're owned by them. They own you now." That's what one of the girls in line told me when I went to apply. She told me, "Once you apply, girl, they're going to *own* you." I said, "Why would they want to own *me?* [laughs] And it's not like they're paying for me." She said, "Well, no, with their taxes and stuff, they're taking care of you." [And I said,] "Well, I understand that. But it's not like I have to jump whenever they offer." But when she said that, it really scared me. Because it meant that if they called me up, I'd have to jump and go to them.

If they sent me here, I had to go whether I liked it or not. She made it sound like "You're in their hands now," like I was born to them.

While AFDC applicants tend to have more intense and specific fears about autonomy in relation to the welfare state, some SSDI claimants also report being concerned about state power. For SSDI claimants, however, these concerns tend to manifest themselves as a vague and general sense of apprehension about "big government." Marie explained, "Anytime you bring government in, I'm afraid. . . . I guess it's maybe because when I was coming up we had this Big Brother thing. [laughs] And that has stuck in my mind, that the government is there with their thumb over you and that sort of thing."

Concerns over the bureaucracy's capacities for surveillance and discipline, and the greater intensity of these concerns in the public assistance tier of the welfare system, both were well illustrated in my interview with Kitty. As a poor divorced parent with a disability, Kitty was eligible for both AFDC and SSDI. After dismissing the possibility of taking her ex-husband to court, Kitty's decision between the two programs turned on issues of privacy and autonomy.

I assumed, and correctly, that I didn't have to deal with a worker as much in SSD[I]. There wouldn't be the imposition in my privacy. They wouldn't be in my face constantly with "What were you doing? Why were you doing it?" I don't have the kind of personality that would work well with AFDC. I'm extremely assertive.

One important side of the political dilemma for applicants, then, is defined by the potential for welfare participation to leave them vulnerable to state surveillance and control. For claimants, however, the potentially harsh terms of welfare receipt must be measured against the conditions that will prevail if they forgo their entitlement. Poverty can produce its own threats to autonomy, both because of its direct debilitating effects on individuals and because of its potential to drive them into unequal and coercive relationships. To understand why applicants claim benefits despite their fears of government, one must take a close look at how poverty relates to power and dependence in everyday life.

Because AFDC has a means test that is set well below the poverty line (Edin and Lein 1997), clients typically experience severe deprivation prior to applying for benefits. Many recipients report experiencing a lack of food, an inability to use transportation, inadequate shelter or homelessness, and significant restrictions on time and energy. In addition to having physical consequences for individuals, these conditions also have important psychological effects. Clients' accounts of the periods leading up to their welfare applications include frequent references to distress, ranging from persistent concerns over making ends meet to more incapacitating bouts of depression and fear.

Because SSDI is not means-tested and hence does not require its applicants to be impoverished, one might assume that SSDI clients do not experience similar conditions prior to claiming benefits. People with disabilities, however, tend to be poorer than the population at large (Howards, Brehm, and Nagi 1980), and studies of client income suggest that social insurance benefits provide a modest standard of living for many who would otherwise live in poverty (Danziger and Weinberg 1994, 40–44). Clients' accounts underscore these observations. Even for middle-class people with disabilities, a loss of work frequently combines with the costs of health care to eat up life savings and drain familial support systems. Joe recalled, "I had one trip to the hospital, and the bill for the hospital alone (not the doctors, just the hospital!) was $22,000. I went broke. Oh, Jesus, about $27,000 we had collected from this [private insurance], every penny of it went to medical bills."

As social citizenship theory suggests, a lack of basic necessities such as food, shelter, and health care can strip individuals of the status and capacities they need to enjoy meaningful membership in their community. Darryl's story offers a striking example of how welfare claims provide individuals with a means to protect themselves against extreme forms of social and political marginality. When I met Darryl, his schizophrenia had been subdued by medication; he was maintaining his own apartment and holding down a part-time job. As he recounted how applying for SSDI gained him access to medical care and a modicum of financial security, he described his earlier periods of destitution and isolation.

I'd be walking the streets because I was homeless. And I would get hungry, and I didn't have cigarettes. So, I'd steal a pack of cigarettes and then go in a restaurant and order a meal. And I'd eat the meal, and then tell the manager, "I don't have any money. I can't pay for this meal." And then they'd lock me up in jail. So, without SSD[I], I would just go back and forth between the street and jail—staying on the street until I got hungry enough to not care about maybe going to jail.

For individuals who confront the extreme hardships associated with homelessness, welfare claiming can offer a path toward greater security, autonomy, and inclusion within the community. This function of welfare claiming, however, is hardly limited to the homeless. To meet their basic needs, people who experience poverty and/or disability frequently have to rely on others. As a result, they may find themselves in a precarious state of informal dependency. The people they depend on cannot always be counted on to serve as unfailing, benevolent, and sufficient assistants. Dependence can give rise to inequalities, support may come with strings attached, and the threat of destitution can trap individuals in coercive and even dangerous relationships. In this sense, it is a mistake to conceptualize welfare-claiming decisions as choices between dependence and autonomy: they are choices about whom and what to depend on.

The concept of independent living—living at home rather than under supervised institutional care—signifies a strongly held value in the disability community. Partly for this reason, many SSDI clients express dismay at arguments that equate program usage with dependence and contrast it with autonomy.[4] Along with many of her fellow SSDI clients, Bridget saw the preservation of independent living as a central goal of welfare claiming: "If I hadn't applied, I would have had to go to a nursing home when my savings ran out. SSDI allowed me to maintain my independent living situation. . . . I didn't want to be stuck in some nursing home depending on other people for everything."

In contrast to the independent living secured by claiming SSDI, many clients portray institutionalization as the alternative and worst possible outcome, the ultimate form of dependence and degradation (Edelman 1977, chap. 4; Goffman 1961). Merton explained, "It's humiliating to be in a nursing home. It's humiliating to be dependent on someone. That's why people need the programs, because otherwise they'd be dependent. They need some help so they can take care of themselves."

AFDC claimants, of course, rarely risk being placed in a nursing home, but they are equally likely to see welfare claiming as a means to escape or evade dependence on others. Prior to applying for benefits, women in AFDC frequently depend on friends, lovers, or family members for assistance. In many cases, these women find that the people who support them financially also expect to have authority over them. The most common coercive relationships involve men in the role of boyfriend or husband. Dependence on a male breadwinner entails a risk of abandonment that can silence women in decisions that affect their well-being. Lashell, for example, felt that depending on her boyfriend's income made her less than equal and left her vulnerable to abandonment. She continued to live with her boyfriend, but she sought AFDC over his objections because "even though he was working, I wanted my own income for me and my baby. . . . AFDC let me get my independence in my own financial situation."

More direct threats to autonomy and physical well-being arise in cases of domestic violence, an experience that is all too common among recipients (Bassuk, Browne, and Buckner 1996; Ehrenreich 1995; Raphael 1995, 1996). Abuse by a man was mentioned, even if only in passing, by almost half the women I interviewed in AFDC.[5]

As feminist theorists have argued, "gender-based violence is, among other things, a problem of democracy. . . . [P]rivate violence affects the community as a public body" (Sapiro 1993, 432, 445). Clients' accounts underscore this insight, demonstrating how private coercion enforces isolation and undermines the physical and psychological security needed to participate in the community.

At the same time, clients' stories also highlight the protective function of the welfare state and the defensive uses of welfare claiming. To women subjected to domestic violence, the threat of social control posed by the welfare agency appears negligible compared to the control exercised by an abuser. To put this unequal comparison in proper perspective, it is helpful to consider a longer excerpt from my interview with Hope.

Well, could you start by telling me what was going on for you at the time you decided to apply? How did you wind up going down there?

My ex-husband was into cocaine. And I heard from my mother and sister that he was using it. And he tried to throw me down the basement steps. And I figured me being pregnant, and having my son in my arms, while he was trying to throw me down the steps, there had to be something seriously wrong. So, I left him on my son's birthday. I packed up everything and left. And there was nothing else for me to do besides AFDC. I was pregnant, and my son was only a year old. First I tried to get a divorce, but they couldn't give me a divorce because I didn't have any funding and because I hadn't been here six months. I had been in [city name], Illinois for a year. So I came down here and went on AFDC. And it was embarrassing. It's not something I really wanted to do. And I was scared. I went down there by myself.

Would you have been able to leave that situation without AFDC?

It was the AFDC that allowed me to do that. Otherwise, I would have been stuck in an abusive situation. My husband wouldn't let me have toys for my son. I made toys out of old clothing and things my friends had—"Ooh, that looks furry. Can I have that?" I made blocks. And I cut tin and made it into a box. And I put a ball in there so that when he shook it, it rattled. That's what he had to play with. And I would watch the clock for when [my husband] would come home, because I had no phone. And as soon as I'd see him walking up, I'd take everything, all the toys, and hide them. All of his toys would flatten out because I made them out of cloth. I'd put them under the mattress.

He wouldn't let you have the toys you made for the kids?

No. "Toys aren't good for boys. They won't grow up to be men if you give them toys." That's what he would say. And if he found the kids with toys, he would beat me. I lost all of my teeth because of the toys. All of my teeth are dead. If the house wasn't spotless, which it almost always was, I'd get beat. I didn't know why he was acting the way he did. Maybe he had a bad day. So, I always made sure everything was just right. He didn't see [the toys]. Pots and pans also worked as toys. But then when [my son] got older, he started pulling out pots and pans on his own. And my husband explained to me that the only reason he's doing that is because he's playing with them during the day. What else are you supposed to keep a baby occupied with? They don't just lay there and sleep.

Clothes—I could not buy clothes for [my son]. He had rags for clothes. Whatever anybody gave me, I used. [My husband] bought nice, good clothes for himself, but I wasn't allowed to buy clothes for myself either. So I kept wearing pregnancy clothes. Anything he wanted, he got. It was very abusive. But I didn't care, up until the point where we had no food in the house. Everything we had, I had bought with a trust fund I had for $10,000.[6] So I bought the furniture. We had no TV. But I bought all the baby stuff. And the $10,000 didn't go far. I didn't know how to make money stretch back then. Things didn't improve much at all. But every time someone would say, "Hey, Hope, this is not the way things should go," I'd push myself back to the situation. I wanted my white house with a picket fence. It was going to work. I was going to prove everyone wrong. This wasn't happening. It wasn't an abusive situation. I wasn't going to let anyone believe it was. But it was.

Did you see it, at the time, as being abusive? Did you just want to hide it from them? Or did you not see it that way at all?

I started seeing it as that I was being selfish. I was maybe being overly— I couldn't recognize a lot of things. I always made an excuse for it. And I went by that excuse. It took me four years from the time I was married to my husband to the time I finally said, "Forget it. I'm getting a divorce." I gave him chances. . . . He raped me right after my daughter was born. And I told him, "This can't happen." That's the only way we could have sex, if it was rape. It couldn't be intimate or anything. I didn't even know what sex was until after I got a divorce from him. I was faithful all the way through. I didn't have any interest in sex anyway, because I was raped also as a child. It was the same thing. So I didn't know what anybody liked in sex. You're hurt; there's pain; you get bit; you get hit; you get beat. I can't see what people like about sex. When I finally left him . . . it was hard because the police would come over and say, "I only see red marks on you. I don't see any bruises. When there are bruises, then call me." I'm like, "Well, can I call you tomorrow? They'll be there tomorrow." "No, they have to be there the same day you call." Well, I don't bruise very easily. I don't get a bruise right away. The bruise comes the next day, or it will come on green. They told me that my husband had every right to be in the house because he was my husband. They told me that if I truly wanted to get rid of him, I would get a divorce.

Like victims of gender-based violence, younger women who have abusive parents or parents with drug and alcohol problems tend to use welfare claiming as a way to obtain greater social autonomy, physical security, and psychological stability. Describing her trip to the welfare agency as a decision to leave her alcoholic and violent mother, Renee recalled, "I didn't want us to have all the family problems and abuse. I wanted to have a safe place for my daughter. I knew if I had my own money, I could make a safe home for her. I did *not* have a safe one at the time."

Even in situations far more benign than the ones endured by clients such as Hope and Renee, welfare benefits offer individuals an alternative to dependence on significant others who may prove unreliable or turn resentful. For applicants, one great advantage of the "impersonal" welfare state is that it can provide relief without making them feel beholden or guilty in their closest personal relationships—without positioning them as vulnerable supplicants in their daily lives. Cheryl, for example, explained that she saw AFDC as the only way to avoid imposing on and becoming dependent on her mother. In this sense, "AFDC was more independent than the other options I had. I don't really know how to say it. My mom's a people. They're not a people, they're an agency. My mom's not an agency. So, can you see where I would feel different there?"

Clients in both SSDI and AFDC echoed Cheryl's desire to avoid feeling indebted to and reliant on family members. Phil, for example, saw SSDI as the only way to spare his parents heavy financial burdens and to achieve the degree of independence from his parents that he expected as an adult.

There was no way my dad could afford to support me. I didn't want to move back home. I was living on my own. I didn't want to be cared for. I wanted to remain independent. And so I felt very funneled into one way— I mean, there was only one way you could really go. And I'm sure a lot of other people feel that way too. . . . I didn't hate the family. I didn't want to get away from the family. But I wanted to be independent. And [SSDI] let me do that. It did let me go live on my own, rent on my own with roommates.

In sum, the first dimension of applicant decision making concerns issues of power and dependence. This dimension not only helps to explain demands on welfare programs but also points toward the deeper political significance of welfare claiming. To be full, equal, and engaged members of a political community, citizens need to have some degree of autonomy and security. Extremes of dependence and vulnerability threaten individuals' abilities to direct their own lives and participate in their community's collective political life. For applicants, particularly those channeled into public assistance programs, the welfare state can appear to be a significant threat to autonomy. In deciding whether to claim benefits, individuals must weigh the possibility that their dependence on the state will turn them into objects of surveillance and discipline. For some people who are eligible for benefits, this threat to autonomy may serve as a significant deterrent to welfare claiming.

Poverty, however, poses its own threats to autonomy and security. Poverty can be physically and psychologically debilitating, and it can force individuals into a vulnerable state of dependence on others. Welfare claiming provides citizens with resources that can be deployed against these threats. In so doing, it offers citizens a way to secure the essential preconditions of social and political involvement. This political function of welfare claiming tends to get lost when observers focus too narrowly on welfare receipt as a form of dependence and on the welfare state as an agent of social control (Fraser and Gordon 1994; Gordon 1988, 1990). Compared to Darryl's life on the streets or Hope's life with her abusive husband, the welfare state's social control seems considerably less oppressive.

For applicants, welfare claiming can raise fears of dependence and vulnerability in relation to the state, but it can also represent a path away from dependence and vulnerability in everyday life. In this sense, welfare applicants do not really face a choice between dependence and self-sufficiency. Instead, they must ask and answer a much more difficult question: "On whom, on what, can I depend?"

Identity and Obligation

The second dimension of claiming decisions revolves around questions of social identity and obligation. Here again, applicants confront a dilemma of considerable political significance. Just as citizens need to possess some amount of autonomy, they also must maintain a degree of respect in their community (Fraser and Gordon 1993; Pateman 1970). According to social citizenship theory, welfare systems offer individuals a source of protection against the isolation and indignity bred by poverty (Marshall 1964). By making demands on welfare programs, citizens can gain the resources they need to share in community life and fulfill the duties that are expected of them as community members. Social control theory, by contrast, suggests that welfare systems may function to degrade the status of those who do not work (Piven and Cloward 1993) or who violate social norms related to gender and the family (Gordon 1994; Mink 1998), turning them into a pariah class.

Taken together, these theories point to the two sides of the applicant's dilemma of identity and obligation. On one side, poverty serves to stigmatize the poor. Research consistently shows that Americans tend to associate poverty with personal deficiency and failure and to hold the poor in low esteem (Feagin 1972; Hochschild 1995; Kluegel and Smith 1986). Moreover, poverty can leave individuals unable to fulfill social responsibilities that are essential for social dignity and positive feelings of self-worth. Welfare claiming offers a way to relieve at least some of this threat to identity, but it can also be a source of stigma in its own right (Goodban 1985). For some, welfare receipt may be seen as the ultimate form of humiliation, irrefutable evidence of personal inadequacy. Balancing these two threats to identity, applicants tend to experience welfare-claiming decisions as an emotionally difficult referendum on self-worth (Nelson 1980).

In deciding whether to file a welfare claim, applicants typically pay a great deal of attention to how this act may be judged, both by "general others" (the public at large, strangers, acquaintances) and by "significant others" (friends, family members, lovers, spouses). As a result, claiming decisions tend to reflect prevailing climates of opinion. Public opinion toward welfare receipt in the United States varies across the two tiers of the welfare system. While social insurance programs enjoy a considerable amount of public support, public assistance programs and their recipients tend to elicit far greater hostility (Gilens 1999; Kluegel and Smith 1986; Page and Shapiro 1992; Shapiro and Young 1989).

Not surprisingly, clients who applied to SSDI were less likely to recall having fears about how people in general would react to their new status than were clients who applied to AFDC. In fact, when it comes to the reactions of general others, SSDI applicants usually worry less about program participation than about the stigma associated with their disability (on disability stigma, see Fox 1996; Livneh 1988; Yuker 1988). As Marie explained, "There's a stigma in society toward disability, but not for [SSDI]." Katrina was typical of SSDI applicants in recalling, "I think I had more fears about my disability [multiple sclerosis (MS)] and how people would react to me as a handicapped person. . . . I didn't think anything of the program." People who filed AFDC claims were far more likely than their counterparts in SSDI to worry that general others would look down on them. Sandra recalled,

I was afraid. And even now—they give you food stamps, and then you walk into the store and you're in line, and the people with checks all look at you like "What are you doing with food stamps?" They look at you like "You're in good health. Why don't you go out and work?" . . . I guess when I applied I was worried about how people would talk about me, and I still feel like they do.

For black applicants, concerns about the judgments of others tend to take on an especially intense and racialized form. Race is a major factor shaping public attitudes toward welfare programs and popular perceptions of welfare recipients in the United States (Gilens 1999; Kinder and Sanders 1996). Single black mothers play an especially prominent role in popular images of the dependent welfare "queen" (Fraser and Gordon 1994; Lubiano 1992). It should not be surprising, then, that race also shapes the way applicants view their welfare claims. Betty, a white woman who applied for SSDI with her African American husband, Tom, argued that regardless of what kinds of benefits an individual claims, "race is the big issue affecting how it's viewed. For black people there is more of a connection with welfare. . . . [White people think,] 'I worked for my money. And those people, those niggers, never worked a day in their lives.'" Explaining why she had reservations about claiming AFDC, Alissa commented, "I think that the fact that I am black allowed people to say 'OK, another black woman with all these children on welfare.' . . . I knew they would look at me as another stupid little black girl with all these kids."

In addition to being concerned about how people in general will react, applicants tend to worry about the judgments of significant others. The intensity of their anxiety, however, tends to depend on their social background. People whose social circle has included very few welfare recipients are the most likely to resist applying for benefits because of a fear that significant others will look down on them. In recounting her experience applying for AFDC, for example, Tina noted, "I was worried about what my family would think. I was the first one. My cousin's on it now, but I was the first one who actually applied for it. And I thought my family was going to look at me like I was a disgrace to the family or a lowlife or something." Likewise, Dizzy, a former athlete and tavern owner who applied to SSDI after developing MS, feared that his friends might think he was trying to "scam the system." He recalled, "I first hurt my back in 1974. I hurt it bad. My friends used to say, 'You're faking,' and all that. So I was concerned when I applied to SSDI that they might be thinking the same thing, even though I have all the medical records to substantiate it."

In many cases, eligible people are hesitant to apply for welfare less because of what others might think and more because of how their own beliefs about welfare clash with the images they hold of themselves. For those who come from poor backgrounds, for example, the act of filing for benefits often represents a symbolic defeat—the fulfillment of a destiny they had always assumed, or at least hoped, they would escape. When Josephine began to consider claiming AFDC, for example, she expected her neighbors to see it as "no big deal." Still, she recalled feeling "very disappointed because I thought I'd be further [toward my goals] than I was then. And I was saying to myself when I was growing up, 'I'll never get on this. I never will.' And then I ended up on it."

Relative to their counterparts in AFDC, SSDI clients are less likely to have known welfare recipients in the past. As a result, they are more likely to view their own application for benefits as an uncommon and shocking turn of events. Some recalled that they had always assumed there was a great moral distance between themselves and the "kinds of people who live off welfare checks." As they considered filing for SSDI, these applicants tended to feel a sense of moral failure. Phil managed a fast-food restaurant before he experienced loss of vision, a serious foot infection, and kidney failure, all within one year. Even with all these hardships, Phil initially decided not to act on his eligibility because he felt that receiving welfare would be too much of a blow to his self-esteem.

> I thoroughly resisted applying for SSI or SSDI or any of the social-welfare programs because I didn't feel right about that. . . . I was brought up in a typical working-class household, and everybody worked for a living. And social-welfare programs were kind of like a taboo. Only people who wanted to steal the system blind were on social-welfare programs. That was the stigma I grew up with from my family. I came from a family of eight kids. We all started working at age fifteen or sixteen and contributed to the family. And Dad worked hard forty plus hours a week. And Mom was a full-time homemaker with eight kids. So the work ethic was very strong. And so to change that to a life of welfare where you just sat at home and collected money was very—was not real tasteful at that time. . . . [My dad] taught his children that you work as hard as you can at what you do. And if you can't work as hard as you can at what you do, then you have to find something else to do. But you can't sit back and accept money for nothing. So there was that whole issue there . . . my own self esteem for having to rely on a social program.

Relative to women in SSDI, men tended to view their inability to provide for their families through employment as a more profound and personal failure. This pattern largely reflects the persistence of gendered expectations regarding the breadwinning role in American society (Basow 1992, 253–55; Gordon 1994). As Emerald explained, "the old-fashioned attitude about making your way says it's OK to be at home waiting on my husband's money, but it's not to sit at home waiting on the government's money." By contrast, men in SSDI felt that to be a father, to be a "normal" man, they needed to be a wage earner. Betty and her husband, Tom, originally applied to SSDI together after doctors told Tom that the factory carbon in his lungs would kill him within a year if he did not quit his job. Betty recalled her late husband's resistance to applying for benefits.

> It was a terrible process for him getting on it. It insulted his manhood or whatever. My husband's family had been on AFDC. And he was not go-

ing to take any form of handout at all unless he had earned it and put it towards retirement. It was very hard for him all through our married life because he had only worked four or five years of our married life. It was difficult for him, having to accept a handout. He wanted to support his family and be more normal like other men.

In addition to signifying a personal failure, welfare claiming is also viewed by many applicants as a rite of passage into a new and unwanted social group. In the AFDC program, applying for benefits means becoming a "welfare mother." Penny summed up this transition when she observed, "You can say, 'these people, these people' all you want to. [But once you apply] you can't exactly separate yourself on that because now you are one of 'these people.'" To the clients I interviewed, becoming an AFDC recipient meant taking on a group label tainted with a diversity of negative stereotypes: laziness and a failure to embrace the work ethic, sexual and reproductive irresponsibility, neglectful or abusive parenting, drug and alcohol addiction, television addiction, exploitation of welfare policies, susceptibility to manipulation by men, ignorance and stupidity, overeating and obesity, a lack of cleanliness, and criminal or violent behavior.

SSDI applicants also tend to view their welfare claiming as an act that confers new and life-defining group labels. As Emerald put it, "It's like you're in the high, medium, and low reading groups in elementary school—the fish, frogs, and whatever. The kids know what reading group they're in." Because the best-known Social Security program is old-age insurance, for example, even young SSDI applicants sometimes complain that applying for benefits made them feel old. Similarly, because SSDI applicants must prove their disability status to obtain benefits, successful claimants tend to feel that they are being stamped with the label "long-term disabled." To Molly, Social Security meant being old and incapacitated, two adjectives she had never associated with herself.

I'm talking to somebody about Social Security. In my head, it was a thing for older folks. "I'm still able to walk from point A to point B. It may not be a straight gait, but I can do it. Why are they saying I should get this?" So, it was a little depressing and a little humbling to realize that they wanted to give me something because of what I had. It was depressing because it felt like I was being put in some category.

To fully appreciate the rite-of-passage quality of welfare claiming, it is helpful to consider an account that is extreme rather than representative. When Starr found that physical limitations kept her from working, she chose to act on her eligibility for SSDI rather than AFDC, in part because only SSDI explicitly acknowledged her disability: "Somehow it brought some clarity in my health status." When the agency deemed Starr to be long-term disabled, however, she was thrown into an emotional crisis. After finding a notice of acceptance and government checks in her mailbox, she called the agency in disbelief.

> Well, I got off the phone, and I just really couldn't believe that they had decided I was really disabled. It was like I never realized before those checks and that phone call that they decided I'm not going back to work. How could they decide that for me? . . . I launched into depression in my mind. I was so angry at the system for determining that my disease (I had both cancer and MS) was so bad that they were going to give me checks every month no matter where I was. . . . I can't tell you how depressed I was. And at 5:30 that night, I attempted suicide. And I came real close to succeeding. Do I blame it on Social Security? No. But it was a trigger. It was the reality that "You're on Social Security Disability [Insurance]." It's a comfort in some ways to not be on it. If you're on [AFDC], you can see it as temporary. They check you monthly. Now, she told me when I called, they probably won't reassess my account for three or four years. I am "long-term disabled." It's like it's time to give up on me. My options are zero. It's like they know something I don't know about this disease or my situation. . . . That label, that thought that I was permanently going to be disabled, it just threw me completely over.

In all these respects, concerns about social identity help to explain why many eligible people resist pursuing their welfare entitlements. On the other side of the applicants' dilemma, however, social identity plays an equally essential role in explaining why clients actively pursue their welfare entitlements.

First, whatever indignities it may entail, welfare participation offers a way to avoid fates that applicants may find more humiliating. Some of these circumstances involve dependence and have already been discussed: institutionalization, homelessness, victimization in domestic abuse, relying on handouts from family and friends. Others provide a more independent source of income but do so in a way that strikes applicants as morally unacceptable. As Kristen Renwick Monroe (1994, 222) points out, "if an option violates a person's sense of self, it is not considered a viable option." Renee, a part-time student, explained that she participated in AFDC because, to her, the alternatives were not acceptable:

> I feel like I don't have a lot of choices. It's either this or that for me. [My only option is that] I can find some way of drug dealing and risk going to jail or sell my body and risk going to jail, doing anything I can do to pay my way to go through school and get day care. So, I feel stuck. I feel trapped. I feel like I don't have a lot of choices.

Second and more importantly, identity is an important motivation for welfare claiming because social roles imply obligations to others (Rosenberg 1990). Resources gained by making demands on welfare programs allow people to fulfill duties to others that they view as essential for respectability. Here, one finds two important functions of welfare claiming intertwined with one another. Welfare benefits allow individuals to meet social obligations in everyday life; by meeting these obligations, clients simultaneously protect themselves against degraded status and diminished self-esteem.

Among AFDC clients, motherhood is typically the social role that generates the most highly valued obligations. Women in AFDC make frequent references to motherhood as a central and valuable element of their sense of self. Almost without exception, the women I interviewed argued that a good mother must do whatever is necessary to provide and care for her children, including swallowing her pride and accepting the indignity of welfare.[7] Nancy, a former military surgical technician who could not find work in her field, felt humiliated by her need for welfare but explained, "All I knew was that I was going to be able to feed my son and clothe my son." Cheryl provided a representative example of how a sense of maternal obligation tends to promote welfare claiming by overriding feelings of shame and guilt.

To have to go down [to the welfare agency] was really scary, but I did it because I had to do it. I knew those kids had to eat. And I knew they had to have clothes. And I knew they had to have food. It was scary for me. It made me feel bad that I have to take taxpayers' money to support my kids. But if I can't support my kids on my own because I don't have an education, I'm going to have to have some help to do it. How are these kids going to eat? Where am I going to live? And that's what AFDC did for me. They gave me a place to live and food and medical insurance for when the kids get sick. Kids need shots, they need this, they need that. Basically, that's what AFDC did for me.

The obligation to care for children promotes welfare claims, not only because it is valued by applicants but also because it is viewed by significant others as a legitimate justification for seeking government assistance. In this manner, the meaning of welfare claiming for the individual and for the social group is transformed from an admission of failure into an expression of parental duty. Shelly, for example, was granted guardianship of her four grandchildren after her son-in-law sexually assaulted them. With this sudden change in family obligations, she could no longer make ends meet on her salary as a merchandiser. She explained her decision to claim benefits by saying,

[AFDC is] there to help me get help for my [grand]children. I don't want to see them starving. I don't want to see them in an abusive relationship like they were in. I don't want to see anyone touch them. . . . I talked to [a friend] about it. I talked to my daughter who had been on it. And I told them that I felt real guilty. And they told me I shouldn't feel guilty because I'm asking for help for the children.

Like women in AFDC, some men in SSDI also see welfare claiming as a means to provide for their children and as an expression of the value they place on their parental obligations. After Michael was laid off from a local factory, for example, he was only able to find a handful of low-wage job prospects. Living alone, he suspected he could have survived on the meager paychecks these jobs provided, but he could not have kept up his child support payments. He recalled, "I had to apply for SSDI because under that program, if you have a child, she will get a check, too, just like the person gets a check. So that's what caused me to get into Social Security. . . . The only reason I did it was because of my daughter. If I didn't have a daughter, I probably wouldn't have done it."

Parental duties are unique in some respects, but they illustrate a function of welfare claiming that takes on a variety of forms. Applicants differ in how broadly they define their social responsibilities. The web of obligations may be restricted to children, or it may stretch outward to include other family members, housemates, friends, or even the broader community. But in each case, welfare claiming provides applicants with a means to fulfill obligations that are important to them and, presumably, to others who might judge them.

Dizzy, for example, had always contributed his paychecks to a common income pool shared with other family members in his household. When his physical difficulties forced him to limit his working hours, it affected everyone in the family. Dizzy claimed SSDI in part because he felt it was his duty to continue contributing his fair share. Similar motives are cited by some women in AFDC who want to contribute income to the household they share with their boyfriend. Explaining why she filed her claim, Lashell commented, "I wanted to contribute to our family as much as [my boyfriend] was doing."

Beyond the household, family and extended kin relationships create a wider network of obligations (Stack 1974). In trying to meet these obligations, the official welfare applicant functions as a representative, asserting an individual claim that articulates the needs of a broader social group. Josephine, for example, did not expect to need AFDC. But when her mother became ill, she saw no choice but to take advantage of the fact that, as a poor woman with a child, she was eligible for program benefits that could be used to help out. Although Josephine's mother did not appear anywhere on her formal application, she was, in a sense, the true beneficiary of Josephine's claim.

I needed to help her medical expenses, so I went on [AFDC]. I was upset about it, and I wouldn't have planned on doing all this. . . . It wasn't much of a choice or much to think about. Who is going to pay for the medical bills? . . . What my mother was getting wasn't enough. And it was real hard, the rent, gas, and whatnot. So, it was pretty much a no-win situation. It wasn't like I was between a rock and a hard place. It was just a no-win situation. So, I had no choice but to sign on to AFDC.

In addition to giving assistance to others, welfare claims also allow individuals to participate in the reciprocal obligations of exchange relationships. By filing a welfare application, individuals gain access to resources they need to be contributing members of the extended kin networks that serve as core systems of social and economic organization in poor communities (Edin and Lein 1997; Stack 1974). In addition to providing an adaptive strategy for economic survival, participation in these networks is often seen as an essential element of adult community membership. Shelly, for example, saw cooperation in such a network as a critical part of daily life in her neighborhood.

You have to barter. That's the way I do things. You have to help each other to survive on AFDC. . . . I can't sew. I have a friend who sews, but she can't bake. So, I'll take all kinds of mending over to her house so I don't have to buy new stuff; and then I'll bake her a cake so she doesn't have to buy one on a birthday. She's Mexican. She can make a better enchilada than I can, but I can cook American food different than she'd cook it. So we exchange food. And that's the way the world is becoming more and more.

Active participation in social networks requires both material resources and time. Welfare participation functions to meet both these prerequisites. It supplies individuals with income that is often comparable to low-wage work (Edin and Lein 1997) while providing them with time needed for unpaid work in their families and communities. Lynn, for example, contributed volunteer work to a social-welfare organization, and because she lived in a high-crime neighborhood, she took on the responsibility of watching over her and her neighbors' children when they returned from school. She went on to point out,

I'm a stay-at-home mom who drives. That's a rare find. I'm on every kid I know's emergency contact for school. If I were in the workforce too, a lot of these moms would end up losing their jobs. . . . There have to be some mothers in the neighborhood who are going to do this, or none of the mothers, even the ones who want to work, are going to be able to work.

The use of welfare claiming to fulfill social obligations is anchored at one end by its most common and highly valued form, the duty to care for close relatives, especially children. At the other end of this continuum, however, there is a small but important group of individuals who define their obligations much more broadly and see in welfare participation an opportunity to contribute to the overall quality of life in their community. J, for example, explained that she stayed in SSDI rather than seeking a job because the welfare benefits permitted her to volunteer her time as a psychological counselor at a free center for social services. Similarly, Starr donated her time to local schools and to organizations serving people with disabilities.

> It's ironic. I think a lot of people in welfare programs or with disabilities contribute a lot to society. I guess I made a decision for myself about fifteen years ago that I would stay as active in my community as I could. That was real important to me. I would say most of what I did at that time was either directly related to volunteering for something with the MS Society or with my kids' schools. There is always a need for some parent out there to come to the schools and help. There are so many two-party [two-parent] working families that those of us who can't work have to make a commitment to do those things.

In sum, the second dimension of welfare claiming concerns issues of social identity and obligation. The need to maintain a positive identity, in one's own eyes and in the eyes of others, adds to the applicants' dilemma in ways that help to explain why eligible people choose to pursue or forgo welfare benefits. The act of welfare claiming, especially in a public assistance program, can be mortifying. The degraded identity it conveys can effectively strip individuals of full and equal community membership. But poverty poses its own threats to an individual's social status. Equal dignity and self-respect cannot last long when an individual is unable to fulfill highly valued social duties. Work is one, but only one, such duty in the United States (Mead 1992, 1997a). However stigmatizing it may be, welfare claiming allows applicants to fulfill a variety of other obligations that are central to their self-esteem and social status. It allows them to make competent contributions to social relationships that they and others deem to be important. In this sense, one might say that citizens depend on the welfare system because they perceive that others depend on them.

Economic Security

For applicants, the economic dimension of welfare claiming is inseparable from the issues discussed in the two preceding sections. To maintain a degree of autonomy, enjoy social dignity and respect, and fulfill their obligations to others, individuals must establish a basic level of economic security. Unlike many

other types of political action, welfare claiming allows citizens to gain immediate access to essential resources such as food, shelter, and health care. In the
short term, applicants use these resources to meet pressing needs and to evade
threats to their well-being. For many applicants, welfare claiming also functions as part of a long-term strategy designed to lift themselves out of poverty.
In both of these respects, applicants tend to see welfare claiming as a path toward greater economic security—a path that can have distinct advantages over
alternatives such as low-wage employment or reliance on informal social support.

The economic value of welfare claiming, however, varies considerably
across the two tiers of the welfare system. Social insurance programs in the
United States, such as SSDI, offer relatively generous benefits that lift a large
percentage of their recipients above the poverty line (Danziger and Weinberg
1994). In comparison, public-assistance programs such as AFDC are much less
effective at combating poverty (Albelda and Tilly 1997). Because program benefits in AFDC are so meager, and because rules prevent the accumulation of assets or outside income, recipients tend to remain quite poor and usually have to
rely on informal assistance from others to make ends meet (Edin and Lein
1997). Given these objective differences between programs, it is not surprising
that people eligible for SSDI are more likely than their counterparts in AFDC
to expect welfare claiming to provide them with immediate economic security.

SSDI benefits are based on a percentage of prior wage deductions: all
SSDI clients make less than they did at work, but people who have made more
in the past receive more from the program. Among the clients in this study, reported monthly incomes from SSDI ranged from $543 to $1,900. Many clients
also earned additional income in part-time jobs or had spouses who served as
additional breadwinners. Clients who received lower payments understandably
were more likely to complain that the SSDI program is not generous enough.
Nevertheless, SSDI clients consistently reported that they expected program
benefits to serve as an effective path toward economic security at the time they
applied to the program.

As a means-tested program administered at the state level, AFDC benefits
vary from state to state and according to the applicant's family size, assets, and
income. On average, AFDC benefits are typically lower than SSDI benefits and
are reduced further if clients report to the agency any wages, gifts, or child support payments. The AFDC clients in this study received monthly benefits that
ranged from $440 to $800. These clients also received food stamps, and many
had unreported income from employment or significant others. Unlike their
counterparts in SSDI, AFDC clients rarely expected welfare claiming to lift
them out of poverty at the time they applied. Based on their own experiences
or conversations with significant others, applicants usually knew that AFDC
benefits would not be high enough for them to make ends meet. When Nancy

considered applying in the early 1990s, for example, she recalled her earlier experience receiving AFDC in a southern state during the 1980s. Her description suggests how little economic security AFDC benefits can provide in a low-benefit state.

> AFDC down there for a family of three was $185 per month. I couldn't even pay my rent. It was an apartment in a house. And it ended up that we had no heat, no water. The landlord didn't evict us because he wanted someone in the building because it had been set on fire before. So he didn't care if we lived there, but he wasn't going to give us any services. So I had kerosene heaters. We were living in one room. We went to my neighbor for water. We had a porta-potty. It was very difficult. We were this close to being on the street.

For applicants, the attractiveness of benefits from a welfare program is usually judged in relation to two income alternatives: wages from immediate employment and informal support from significant others. As an overview of this three-sided comparison and its relationship to issues described in the preceding sections, it is helpful to begin with a closer look at a single person's story.

Debber began to seriously consider applying for AFDC when her abusive husband tried to throw her and one of her children down a staircase. She explained, "I was with him for nine years. I couldn't take it anymore. You know the old saying, 'You never know how much enough is until you've had too much?' Well, that's what it was. When he threatened to take my life, me and the kids, I said 'You are not my husband no more.' And I took the kids and left." As soon as Debber left, however, she confronted the same economic dilemma that forces many women to go back to their abusers (Raphael 1995, 1996). Her husband's job had been providing the larger of their two incomes as well as health insurance for her and her children. Debber's job as a cook and cashier at a family restaurant paid only minimum wage, with no additional benefits.

In the following excerpt, Debber recounts her efforts to find a viable solution to her dilemma. Her account is representative of most claiming decisions in several respects. First, she weighs three types of options: employment, informal support, and welfare claiming. Second, she does not expect AFDC to offer a high level of economic security. Third, her search for a solution takes the form of a process of elimination: the AFDC program is the last candidate left standing. Fourth, her search has a tone of desperation and ends with a resigned acceptance of welfare claiming as a last resort: "I had no choice. [Claiming AFDC] was something I had to do for me and my kids to survive."

> I had a job; I was working. And when I left my husband, there was no way I could afford day care for my children. They were just babies, and I had

three of them. The oldest was in school, but I had two younger ones at home. And there was no way I could afford it making minimum wage. Plus rent and everything else, it was impossible. . . . I was in pieces. I knew welfare would only give me enough to make it, and it's a hell of a way to live. At the end of the month, you run out of food. You run out of soap. And you've got to borrow money just to make it. Even when you do get your check, a lot of it you've got to go buy food with because you don't get your food stamps until two weeks later after you get your check. It's terrible. . . . I talked about it with my mother and my auntie. They're not rich. They're middle-class people, just making it. And they couldn't help me out financially. . . . [AFDC] was my only path.

To understand the process of elimination described by Debber and other clients in both SSDI and AFDC, one must begin with the perceived limits of employment as a source of economic security. There are, of course, observers who argue that people who claim welfare benefits do so despite access to adequate work opportunities (Mead 1992). Recent poverty scholarship, however, points to a variety of ways in which low-wage jobs can keep workers poor and push people toward welfare programs (Edin and Lein 1997; Handler and Hasenfeld 1997; Newman 1999; Schwarz 1997; Solow 1998). Although interviews do not provide a basis for assessing work opportunities as an objective feature of claimants' environments, they do suggest that an adequate understanding of claiming decisions requires some appreciation of how the problem of work appears to applicants. People who apply to SSDI and AFDC are, in most cases, workers who see no way to meet their needs through their current jobs or through positions available in the labor market.

Among SSDI claimants, the most important barriers to achieving economic security through work arise as a direct result of physical limitations and health problems. Some applicants simply cannot work because they suffer from advanced disabilities. For others, however, health problems pose a barrier to employment primarily because available jobs do not appear to offer accessible work environments, adequate health coverage, or policies that allow for leaves during health crises.

People who need ongoing medical care tend to view jobs that do not offer medical benefits as essentially unworkable. And even when employers provide health plans, individuals sometimes find that their conditions are not covered. Holly, for example, applied to SSDI after her employer's new insurer excluded her MS from coverage as a preexisting condition.

At the time I went into the program, a medical insurance company wouldn't pick you up. My employer was changing insurance companies [and the new company] wasn't going to accept me because of a preexisting condition. And at that time, I was having a lot of CAT scans, MRIs, and expensive things. . . . I needed medical care, and I was getting stuck all over.

In addition to reasons associated with health coverage, SSDI applicants are also likely rule out the employment option because of disabling work environments. In some cases, applicants turn to SSDI when they find that their employers are unwilling to change procedures to accommodate employees with different abilities. Holly, for example, had more than just health insurance problems at the job. Her employer also refused to meet her visual needs by changing the color setting on her computer screen or to accommodate her limited mobility by letting her use the shipping and receiving elevator to get to her desk on the second floor. Taken together, these problems led Holly to claim welfare benefits despite her continuing ability to work. Similarly, Donna left her job as a reference librarian when her employer refused to accommodate her disabilities. Recognizing that she could either pursue a legal complaint or claim welfare benefits, Donna chose the less costly and faster course of action offered by government.

> It wasn't practical. Behind the reference counter, there were tons of desks. There wasn't any way you could get a scooter through without having major disruptions. And as far as going up the stairs to the upper part, there was no way. So, after talking with them, I either had the option of pursuing something about the ADA with the MS Society—and I didn't want to get into that hassle—or go strictly with the disability insurance.

Like their counterparts in SSDI, AFDC applicants also turn to government, in part, because they conclude that they cannot achieve economic security through work. The most basic problem is that most low-wage jobs do not pay enough to support an adult and one or more children (Albelda and Tilly 1997; Edin and Lein 1997). Minimum-wage jobs make up most of the employment prospects available to the people who claim AFDC benefits (Spalter-Roth and Hartmann 1994). In addition to failing to lift families above the poverty line, these jobs also impose additional costs on women relative to what they would spend as AFDC clients: transportation to and from work, child care, medical care, and work clothing, to name only a few (Edin and Lein 1997). Thus, to understand why claimants may be attracted to AFDC's subsistence-level benefits, one must begin with the meager wages available to the working poor (Handler and Hasenfeld 1997; Schwarz 1997).[8]

In addition to paying poverty wages, most jobs available to AFDC recipients lack health benefits. People who apply to AFDC are, by definition, parents with children. They generally need health care for themselves and see it as their responsibility to obtain it for their children. Many women turn to AFDC as a way to gain access to prenatal care during their pregnancies or pediatric care after their child is born. Tina, for example, had no health benefits in her job as a grocery cashier, and as her pregnancy advanced she found that her employer became less willing to give her a full schedule of shifts. When her son was born with health complications, she could not afford the basic costs of caring for him, let alone the costs of medical care or private health insurance. She recalled, "After I got him out [of the hospital], he was on a monitor. And it was about $2,000 a month just to have that monitor. . . . I didn't have health insurance. So that's what pushed me to go on AFDC. So, I went down and applied for that so I could get the medical."

Like people with disabilities who turn to SSDI, parents in AFDC also turn to government after concluding that available jobs do not offer features designed to meet their particular needs. Most minimum-wage employers do not provide accommodations for pregnancies, parental leaves of absence after childbirth, flexible hours needed to raise young children, or child-care facilities. The majority of recipients who try to balance work and parenting find that the costs of child care during work hours can eat up the bulk of minimum-wage earnings (Albelda and Tilly 1997). In addition, some applicants simply place a higher value on the unpaid work of parenting than on paid work in minimum-wage jobs; these women apply to AFDC, in part, because they consider it irresponsible to leave infants or young children with others for long stretches of time during the workday.

For women at the low end of the labor market, decisions about work and welfare can also raise questions of personal safety. Just as AFDC claims allow women to escape domestic violence, they also provide an alternative to jobs that might put these women at physical risk. Prior to claiming AFDC, for example, Lynn spent a year working as a live-in domestic worker and was assaulted repeatedly by her employer. "I was raped every day. It was a horrid, horrid thing. So I ended up trying to kill myself." Nancy's job required her to work alone throughout the night, a position she felt left her too open to physical assault: "I was working at a convenience store and gas station, a very difficult and dangerous job. I was working third shift. I was really starting to get scared about it. I had been robbed several times, had a gun put in my face, a knife in my face, been punched." By comparison, full-time parenting supported by AFDC benefits appeared to Nancy to be a safer and more sensible course of action.

In addition to these problems, some clients in both AFDC and SSDI believed that they had encountered discrimination on the job market. In describing their efforts to find work, clients frequently suggested that employers backed away once they found out about pregnancies, young children, disabilities, or welfare histories. These barriers, of course, would have added to any discrimination individuals might have encountered on the basis of gender, race, age, or sexual orientation. For all of these reasons, local job openings strike many applicants as an illusory or inadequate path to economic security.

The second source of income applicants considered was informal assistance from family members and friends. Most clients report that they relied on support from significant others prior to claiming benefits, and many continued to receive support after they became program participants. But while this informal assistance may help to make ends meet, it is simply not enough to make welfare claiming unnecessary (Edin and Lein 1997). For people in SSDI, health-care costs and normal monthly expenses typically add up to more than they and their significant others can absorb, even if they come from middle-class backgrounds. In some cases, medical bills alone devour an applicant's life savings and significant amounts of relatives' assets immediately after loss of employment.

Women in AFDC usually receive help from parents, siblings, friends, or the fathers of their children (Edin and Lein 1997). However, because poor women are more likely to come from poor families and poor neighborhoods (Beeghley 1989; Behrman and Taubman 1990; Massey and Denton 1993; Solon 1992), they are unlikely to have friends or family who can provide large amounts of support over an extended period of time. And even if significant others are able and willing to offer financial support, they do not have the means to provide health care. At best, then, support drawn from social networks offers poor women with children a way to supplement the income they can bring in from AFDC benefits and work (Edin and Lein 1997; Stack 1974). Support from significant others does not offer a viable path toward economic security in its own right and, as discussed earlier, it can leave women dependent on those who supply their means of survival.

Thus, in the immediate context of their welfare-claiming decisions, individuals tend to see two alternative paths of action, wage work and informal support, neither of which appears to offer an adequate source of security in its own right. Welfare claims provide applicants with either their only means of financial support or with a way to augment the meager income they receive through wages and informal assistance. This, in a nutshell, is the short-term economic logic of welfare-claiming decisions.

To adequately grasp the economic dimension of claiming decisions, however, one must also ask how welfare participation functions within applicants' long-term strategies for economic security. Although welfare claims are usually viewed by applicants as a stopgap measure needed to satisfy immediate needs, they also can represent a first step toward a more sustainable or, in some cases, ambitious strategy for economic security. In these long-term considerations, one can see clearly how the three dimensions of welfare claiming intersect. The application for welfare benefits functions as part of a broader effort to gain the security needed to avoid dependence and to fulfill obligations over the long haul.

Long-term strategies are psychologically important for applicants because they imbue welfare claiming with a more hopeful and morally acceptable meaning. Indeed, the reason why the label *long-term disability* leaves so many SSDI applicants feeling defeated is that it seems to suggest that welfare claiming is not a means to some future end. The phrase *long-term* makes welfare claiming seem like the end of the line. Marie recalled,

> I thought of [applying to SSDI] as that I would never have goals again. I wouldn't have the life that I had set goals for previously. That was all gone. And I would never have goals that I could set again. And that's the way I perceived it, like my life was ending.

Despite the frequency of these feelings, welfare claiming in SSDI does function for many clients as part of a long-term plan. The most common strategies can be grouped in three categories. First, there is the "income bundling" strategy. Unable to rely solely on work or informal support, SSDI applicants frequently hope to combine these two income sources with welfare benefits to form an overall package of resources. In fact, the eligibility rules for the SSDI program encourage applicants to consider this strategy, allowing them to bring in for an indefinite period some part-time wages and informal assistance without losing benefits. As a result, many SSDI applicants view program benefits as one element of a broader strategy for economic security over the long haul.

Second, SSDI claims may be advanced as part of a "holding pattern" strategy. For people who have marketable skills and strong job histories, eligibility for SSDI sometimes offers a way to wait out hard times while hoping for a more suitable job opening. J, for example, had a master's degree in social work and worked as a social worker until she began having what she called "scary thoughts" (for example, special messages in the newspaper intended only for her). After stabilizing her condition with medication, J could only find cashier positions in a grocery store and a secondhand clothing store. There seemed to be nothing in her field. In her own eyes, J was an unemployed social worker; she did not think of herself as a cashier and did not want to abandon the career she had chosen for herself. SSDI benefits allowed J to volunteer full time as a psychological counselor at a free clinic while searching for a paid social work position.

> There are a whole lot of low-paying jobs and only a few high-paying jobs. And in some ways, I'm overqualified to earn money in the jobs that are available. If I was a factory worker, I would know where to go right now. But I'm more of a computer person. There are few jobs that are both high paying and available. And in social services, my field, it's going from bad

to worse. So it's hard. I would rather have a job than do this. And I've been looking for a long time. But there aren't any jobs in my field.

Third, welfare claiming in SSDI is also pursued as part of a "stepping-stone" strategy. By relying on government aid, SSDI claimants are able to leave the labor market for a spell and return later with stronger job credentials. Francis, for example, saw his application to SSDI as a means to obtain both short-term and long-term independence. Program benefits not only allowed him to live on his own right away but also permitted him to pursue a college degree. Thus, while Francis looked down on welfare claiming as a form of dependence, he also recognized it as a short- and long-term path toward independence.

[I thought that welfare participation] would be a stepping stone to where I could be living my life of independence. . . . Eventually, I got a place on my own, and I got to go to school and get an education. I was living with my family; and I wanted to get into the program to get a place with room-mates and get an education and then eventually to get a job and place of my own. My goal still to this day is to not be dependent on any govern-ment money at all, to be self-supportive.

Because AFDC claimants rarely have had high-status jobs, they are less likely than their counterparts in SSDI to pursue a holding-pattern strategy. Instead, they are more likely to view AFDC participation as part of an income-bundling or stepping-stone strategy.

Partly because AFDC benefits are so low, most recipients cobble together a sustainable economic package out of government assistance, informal support, and either reported or unreported wages (Edin and Lein 1997; Spalter-Roth and Hartmann 1994; Stack 1974). Unlike SSDI, however, the AFDC program does not allow clients to earn income without losing benefits. As a result, most clients combine work and welfare either by concealing their wages or by cycling back and forth between stints of AFDC participation and work (Spalter-Roth and Hartmann 1994).

Some AFDC recipients work and voluntarily report their wages to the agency. This bundling strategy may strike some as irrational because, relative to taking AFDC and not working, it sacrifices time at home without producing a gain in income. But this appearance of irrationality only arises if one assumes, incorrectly, that AFDC clients view work and welfare purely as sources of income. A job, even a part-time job with low wages, holds a symbolic value for many women that cannot be captured in a dollar-for-dollar comparison with AFDC benefits. Work can bolster feelings of self-worth, offer a regular activity outside the household, and provide evidence to significant others that one does not fit the welfare stereotype. For women who value work in these ways, welfare benefits may be viewed as an income supplement—as a way to fill the gaps left by jobs that offer inadequate wages and no benefits.

Cheryl, for example, could not find a job that would pay adequate wages and give her enough time with her children. But she also did not want to give up work entirely in favor of welfare receipt and stay-at-home parenting. Even though she made no more income than she would have from AFDC alone, she combined AFDC and part-time employment so that she could pursue a more satisfying mix of activities: part-time work, an educational program, parenting, and volunteering at Head Start. She explained,

> I'm only working because I don't want to be on the couch. I don't want to be stagnant—not doing anything. So I go to school in the morning and raise my kids and work three or four days out of the week at the grocery store. But I have to pay child care for those four nights. And after day care is paid, my job gives me enough money to buy cigarettes. I work between fifteen and twenty hours a week and make enough money to buy a pack of cigarettes.

I found some of the most elaborate examples of bundling strategies among adult residents at the shelter for homeless families. Most families at the shelter survived on a mixture of wages, support from significant others, shelter services, government benefits, and community programs. Many residents worked sporadically in temporary jobs that offered low wages, no benefits, and little continuity of employment. By moving from shelter to shelter, they found beds for their children without incurring the unaffordable costs of an apartment and obtained some free child care from shelter staff during the workday. By claiming AFDC, they added health insurance and a more reliable source of income. Each element of the income bundle filled gaps left by the others.

Like their counterparts in SSDI, AFDC applicants also use welfare claiming as a path toward better jobs and greater economic security. To some applicants, welfare claiming is a form of investment in the future, part of a long-term strategy for escaping the dead-end world of low-wage employment. As Celina explained, "It was like a stepping stone for me. . . . I want to use it until I get through college. And then I'll be a taxpayer. And they can take it out of my check if they want to. I just wanted to be able to stay in school, get out on my own, and raise my child." This stepping-stone strategy has also been found in earlier research with AFDC clients. Kathryn Edin explains the process as follows:

> From their experience in the low-wage labor market, the unskilled and semi-skilled mothers in our sample absorbed two seminal lessons. . . . [T]he kinds of jobs they could get didn't make them any better off [and]

no matter how long they stayed at the job or how diligently they worked, jobs in this sector did not lead to better jobs later on. . . . [T]he women we interviewed had come to consider work in the "$5 an hour ghetto" as poor future planning. Respondents emphasized that they traded low-wage work for welfare as part of a strategy to achieve their long-term goal of economic self-sufficiency. (1995, 4, 7)

AFDC clients consistently describe education, rather than an entry-level job, as the best way out of poverty. But full-time work and parenting leave little time to invest in education. For some applicants, welfare claiming offers a way to be an attentive parent and a student.[9] Elizabeth, for example, hoped that a combination of welfare and school might lead her eventually to a better job and what she thought of as full personhood.

I worked for a time at [the] hospital, for about three to four years. I was a housekeeper, a position with no advancement. Or even if there was advancement, at that point in time I thought about my age and wasn't patient enough. And I also felt that education was a key to me one day obtaining a full circle, being a full person. I come from a family of people who have achieved those goals. Those were my aunties. So I always looked at those people, and I made the decision to go back to school. I believe it was in '89. I quit my job—I quit my job, knowing that I would have to go back on the welfare. But I always felt that was the way out that I had. Since the opportunity was there for me, I took it.

For Elizabeth and many other clients, welfare claiming expresses an unwillingness to accept a lifetime of alienating, poverty-wage work. In a society that prizes wealth and professional achievement as elements of the American Dream (Hochschild 1995), welfare claiming can be seen as a last-ditch effort to hold on to higher aspirations for a respectable and meaningful occupation. Renee, a young AFDC client and part-time student who hoped someday to become a psychologist, asked, "[Should you just] work yourself to death forever, for the rest of your life, on something stupid and meaningless?" Sandra was working part time in a grocery store and pursuing a high school diploma when the store was closed down for violating safety standards. In deciding whether to seek out another minimum-wage job or claim welfare, it seemed clear to Sandra that the former rather than the latter represented giving up.

They closed the store down, and what could I do? I was still going to school. What was I supposed to do, just give up and take a bad full-time job? I applied [for AFDC] mainly because I felt I had to continue in school and because I had to have something to live on while I was doing it. And since my brothers and sisters had all been scattered in foster homes, I had no family to turn to. The aid was my only survival.

Thus, the economic dimension of welfare claiming has both short- and long-term elements. Although work and informal support are often available to individuals as they make their claiming decisions, these income options frequently prove to be unreliable and inadequate. For many who apply to SSDI, especially those who have made higher wages in the past, welfare claiming provides a solid floor of economic security that keeps them out of poverty. As Dizzy put it, "At least now I get to live from month to month. I don't get to go out to eat or do anything fancy like that, . . . but that's OK." For AFDC applicants, the low level of public assistance benefits combines with low-wage jobs and low-resource social networks to create a less tractable predicament. As Renee lamented, "There's blockades here *and* there." Without a single income source that can offer a guarantee of economic security, many applicants recognize that they do not confront a set of mutually exclusive paths. Instead, welfare claiming, work, and informal support are resources that can be drawn on in a variety of ways to fulfill short-term needs and responsibilities while maintaining long-term aspirations.

Welfare Claiming: Functions and Dilemmas

The official forms that applicants fill out at welfare agencies suggest a simple portrait of welfare claiming. There is an individual listed as the primary beneficiary, and there are financial benefits supplied by government. Looking at these applications, it is easy to see the claimant as an individual economic actor and imagine the attraction that welfare benefits must hold as financial ends in themselves. Virtually nothing exists in the official record to suggest the broader social origins and deeper political significance of the citizen's demand on government.

A very different view of welfare claiming emerges from clients' accounts. From this standpoint, it is easier to recognize that formal demands on welfare agencies have deep roots in the informal social and political relations of everyday life. To understand why eligible people pursue or forgo their welfare entitlements, one must look to the functions and meanings of welfare claims within these day-to-day relationships. Here, it is possible to see the difficulty of the applicant's dilemma with greater clarity. As they struggle to achieve some autonomy and economic security in their daily lives, as they attempt to fulfill their obligations to others and maintain their self-respect and social dignity, eligible people confront a contradictory mixture of reasons to seek out and resist welfare participation.

In welfare-claiming decisions, sociological complexity gives rise to psychological ambivalence. For applicants, a welfare claim may be a symbolic admission of economic failure and an expression of hope for economic success. Claimants may resist welfare participation as a form of dependence but also see it as the best way to gain independence in their daily lives. They may fear the welfare state as an agent of surveillance and social control while embracing it as a haven from coercion or violence. Caught in a complex web of social expectations, applicants may see welfare claiming as a noble form of self-sacrifice and as a demeaning personal defeat.

By recognizing these dilemmas, it becomes easier to understand why, despite the financial incentives, eligible people may hesitate or fail to pursue the cash benefits offered by welfare programs. Similarly, if one attends to the functions of welfare claiming in everyday life, it does not seem strange at all that sensible people actively seek out the potentially stigmatizing and disciplinary "interventions" of the welfare state (Gordon 1990). Finally, in each of the three dimensions of welfare claiming, one can find important explanations for why a higher percentage of eligible people pursue welfare benefits in social insurance programs than in public assistance programs.

Relative to AFDC, the SSDI program offers a more complete realization of the goals identified by social citizenship theory. In both tiers of the welfare system, benefit claims offer a means for citizens to maintain their autonomy, social status, and economic security. But the AFDC program serves these functions in ways that are decidedly inferior to (and hence less attractive than) the SSDI program. In comparison to SSDI, the design of the AFDC program raises more concerns about privacy and autonomy. The stigma associated with AFDC participation also poses a greater threat to social status and feelings of self-worth. And critically, AFDC benefits are so low that they do not lift recipients out of poverty. That is, AFDC benefits do not fully relieve clients of the vulnerability that comes with dependence on significant others, the inability to meet important social obligations, and the ongoing struggle to cover the costs of basic necessities at the end of each month.

In addition to shedding light on individuals' decisions to make demands on welfare agencies, the analysis presented in this chapter also points toward important questions that must be asked when policymakers consider removing or cutting back welfare programs. In the absence of this government assistance, how will community members fill the income and benefit gaps left by low-wage jobs? How will they gain access to the training and education they need to pursue career aspirations and escape working poverty? Will single parents have access to scholarships and child care so that they can balance school and child rearing? What means of escape will be available to those who suffer domestic abuse? The list can go on, but in each case the point is the same: To responsibly debate changes in welfare policy (whether they involve program additions or subtractions), policymakers and citizens need know what welfare participation accomplishes and means for community members. This sort of knowledge requires looking beyond the correlates of program usage to ask clients about their reasons for turning to government.

The preceding analysis has identified a range of reasons why citizens might pursue or forgo welfare claiming. The origins of welfare claims can be traced to a complex mixture of social and political motives: the struggle to escape dependence and achieve autonomy, the desire to be respectable to and fulfill one's obligations to others, the necessity of meeting short-term needs, and the refusal to give up on long-term aspirations. Recognizing this diversity of motives does more than just allow for a more coherent understanding of welfare claiming. It recovers the agency of people who seek to mobilize their government's welfare institutions and allows us to recognize their claims as social and political actions.

CHAPTER 4

Welfare Claiming as Survival Politics

A political analysis of welfare claiming must explain not only why individuals make demands on public benefits but also how people win benefits from government. In the preceding chapter, I argued that welfare claiming serves important political functions for citizens. It provides them with a means to protect their autonomy and status, fulfill social expectations, meet short-term needs, and pursue long-term aspirations. To serve any of these purposes, however, welfare claims must be successful—that is, individuals must act on their program eligibility and do so in a way that produces tangible resources. The U.S. welfare system is not designed to locate people in need, inform them of their eligibility, or ensure that they receive aid. Like other government institutions that serve as sites of demand making, the welfare system tends to ignore the quiescent; it responds primarily to those who vocalize their needs and act on their interests.

The goal of this chapter is, in a sense, a traditional one in the study of political action: to illuminate the process by which personal stresses become or fail to become the basis for demands on government (Cornelius 1978, 32; Mills 1959; Schlozman and Verba 1979, 1). Regarding this process in the welfare context, two important points can be inferred from existing statistics. First, the process includes pitfalls that prevent many eligible people from converting their needs into successful claims on government. Although public concern tends to focus more on "excessive" welfare usage, nonparticipation by eligible people is by far the more common occurrence (van Oorshot 1991). In the AFDC and food stamp programs, in fact, only a minority of those who become eligible receive benefits (Blank and Ruggles 1993). Second, citizens' abilities to negotiate the claiming process appear to be quite sensitive to context. The rates at which eligible people claim AFDC and SSDI benefits, for example, vary widely over time and across the fifty states (Kronebusch and Tiehen 1996; Soss and Keiser 1999; U.S. House of Representatives 1998).

Despite their political importance, little is known about the processes that give rise to these participation patterns. Most research on program usage begins from the perspective of welfare providers, asking who is served by government programs, for how long, and other questions that can be answered by analyzing the correlates of welfare receipt (Bane and Ellwood 1994; Blank

1997; Ellwood 1988). Few researchers adopt the standpoint of the eligible citizen who asks, "How do I get to there from here?" (Nelson 1980; Schram 1995). How do citizens convert their eligibility into successful benefit claims? What factors facilitate or impede this effort? To answer these questions, one must take a closer look at actual efforts to negotiate the welfare-claiming process.

The successful advancement of a welfare claim is no small feat. To win resources, individuals must recognize their eligibility, initiate contact with government, negotiate complex agency procedures, and, in some cases, persevere in the face of administrators' efforts to deter them (Bennett 1995; Lipsky 1984; Nelson 1980; Prottas 1979). Potential applicants may not realize that they are eligible for benefits, they may not know how to act on their eligibility, or they may resist doing so out of fear or shame. In addition, the conditions that make people eligible for welfare programs (such as poverty or disability) can also strip them of the capacity and energy needed to pursue a complex process of formal demand making. How, then, do some eligible people manage to claim welfare benefits while so many of their counterparts do not?

In what follows, I suggest that an answer to this question can be found by following a thread of participatory-democratic theory described in chapter 1. To explain formal demands on government, one must draw them into a broader frame of analysis that encompasses informal political processes embedded in communities (Hardy-Fanta 1993). In the political lives of claimants, the formal and the informal are two parts of a coherent whole. Welfare claiming is a paradigmatic example of what Carol Hardy-Fanta calls "survival politics" (1993, 46–51). It emerges out of interpersonal processes of mobilization and takes root in informal community networks that provide individuals with resources needed for survival.

Welfare demand making hinges, of course, on individuals' ability and desire to press their claims. But ability and desire are not merely precursors to politics, they are products of politics. They depend, in the short term, on the extent to which individuals are cajoled, advised, and abetted by others. In this chapter, I suggest that the roots of successful welfare demands lie, at least in part, in the social networks that mobilize and assist potential claimants. Extended kin networks, service professionals, and community organizations make individuals more effective agents in relation to the welfare state. Their efforts to assist and recruit claimants play a critical role in the process that converts "personal troubles of milieu" into successful public claims on government (Mills 1959).

In the 1960s, the NWRO premised its "crisis strategy" on exactly this insight: rates of welfare participation depend not only on eligibility and need but also on the mobilization of demands (Piven and Cloward 1975, 89–126). The goals of the NWRO's "massive drive to recruit the poor onto the welfare rolls" extended beyond survival politics. By inducing the poor to demand relief in greater numbers, activists sought to create a fiscal and political crisis that would force policymakers to pass a national income standard. Looking back on that period of confrontational politics, it is apparent that welfare claims emerged out of mobilization processes and served political purposes. This chapter offers an analysis of welfare claiming under less turbulent conditions, when welfare demands are used for survival politics rather than confrontational politics. My thesis is that welfare demands during a period of survival politics continue to emerge out of processes of recruitment and assistance that take place at the community level.

I do not attempt here to test causal claims about the types of people or conditions that produce success and failure in welfare claiming (a goal that would be better pursued by comparing successful and unsuccessful claimants). Instead, this chapter offers an inductive analysis intended to illuminate the types of activities that make up welfare claiming, specify the points of contingency in this process where alternative outcomes are made possible, and identify the range of actors who may exert influence at various points in the process (Becker 1998, 32–46). In addition to offering a more coherent understanding of the claiming process, this analysis provides an empirical basis for suggesting factors that may account for broader patterns of welfare demand making.

Welfare Claiming: Oversocialized and Undersocialized

The role that social networks play in facilitating demands on government is rarely acknowledged in studies of program usage, but it is a key piece of conventional wisdom in research on political action (Eulau 1986; Huckfeldt and Sprague 1993, 1995; Knoke 1990; Sheingold 1973). Social ties, for example, are widely recognized as essential for the recruitment of individuals into social movements (Gould 1993; McAdam 1982; McAdam and Paulsen 1993; Piven and Cloward 1977). By supplying resources and serving as vehicles for mobilization, networks also shape the universe of participants in traditional forms of political action such as voting (Rosenstone and Hansen 1993; Verba, Schlozman, and Brady 1995).

Because welfare institutions have rarely been studied as sites of political action, researchers have paid little attention to the social processes that support demand making in this context. Most models of welfare participation bypass social interaction entirely, embracing an image of the applicant that is either "undersocialized" or "oversocialized" (Granovetter 1985). On one side, undersocialized explanations treat applicants as unencumbered individuals who try to maximize personal utility in light of personal tastes and an environment of incentives and constraints (Blank and Ruggles 1993; Gottschalk, McLanahan, and Sandefur 1994; Hutchens 1981; Moffitt 1983). On the other side, oversocialized explanations describe applicants primarily as objects of group socialization. Welfare claiming in these accounts is a learned behavior; it is an individual enactment of cultural values and behavior patterns (Mead 1992; Mincy 1994). Although they differ from one another in important ways, the two approaches converge on a "conception of action and decision carried out by atomized actors":

> In the undersocialized account, atomization results from narrow utilitarian pursuit of self-interest; in the oversocialized one, from the fact that behavioral patterns have been internalized and ongoing social relations thus have only peripheral effects on behavior. That the internalized rules of behavior are social in origin does not differentiate this argument from a utilitarian one. [The two accounts] thus merge in their atomization of actors from immediate social context. (Granovetter 1985, 485)

To investigate welfare claiming as a mode of political action (as an instrument of survival politics or confrontational politics) is to suggest the need for a different view of social context: a view that acknowledges the ongoing, informal political processes that take place in communities. In welfare claiming, as in other modes of political action, individuals "do not behave or decide as atoms outside a social context, nor do they adhere slavishly to a script written for them by the particular intersection of social categories they happen to occupy. Their attempts at purposive action are instead embedded in concrete, ongoing systems of social relations" (Granovetter 1985, 487).

In the remainder of this chapter, I analyze how these "ongoing systems of social relations" facilitate citizens' demands on welfare institutions. The section that follows draws on clients' accounts to construct a general model of welfare claiming as a political process. Each of the five parts of this model identifies an obstacle that citizens must negotiate to convert their program eligibility into benefits. In the second section, I explore the range of actors who participate in this process, showing how welfare claims emerge out of ongoing interactions with family members, friends and neighbors, service professionals, community organizations, and government personnel. These five types of actors tend to differ both in the kinds of contributions they make to the claiming process and in their importance for particular categories of applicants. Taken together, however, they make up the loose networks that generate demands on the welfare system.

The Claiming Process

How do eligible people become recipients of public welfare resources? The process described by any one client differs in important respects from the experiences of others. By organizing the details of these accounts into more abstract categories, however, it is possible to reconstruct the underlying logic of the claiming process (Becker 1998). To do so, I compared clients' stories both to general models of how personal strains become the "stuff of politics" (Cornelius 1978; Schlozman and Verba 1979) and to the smaller number of models that deal specifically with welfare claiming (Kerr 1982, 1983; Nelson 1980). Out of these existing works, clients' accounts of the claiming process bore the closest resemblance to Nelson's (1980) eight-step model of "help-seeking." Nelson summarizes the model as follows:

> First, an individual must translate his or her perceptions of objective *conditions* into a *definition of a problem*. At this point, the individual tests the *adequacy of the chosen problem definition* by presenting it to others for their concurrence. Next, the individual begins to *review and choose among potential response agents*. Then the person begins to *anticipate the response of the public agency,* that is, to evaluate the cost of seeking aid relative to the certainty of receiving benefits or services. *Perceptions of situational factors* (e.g., no available transportation) *limiting access to service deliverers* further refine the likelihood of initiating help-seeking. However, even an individual whose environment facilitates public help-seeking may never contact a public care agent. If other *competing needs* are perceived as too pressing, the person may never *initiate help-seeking* from a public agency. (1980, 181; emphasis in original)

Guided by Nelson's model, I have organized the process described by clients into a simpler group of five tasks: defining problems, gathering information, deciding to act, making a claim, and gaining agency responsiveness. This model extends beyond Nelson's to include individuals' efforts after they file their initial applications and is organized to shift the focus from the individual to social interaction. Both of these changes, however, should be viewed as incremental revisions to a model that proved, on balance, to be a very good match with clients' descriptions of the claiming process.

The first three tasks in the claiming process may be viewed as more social-psychological, while the last two are more action oriented. Each suggests a set of barriers that can prevent the successful advancement of a welfare claim. First, eligible people may define their circumstances as something other than a problem that can be addressed by making a claim on government. Second, they may lack information about the existence of welfare benefits, about their own eligibility, or about how to file a claim. Third, deterred by social stigma, fears of government, or any number of other factors, they may decide not to act on their eligibility. Fourth, they may lack the skills, time, resources, or assistance needed to make a claim for benefits, or they may be dissuaded by the conditions of the application encounter itself. Fifth, when people who qualify for benefits have their initial applications rejected, they may give up and fail to pursue application or appeals procedures that would force the agency to grant their entitlement.

Defining Problems

People can endure tremendous hardship without pursuing any form of remedy. Conditions that would lead some to pursue individual or collective action may be perceived by others as an unfortunate but natural and expected part of life. Oppressive group conditions, for example, are unlikely to give rise to social movements unless they are interpreted in a way that "inspires and legitimates" collective action (Gamson 1992; Snow and Benford 1992; Snow et al. 1986). Similarly, litigation is unlikely to emerge out of a personal injury if individuals fail to "name" their situation in a way that implies the need and potential for a legal remedy (Felstiner, Abel, and Sarat 1981). In the same way, people who are eligible for welfare benefits may fail to perceive their life conditions as problems that need to be addressed at all, let alone by turning to government.

Welfare claims do not emerge directly from objective hardships or even from subjective experiences of need; they depend on the particular frames of reference people use to understand these circumstances (Simon 1985). As a result, it is a mistake to assume that a particular condition—such as limited access to food, shelter, or essential medical services—will be perceived as a problem that requires or legitimates a welfare claim. As Nelson points out, it is often easier for welfare providers and policy analysts to ignore this distinction, but doing so produces a distorted understanding of the dynamics of program usage.

> The importance of the difference between conditions and problems cannot be overemphasized. The crucial distinction is that the same set of negative conditions is likely to be interpreted differently by different individuals. Many of the difficulties with research on poverty generally, and service utilization specifically, are a direct result of not insisting on this distinction. In addition to being paternalistic, the exclusive use of arbitrary, objective standards by planners without adding subjective descriptions of problems is a major cause of inadequate estimates of program utilization. (1980, 182–83)

Interpretations of life conditions that support or dissuade welfare claiming tend to emerge through social interaction and become agreed-upon definitions of reality (Berger and Luckman 1967; Goffman 1974). Clients consistently report that in the period before they sought benefits, they attempted to make sense of their situations through discussions with others. In many cases, eligible people actively solicited the opinions of trusted allies, asking whether a situation seemed "serious" and, if so, what should be done about it. In other cases, a casual conversation with a friend or family member suddenly redefined an everyday difficulty as an acute problem that could not be tolerated any longer. Finally, in some cases, welfare claiming was pursued only after significant others intervened to suggest new interpretations of the applicant's situation.

In all these ways, community members participate actively in individuals' efforts to understand their life situations and shape the problem definitions that produce welfare claims. Friends and relatives suggest that domestic conflicts have changed from ordinary relationship problems into a life-threatening pattern of abuse. They argue that a routine inability to pay for food and utilities is not a natural part of being poor but constitutes an unacceptable threat to a child's well-being. They insist that difficulties with pregnancies, child care responsibilities, or disabilities are no longer sustainable and that work is no longer possible.

When I asked clients why they waited so long to act on their eligibility or why they did not apply during an earlier eligibility spell, they frequently pointed to a failure to define their situation as a problem that warranted significant action. The hardships that eventually led to a benefits claim had seemed, at an earlier time, to be sustainable or even normal. They did not seem to require or legitimate a welfare claim. In some cases, these interpretations stood up for a time because clients were reluctant to discuss their personal situations with others. In other cases, clients recalled that significant others had agreed, or even convinced them that their troubles were normal or that taking action to solve them would make matters worse.

During the eligibility spells in which they successfully apply, most clients experience one or more conversations that serve as catalysts for action. In these conversations, they or someone else reconsider a situation that previously has appeared workable and identify it as a crisis that requires an immediate response (Edelman 1977). This new definition is usually expressed to others, who endorse it or refine it by pointing out additional dimensions of the problem. Eventually, a new interpretation is validated as reality, and seemingly normal conditions are recast as problems needing solutions.

Gathering Information

Although they may perceive a need for action, individuals can easily be thwarted in the claiming process if they do not know about public programs or their own eligibility. Like other types of political action, welfare claims depend on information (Ferejohn and Kuklinski 1990; Kuklinski 1990). People who qualify for benefits have to identify a channel for action that will allow them to influence government allocations (Cornelius 1978, 40). This task can involve gathering information about the existence of a welfare program, its jurisdiction over one's problems, the kinds of aid it offers, its conditions of eligibility, and the procedures that applicants have to traverse to become clients. Some knowledge is essential for welfare claiming, but if information about application procedures or program rules arouses anxieties, it also may serve as a deterrent (chapter 3). As a result, information is a major influence on whether an eligible person will make a claim and, if so, what institution will serve as its target (van Oorschot 1991, 25).

Because welfare agencies do little to advertise their services or seek out potential clients, individuals may have little idea where to start in looking for assistance. Social networks provide both a repository of information for welfare claimants and a source of assistance in gathering information. Although some of what claimants hear from others may be vague or incorrect, familiar social relations offer an accessible and trustworthy shortcut for obtaining information (Calvert 1985; Carmines and Kuklinski 1990; Huckfeldt and Sprague 1993; Mondak 1990). Knowledge about where one can get help during a crisis is a valuable resource exchanged in disability communities and in poor communities (Edin and Lein 1997; Oliker 1996; Stack 1974). Survival politics is accomplished, in part, by making the interpersonal connections that get this information to those in need (Hardy-Fanta 1993).

Long-term exchanges of information over a lifetime allow some applicants to enter the claiming process with greater knowledge. Everyday conversations with family members, friends, coworkers, schoolmates, and other associates yield a rich mix of more or less accurate information and tall tales. These long-term exchanges of information provide eligible people with resources they need to pursue the claiming process and occasionally with reasons to avoid it. Not surprisingly, people who come from social contexts where poverty and/or disability are more common tend to know considerably more about specific programs prior to their own eligibility spells. On balance, this knowledge allows for more informed decision making and lessens the need to gather information as part of the claiming process itself.

Many applicants, however, enter the claiming process with almost no knowledge and have to gather and exchange information along the way. Merton, for example, had not even heard of the SSDI program: "I didn't even know the program existed at that time. There were no billboards up anywhere saying 'Apply if you're disabled.'" Penny was equally short on information when she became eligible for AFDC: "I didn't know anything about [AFDC]. As far as I knew, I'd just stay home and take care of [my baby]." For these and other applicants, information gathering is an essential task in the claiming process. Eligible people tend to learn about welfare programs and discover their own eligibility by asking around and by receiving unsolicited advice. Significant others also may investigate channels for assistance on their own and report back to the claimant on what resources are available and how to get them. In these and other ways, social networks allow successful applicants to surmount the informational barriers to welfare claiming.

Deciding to Act

In addition to supportive problem definitions and information, welfare claiming also requires a decision to act. This stage of the claiming process and the complex social considerations that go into it were described at greater length in the preceding chapter. What is important to add here is that welfare claims tend to emerge out of small-group decision-making processes. As they sort and weigh their obligations, fears, and hopes, eligible people usually rely, at least in part, on conversations with others. They also draw on others' opinions as guides for evaluating and ruling out alternative paths of action. Most clients recall a particular discussion in which the decision to apply for benefits was made with, or even by, people close to them.

Some people who have more background knowledge decide to claim benefits without much discussion and consult with others only after they have made their decision. But in most cases, the decision to go to the agency is made with and validated through consultation with others. Some clients describe a period of hesitation after learning about their program eligibility that ends only after a crystallizing conversation in which significant others agree that welfare claiming is morally acceptable and the "only choice." Marie, who could not work because of her multiple sclerosis (MS), recalled, "I was encouraged by my doctor and by my family to start the application for SSD[I]. . . . [My doctor] spent a lot of time with me. But I also talked with my family. And it was agreed that economically it was a 'have to' situation. There just wasn't any other way around it."

Decisions to apply were usually made in consultation with a few other people or through a sequence of discussions. Phil, for example, considered applying to SSDI but could not overcome his own resistance to "welfare dependence" until a number of people close to him agreed that he should apply. He decided to act only after extensive

> conversations with my wife (then girlfriend, now wife), my father, mother, a lot of my friends, a couple of people I knew in the [disability] community. There was a particular gentleman who I met who was a DVR [Department of Vocational Rehabilitation] counselor, and he was also blind. And somebody gave me his name when I started to lose my eyesight. And I talked to him, and he gave me some advice. And I thought he gave good advice. So, it was a lot of different opinions from a lot of different places, not just one thing.

Making a Claim

It is one thing to decide to claim benefits and another to do it. Potential applicants may have trouble getting to and from the agency or securing child care. They also may have to forgo activities that normally allow them to support themselves and their children. And in addition to these material and opportunity costs, making a claim may also entail psychological costs in the form of fear, stigma, or embarrassment brought on by experiences at the agency. As I discuss in chapter 5, applicants may find agency procedures to be confusing, intimidating, or humiliating. They may also have difficulty collecting the personal records that must be submitted to document their claims. Overcoming these obstacles constitutes a fourth task in the welfare claiming process.

Even eligible people who have lived around welfare recipients most of their lives rarely know very much about the nuts and bolts of filing an application. Significant others fill the gap by telling claimants where to apply and how to improve their odds of acceptance. They gather documents required for the application and identify sympathetic doctors or lawyers who can help substantiate claims. They help out by watching children, offering a ride to the agency, or providing emotional support during the long hours in the waiting room. They may even fill out the application if official claimants are confused by the forms, limited by a disability, or worried that seemingly insignificant word choices might mean the difference between acceptance and rejection.

As individuals, applicants frequently do not have all the skills and resources needed to apply for benefits. In addition, by the time they try to file a claim, applicants are often in a debilitating state of personal crisis. As a result, social ties tend to play a critical role in converting decisions to apply into claims on government. Two SSDI clients, for example, recalled earlier periods of homelessness when they had not been able to obtain benefits because they did not know how to pursue the application process or how to obtain the necessary documents. They attributed their later successes to the fact that professional counselors had guided them through this process, drawing on superior skills, information, and social contacts to advance their claims.

Younger women in AFDC frequently reported delaying claims until someone could accompany them to the agency. They feared going by themselves to confront the workers and other applicants they expected to find there. On several occasions, women did not act immediately on their decisions to apply because of the danger of walking to the agency or waiting for the bus in harsh winter weather with their children. Despite their need for assistance, applying for welfare had to wait until someone could watch the kids or provide transportation to the agency. Although applicants differ in the types of help they need, the vast majority gratefully recall assistance provided by others at the time they applied.

Gaining Responsiveness

For many successful applicants, waiting is the only activity between filing a claim and receiving welfare benefits. But if the claimant's initial application is rejected or if the waiting period goes on for too long, there may be a final task to complete in the claiming process. Gaining responsiveness involves overcoming resistance, rejection, or inaction on the part of the bureaucracy and can require putting pressure on specific personnel, appealing an agency decision, or filing a new and separate claim for benefits. Formal appeals processes are more commonly pursued by SSDI applicants, but AFDC clients are just as likely to pursue informal means of influence. For many people who legally qualify for benefits, bureaucratic foot-dragging or an initial rejection may lead to failure in the claiming process. Some claimants, however, overcome these obstacles by drawing on assistance provided by friends, family members, service professionals, local organizations, or government personnel.

Applicants who are rejected in the SSDI and AFDC programs, for example, may retreat for a time and then later file new claims. In other cases, applicants may respond to a rejection by initiating appellate procedures. In the SSDI program, for example, approximately 51 percent of claimants fail in their initial application to the program; of these rejected claimants, a full 57 percent continue to press their claims by requesting a formal reconsideration; and some of those who suffer a second rejection continue to push their cases by demanding reviews conducted by administrative law judges, the federal Appeals Council, and eventually a federal district court (Soss and Keiser 1999). Throughout these efforts, claimants rely heavily on assistance from lawyers, doctors, social workers, and local organizations.

Responsiveness from a welfare agency may also be pursued through less formal methods. Some claimants try to hasten or influence agency decisions either on their own or by mobilizing others on their behalf. While applicants may possess little influence themselves, they are sometimes able to use their roles as constituents of elected officials or as clients of service professionals to involve others who have more skills and better connections. Social ties to community members and local organizations can also be used to try to influence agencies. In her study of social connections and survival politics, for example, Hardy-Fanta (1993, 39) notes that one woman in her sample was particularly fond of using "her influence with government officials to extract benefits for Latinos in the area of welfare and child care."

Welfare-claiming experiences come in all shapes and sizes but tend to share a common process. Social ties allow claimants to find the assistance they need to successfully complete this process. Welfare claiming usually is not accomplished through an organized form of social interaction: it bears little resemblance to a consciously formulated collaborative project. This, of course, is one of the major differences between welfare claiming as an instrument of survival politics and welfare claiming as an instrument of confrontational politics. In the latter case, community activists with collective goals recruit eligible people to claim benefits as part of a larger political strategy (Piven and Cloward 1977). In survival politics, applicants draw on a loose but effective collection of social ties to negotiate the claiming process. The people involved in the process may have very different relations to an applicant and may not share broader goals. What is shared across the two modes of welfare claiming, however, is the critical role that social interaction plays in converting objective needs into demands on government.

Actors in the Claiming Process

Social networks provide active participants in the claiming process who supply individuals with critical resources: information, encouragement, reassurance, and material assistance. The resources that facilitate most forms of political action are more likely to be found in networks of people with higher socioeconomic status (Verba, Schlozman, and Brady 1995). By contrast, the resources that assist in welfare claiming tend to be distributed more widely. For example, while the types of knowledge needed for many kinds of political action are typically concentrated among those with higher education levels (Delli Carpini and Ketter 1996), formal education tends not to be associated with greater knowledge of welfare programs or higher claiming rates (Hasenfeld 1985; Soss and Keiser 1999).

Depending on their composition, social networks offer individuals different types of advantages in the claiming process. The strongest repositories of knowledge and most supportive attitudes are likely to be found in social settings where program participation has been most common. Thus, people who are eligible for programs that serve poor families and people with disabilities are likely to have some advantages in the claiming process if they come from economically disadvantaged backgrounds (Edin and Lein 1997; Howards, Brehm, and Nagi 1980). By contrast, networks that include the well off and well educated are more likely to supply individuals with access to transportation and skilled assistance in gathering documents and completing forms. Finally, regardless of their immediate social ties, claimants find that some types of assistance can be supplied only by professionals, organizations, or government personnel who have greater expertise or authority.

Thus, the actors who participate in the claiming process vary in the roles they play, in their abilities to play them, and in their relevance for particular categories of applicants. Based on the recruiters and assistants who were most prominent in clients' accounts, I focus here on five categories of actors: family members, friends and neighbors, service professionals, workers in community organizations, and government personnel.

Family Members

Family relations are a frequent topic of welfare research, but most studies begin with problems of poverty rather than questions of political action. Families are studied as important determinants of life chances or as agents of long-term socialization. The possibility that family members might contribute to the odds that an individual will turn to a welfare program is considered most often in terms of the culture-of-poverty thesis: the claim that values transmitted through families produce cycles of self-defeating behavior that trap succeeding generations in poverty and welfare dependence (Banfield 1974; M. Katz 1989; Leacock 1971; Lewis 1966; Rainwater and Yancey 1967). Thus, a considerable amount of research is devoted to the question of whether particular family backgrounds enhance an individual's chances of needing public aid (Albelda and Tilly 1997; Gottschalk, McLanahan, and Sandefur 1994; Luker 1996; McLanahan 1988).

If welfare claiming is viewed as a political process of demand making rather than as a direct outgrowth of poverty, however, family members' contributions can be seen in a different light. Research on political action suggests that family members tend to be key partners in political communication and major influences on political behavior (Huckfeldt and Sprague 1995; Huckfeldt et al. 1995, 1027). Consistent with this broader pattern, community research suggests that extended networks of family and kin are primary units of survival politics: they are the most proximate "connections" that help poor people accomplish the activities that fulfill their basic needs (Edin and Lein 1997; Hardy-Fanta 1993; Oliker 1996; Singerman 1995; Stack 1974). Not surprisingly, family members were key actors in the stories of welfare claiming told by clients in this study.

Regardless of their program or personal backgrounds, clients almost always recall some form of deliberation with family members prior to claiming benefits. These conversations play a pivotal role in defining problems, acquiring information, and deciding to act. Family members also figure prominently in efforts to file an application. They are less frequently linked to claimants' efforts to gain a response from the agency. Family members' roles tend to vary according to their past exposure to and attitudes about welfare programs. Relatives who have received benefits in the past or known other recipients tend to have a superior quantity and quality of knowledge to share with applicants. They are also more likely to suggest the possibility of claiming benefits and tend to be more supportive of the idea that individuals should act on their eligibility.

People who are eligible for AFDC and SSDI benefits usually turn to siblings or parents to talk about the problems that push them toward welfare claiming, such as health concerns, relationship problems, financial hardships, problems at work, and concerns about meeting children's needs. These family members frequently suggest the idea of seeking public benefits. Clients in both programs, especially younger clients, also identify family members as an essential source of emotional support and material assistance in their efforts to file a claim. Celina, a nineteen-year-old AFDC client, recalled that she was very scared on the day she applied and remembered that she held her mother's hand throughout the encounter. Vanessa, a twenty-year-old client, recalled that an older niece walked her through the process.

> My niece helped me. My niece showed me how to do everything, because she was also leaving to go back [to another state]. Everybody was leaving me here. She didn't want me without anything, and her not being here. So she helped me go down there and apply before I went in to the shelter. And all my AFDC papers were going to my auntie's house.

SSDI clients also tend to rely on family members as assistants in their attempts to file a claim. Lee-Ann, for example, felt that she was only able to get into the program because of her family's efforts.

> [I talked about it] with my father. And he tried helping out as much as he could by taking me there and sitting with me, and everything like that. . . . My sister at one point went down with me, and she was filling the form out with me. She would just ask me the question, and I would answer, and she would circle or write down the response. I will say this much: I do have a supportive family.

Although family members are equally likely to help AFDC and SSDI clients in defining problems and filing claims, the families of AFDC applicants are more likely to have useful program knowledge. The biggest disparities arise in the background knowledge claimants derive from their families prior to their eligibility spells. In AFDC, applicants usually know something about the experiences of a female relative. This information may be limited to the fact that a program offers aid to poor women with children, or it may include details about where and how to apply for benefits. Lashell, for example, recalled, "Some of the members of my family were in it [so] I knew the deal." Likewise, when Cheryl found herself with little education and few job opportunities, she looked to her mother for a model of how welfare claiming could help her balance parenting obligations with the pursuit of long-term employment goals.

I suppose I did know about it from my mom. I knew about food stamps and Title 19. And I knew my mom got a check every month to take care of us. But I don't want to be on it the rest of my life. I suppose I'm a lot like my mom. She took it because she had to because of the kids, to make sure they were well. And then, when the kids got old enough to be in school all day, she went and finished her education to get a better job so she doesn't have to rely on AFDC. So I suppose I'm a lot like my mom in that. I'm doing exactly that same road she did.

As AFDC claimants decide whether to act on their eligibility, family members tend to provide a critical store of information, encouragement, and affirmation. Anna recalled, "My sister told me to apply for AFDC. So, I went in and applied. . . . My sister said when you're pregnant, they have to help you." Remembering her ambivalence at the time she applied, Alicia recalled feeling more certain of her decision after her family said, "Right now, you need it to help you out."

SSDI claimants who have family members with serious health problems tend to rely on them for information in a way that mirrors their counterparts in AFDC. Dizzy, for example, noted, "My father and one of my older sisters was on SSDI, so I knew about it way before [I needed it]." When he began considering SSDI, his family offered critical advice and support. When I asked Dizzy if he talked about his decision with anyone, he replied, "My mother and my sister and my brother-in-law. . . . [My mother] saw me on a daily basis. . . . [My sister] said 'Don't worry about it. There's no way they can deny you. You're getting worse every day. You cannot work, whether you like to hear that or not.' I said 'Yes, I know.'"

In most cases, however, the families of SSDI clients are less able to provide background knowledge of the program or suggest welfare claiming as a path of action. Katrina captured the typical story: "[I talked with] my family, but they couldn't really tell me what to do." Lack of knowledge, however, does not prevent family members from going out and gathering information about the program on behalf of those who are eligible for SSDI. Such assistance is particularly critical for people with more severe disabilities. Lee-Ann recalled that her father figured out where and how to seek government benefits: "I had heard of [SSDI], but I had never really looked into it or anything. My father was the one that really checked everything."

Thus, family members tend to play key roles in generating and advancing welfare claims. In both programs, families help to define problems, make decisions to act, and file applications. Disparities in knowledge make some families more useful sources of information than others, and these families are more common in AFDC. But even if they have no personal knowledge, family members tend to assist claimants by seeking out information. In all of these ways, family ties facilitate the conversion of personal hardships into demands on government.

Friends and Neighbors

Like families, friends and neighbors also receive considerable attention in welfare research. A variety of neighborhood characteristics have been shown to influence the odds that an individual will claim welfare benefits (Jencks and Mayer 1990; Jencks and Peterson 1991; Mincy 1994; Osterman 1991). But as with families, most of the literature in this area tends to interpret the link between neighborhood and welfare claiming in terms of value socialization or the distribution of economic opportunities (Mincy 1994; W. Wilson 1987). Less attention is given to the role that friends and neighbors play in the extended networks that bring resources into communities and distribute them among community members. As essential elements of survival politics, the social ties of neighborhood and community play a key role in facilitating demands on the welfare system.

The category of friends and neighbors runs the gamut from individuals who enjoy a kin status that verges on family membership to community members who are little more than acquaintances. Like family members, friends tend to help informants in almost all the claiming tasks and to vary in their ability to offer assistance depending on their own experience and knowledge. Most SSDI claimants report that they receive some assistance from friends, schoolmates, coworkers, or members of disability support groups. AFDC applicants, however, usually derive greater assistance from neighbors, reinforcing their family-based advantages.

The social ties that help AFDC claimants win public benefits are usually grounded in neighborhood communities but also may arise through low-wage workplace relationships. Both of these locales tend to supply claimants with people who have program knowledge and who can suggest and encourage an application for benefits. Elizabeth, for example, recalled that her coworkers at a local hospital were the first to raise the possibility that she should apply: "Well, when I was working, they would say, 'Elizabeth, if your income is not enough for this and that, you know you can still get food stamps, you can still go down [to the welfare agency].'"

Neighbors are especially helpful to AFDC applicants as a source of information. Because AFDC is a salient issue in poor communities, it tends to be a frequent topic of casual conversation (Huckfeldt and Sprague 1995). As a result, most people who come from poor neighborhoods know about AFDC before they become eligible for it. Lynn told a common story: "I had heard about AFDC from other people because I lived in a poor neighborhood. So, it was like people knew about it. It wasn't any big secret." Poor neighbors can also provide potential applicants with answers to specific questions about eligibility rules and the claiming process. Renee recalled, "Oh, I just asked around. I'd say, 'How many months [pregnant] do you have to be before you can apply for AFDC?' Mostly everybody knows."

Neighborhood connections also provide applicants with partners in decision making, a source of emotional support, and help negotiating agency forms and procedures. Tina received all of these forms of assistance from an older neighbor. Her story provides an example of recruitment, in which a community member shepherds the applicant throughout the claiming process.

> One of my neighbors, she was kind of like a mother figure in a way. She basically told me I should just try it. She told me that they would probably turn me down since I was so young and had to have a guardian's consent to be on it. But she helped push me through. She helped get me on it. . . . She was on the program. She was also a single mother, and she was on the program. And then she got off. They helped her get a job. She was working at the bank. . . . I went down there the first day with [her].

At the shelter for homeless families where I conducted fieldwork, residents tended to help one another through the claiming process in ways that mirrored the assistance offered by neighbors. The new arrivals at the shelter who were not already in AFDC (roughly 20 percent) were typically eligible to receive benefits. For these women, the shelter substituted for neighborhoods as a place where they could talk with current recipients. Residents typically discussed new arrivals' problems and offered advice about what to do. In many cases, residents explained AFDC eligibility rules and gave advice about where and how to apply for assistance. Residents at the shelter also offered to go the agency with applicants or watch their children while they went alone.

While poor people tend to live near one another in concentrated areas of poverty (Jargowsky 1997), people with disabilities are less likely to live in a shared neighborhood. As a result, they tend not to learn about the SSDI program through neighborhood conversations. In addition, many people who qualify for SSDI benefits have had little contact with the disability community prior to their spell of eligibility. For both of these reasons, individuals who suddenly develop an acute health problem are particularly unlikely to know about the SSDI program or to have a friend who can provide them with reliable information about it.

By contrast, people who have long-term health conditions may draw considerable assistance from the disability community. Although it is widely dispersed, the disability community offers SSDI clients support that resembles what AFDC applicants find in their neighborhoods. People with long-term vision problems, for example, have access to special schools, sheltered workplaces, support groups, and recreational clubs that offer opportunities to make connections with other people who are legally blind. Thus, unlike most SSDI applicants, Mike knew about SSDI well before he considered seeking assistance: "Through other people, I knew [about SSDI]. They were people I knew through the ski club and other groups for people who are blind or have other disabilities." Similarly, Francis first heard about SSDI while attending a school for blind people. Later, coworkers at a sheltered workshop recommended the program to him and encouraged him to apply. He recalled, "It was mainly just being around the environment of blind people. All the time I was in high school, there were kids getting checks. . . . That's where [my information] came from. It was mainly just hearing about it, that it existed, and a little bit about what it was like. I thought, 'Hey, they're doing it, so maybe it's OK if I do it.'"

In sum then, social ties of friendship and neighborhood play an important role in the claiming process. Just as AFDC applicants are more likely to have knowledgeable family members, they are also more likely to benefit from their contacts with friends and neighbors. Nevertheless, people from both programs recalled relying on friends and neighbors as they tried to make sense of their situations, as they decided to act, and as they filed applications. All of these types of assistance were well captured in the story told by Starr. Like Tina, the AFDC applicant who relied heavily on her older neighbor, Starr had a "shepherd" who encouraged and assisted her in applying to SSDI.

> I really went about my life thinking this [MS] was a temporary thing. But about a year and a half after my son was born, I was over at my next-door neighbor's house, and I was talking about some problems I was having with my health. And she said, "Why don't you go on Social Security?" I said, "Well, I don't think I qualify because this disease comes and goes." And she encouraged me to go to the office. In fact, I didn't drive at the time, and she gave me a ride to the office on the near south side. And she watched my kids in the car while I went in and went through the application process.

Community Organizations

In debates over welfare usage, community organizations are usually identified as an alternative to the state as a source of aid for the poor. Conservative critics of welfare, in particular, tout the organizations of civil society as sites of self-help and mutual aid where the poor receive assistance without falling into the trap of "welfare dependence" (Fukayama 1995; Green 1993; Olasky 1992). Here again, though, the concept of political action encourages a different view of how local organizations might affect patterns of welfare usage. Scholarship on civil society and democracy generally holds that secondary associations enhance citizen's abilities to engage and influence government (Edwards and Foley 1998; Putnam, Leonardi, and Nanetti 1993). Of course, when proponents have argued that civil society organizations make "government" more responsive to citizens' interests and needs, they typically have not meant government's administrative institutions (Anechiarico 1998). But the general argument can easily be extended to suggest that community organizations may play an important role in facilitating demands on the welfare system.

Disability associations, labor unions, activist groups, community development organizations, shelters for the homeless, and a variety of other organizations encourage and assist welfare applicants. Together, these groups might even be thought of as a loose infrastructure facilitating welfare demands. Local organizations accumulate ready stores of information about public programs, provide sites for current and potential welfare clients to interact with one another, and, in some cases, even employ individuals whose primary responsibility is to advise and assist people in the claiming process.

Some community organizations are overtly political and forge links between survival politics and more confrontational politics. During the period of my study, for example, a local welfare rights organization was actively encouraging and assisting eligible women to claim their AFDC entitlement. Although this group's efforts were quite small compared to the NWRO's mobilization campaign in the 1960s, the group continued to link welfare claiming to a language of rights and to the idea that poor people should make demands on government without feeling a sense of shame. Activists in the group disseminated information about public programs, assisted claimants through the application process, and supported clients who had conflicts with the agency.

Most organizations, however, assist claimants without necessarily sharing this political agenda. The shelter for homeless families where I conducted ethnographic fieldwork provides a good example. As described earlier, the shelter offered a location for eligible women to learn about AFDC from other residents. It also provided a full-time staff devoted to helping residents find permanent living situations. To prevent families from returning to a state of homelessness or a violent home environment, staff members frequently asked and advised residents about their immediate plans for income. When new residents had no other source of income, staff members routinely urged them to seek AFDC and provided information on how to do so. In a number of cases, staff members (including myself) drove residents to the agency and walked them through the application process.

Because people who are eligible for SSDI are less likely to have knowledgeable family and friends or personal experiences with welfare programs, local organizations tend to play an especially important role in efforts to claim SSDI benefits. For many SSDI claimants, community organizations serve as essential sources of detailed program information. When Bridget left her job as a music teacher, for example, her labor union told her about SSDI benefits and how to apply for them. She recalled, "It was the [teachers' union] that came and explained the SSDI program to me. They told me about the program and told me a specific representative to call at the Social Security offices. They kind of told me about the ins and outs of the program."

The local chapter of the National Multiple Sclerosis Society provides an especially good example of the many ways in which community organizations facilitate welfare claiming. The MS Society hosted monthly disability support group meetings. At these meetings, I watched current recipients advise potential applicants about claiming benefits. I also attended several meetings in which representatives of the organization conducted question-and-answer sessions that covered eligibility rules, strategies for documenting a disability, and ways in which the MS Society might help claimants. As Molly noted, members of the group encouraged one another to persevere in the claiming process and to appeal denials: "We have talked over the last two years about people [in the group] being turned down or in the process of applying. And we have talked about it particularly when a person has been turned down. We tell them to go back and talk to who you need to talk to to get the wheels in motion again." If a regular participant in the group began to consider claiming SSDI benefits, the MS Society offered extensive assistance. Patty recalled,

> [The MS Society] explained all of these things to you about Social Security. They told us where to apply, what things to emphasize, and what doctors to go to. They told me to go to the low-vision clinic and the neurologist. At that time, fatigue had just become an allowable factor in Social Security applications, so they said, "Be sure you document the fatigue factor." And they told me how to go about applying and what was going to happen and how much it would cost me. They went through the whole thing. . . . They gave me a lot of support to press ahead and also a lot of information and advice on how to do that.

In addition to helping members of the support group, the MS Society also offered a first line of assistance for newly diagnosed people who knew almost nothing about the SSDI program. Its existence in the community served as a resource on which individuals could draw for information and assistance in the claiming process. Holly recalled,

> I called the MS Society. I can't remember the woman's name, but she was the best. She actually walked you through all the steps. She was really good. She knew her stuff. . . . She told me how to fill out the paperwork, where to go for it, how to get it—everything. . . . I would call her with ques-

tions, and she would help me answer them. She reminded me not to forget a lot of things on the forms. You really have to write down everything you do. So that was a big help. [The MS Society] sent me pamphlets and letters and everything else. I'd say that me getting in [to the SSDI program] was about half and half: half because of me, and half because of them.

To test this assistance, I called the organization to ask if they had any materials that might help me apply for SSDI benefits. Within a week, I received a packet in the mail containing the following:

1. A pamphlet from the Social Security Administration (SSA) detailing the rules and goals of SSDI.

2. A sample of the SSA's disability report form.

3. A detailed seven-page primer on physicians and attorneys that included advice on how to choose among these service professionals, how to document a disability when making a claim, how to enhance the chances of winning an appeal, and suggestions for self-presentation when advancing claims or appeals.

4. A detailed four-page primer outlining nine helpful rules for dealing with the SSA's teleservice center. This pamphlet included tips about the best times to call, what questions to ask, what questions to avoid asking, how to deal with missing information, and a variety of ways to gain agency responsiveness.

5. A recent report on fatigue as a disabling symptom of MS and on how the fatigue provision could be used to claim SSDI.

The union, the shelter, and the National MS Society all illustrate how community organizations typically facilitate welfare claims. There are, however, more extreme cases in which organization personnel essentially advance the claimant's application themselves. When nominal claimants have severe mental or physical disabilities, organized assistance may be the only way they can hope to gain access to their entitlement. Mark, for example, suffered from paranoia and schizophrenia that emerged after he took LSD in his early twenties. At the time of our interview, he was receiving medication through his daily contact with a community center that served people with mental problems and felony convictions. When I asked Mark about applying for SSDI benefits, he explained,

[My caseworker here at the center] informed me of the benefits. . . . She did all the paperwork. I just did the signing part. And she let me know where to sign them. . . . Because I was at [the center], I saw the doctor there. [It] had everything we needed to apply. . . . I wouldn't have been able to [apply] without [the center]. I don't really understand about SSD[I], what it's about. I just know it comes from Social Security. They're just words. I don't know what's behind it or how people get it. [The center] took care of all that. She had a form and everything. But she didn't really go through everything with me. She didn't explain it totally. I wasn't necessarily eager to find out about it anyway. [laughs] She just determined I could benefit from it.

In sum, local organizations provide a key source of recruitment and assistance that encourages demands on the welfare system. As suggested by theories of civil society, a well-developed network of community organizations serves to make citizens more effective agents in relation to the welfare state. Local organizations tend to possess substantial resources in the forms of reliable information, expertise, and personnel. They have the capacity to offer a level of support that differs qualitatively from that provided by individual community members. As a result, the strength of community organizations is a key factor explaining differences across locales in the rate at which demands are made on welfare agencies (see Soss and Keiser 1999).

Service Professionals

Service professionals such as doctors, lawyers, and social workers tend not to be viewed as important political actors facilitating demands on government. Professional efforts to provide services for individuals, however, can often lead to a recognition that clients' "personal problems" are shaped by broader social or political forces (Hartman 1993). A doctor or social worker, for example, may be uniquely situated to recognize that poverty conditions are threatening an individual's physical or mental health. In these instances, individual values and social norms may motivate service professionals to act on behalf of their clients in ways that go beyond their formal duties (Lipsky 1980, 72).

For women who are eligible for AFDC, doctors and social workers sometimes play an important catalyst role. They suggest, for example, that a difficult pregnancy will no longer allow for work or that young children are getting insufficient nutrition and care. These assessments serve to redefine conditions as problems and to push women to begin searching for solutions. In some cases, these professionals may also suggest applying for welfare benefits and provide information about how to file a claim. Anna, for example, recalled that even before her sister encouraged her to apply for AFDC, she received similar advice and information from her nurse-practitioner and obstetrician:

[I talked with] my doctor. She's the one that told me to go down there and all of that—my obstetrician. And the person at Planned Parenthood, where

I found out about the pregnancy, also talked about it with me. From there, they told me to get help with the doctor. And the doctor also talked with me about AFDC.

Relative to AFDC claimants, however, people who are eligible for SSDI are far more likely to be guided toward welfare claiming by service professionals. To begin with, the limited help available to SSDI claimants in their immediate social circles makes them more likely to need and seek the advice of professionals. In addition, because SSDI claimants are more likely to have had chronic health problems, jobs that provide health coverage, and middle-class incomes, they are more likely than AFDC claimants to have ongoing relationships with professionals such as doctors, lawyers, and therapists.

Doctors who have long-term relationships with patients frequently extend their diagnoses beyond narrowly defined physical or mental problems to address related life conditions and options for improving them. At a minimum, doctors tend to play a key role in decisions to stop working and seek an alternative source of income. J, for example, was told by her therapist and psychiatrist that her depression and anxiety were too severe for her to work and was asked to consider income alternatives. The doctor who was treating Emerald for arthritis was even more blunt: "My physician gave me a choice: either quit the job in a month, or he would call my employer and tell them I couldn't stay there anymore."

In many cases, doctors go beyond questions of work to explicitly direct their patients toward the SSDI program. For example, when Holly mentioned to her doctor that her employer had refused to accommodate her physical limitations, "the doctor got irate about it. And he told me 'That's it. Your last day of work is January 3.'" After demanding that she quit work, the doctor instructed Holly to apply to SSDI, an option she had not previously considered: "The doctor decided 'You're going on [Social Security] Disability [Insurance], because you can't work if they won't allow certain things.' . . . I knew nothing about [the SSDI program], absolutely nothing at this point."

Service professionals such as Holly's doctor sometimes advocate welfare claiming, but they are especially likely to serve as a conduit for reliable information about what program benefits exist and how to obtain them. Because they consistently deal with disability issues, some service professionals are uniquely situated to provide clients with an informed source of advice regarding government programs. The following exchange with Marie captures the sort of experience recounted by a number of SSDI clients:

How did you find out about [SSDI]?

I guess originally from my doctor, probably because he dealt with MS and chronic illness before. And so this was an avenue that he knew was there.

And did he recommend that you apply?

Yes, that I start the process.

Had you known, at the time, any people who had been in the program?

No, I didn't. Not at that time. Even when I was working as a nurse, I never knew any of my patients as being in SSD[I] or any of the other things because that wasn't part of their medical record, where their income came from. I really didn't know anyone.

Service professionals also provide assistance in the final task of welfare claiming, gaining agency responsiveness. Typically, this assistance is part of formal appellate proceedings. Health professionals, of course, are called on to vouch for individuals' disabilities, but the major contributors at this stage are attorneys paid through contingency fee arrangements. Because severe health problems can quickly lead to financial ruin, the contingency-fee system plays a critical role in allowing applicants to obtain legal assistance in the claiming process. As Patty explained,

> The amount is set. The lawyer can only take something like a quarter of what money you have coming. Of course, I'd been off for a whole year by then, so he got a pretty good paycheck out of it. By that time, unfortunately, my husband also got laid off, and we went through every penny of savings we had. We got down to the point where we were behind on one house payment. That was the only thing we actually got behind on. Everything else was paid up. But I learned to stretch pennies. I squeezed them real tight and got three or four meals out of a chicken, things like that. You do what you can.

Clients who went through the SSDI appeals process overwhelmingly attributed their success to the assistance they received from lawyers. Dizzy, for example, believed that "you have to have an attorney. You don't get anywhere without an attorney." Research offers mixed evidence for this perception. Legal representation clearly is not necessary for a successful appeal: roughly half of all unrepresented appellants succeed in their attempts to claim SSDI. Nevertheless, legal representation does significantly improve a claimant's chances of winning resources from the program. Almost three-quarters of appellants who are represented by lawyers successfully negotiate the appeals process (see Kritzer 1996, chap. 4). Thus, clients appear to underestimate their odds of succeeding without representation, but they are largely correct that legal assistance increases one's odds of prevailing in the claiming process.

On the whole, then, service professionals are well situated to facilitate welfare demands on government. Such professionals tend to develop close relations with clients, accumulate knowledge about government programs, and have the authority and trust needed to influence claiming decisions. Professional efforts to assist claimants may fit easily into official duties, may take forms that go beyond these duties, or may even become overtly politicized. Many service professionals see important links between their professional work and broader efforts to promote their clients' well-being (Freedberg 1989, 34; Hartman 1993). Social workers, doctors, and lawyers may place a high priority on helping community members overcome problems associated with poverty and disability; some may even view collective political efforts as a logical extension of their work with individual clients (Solomon 1976).

During periods of confrontational politics, professionals can play a key role in the mobilization of demands. Poverty lawyers, for example, were essential participants in the NWRO's 1960s' campaign, working diligently to mobilize welfare claims and fighting to remove the agency rules and practices that blocked these claims (Davis 1993). During periods of survival politics, professionals aid claimants on a more piecemeal basis but continue to serve as important assistants who push eligible people to make demands on government and help them prevail.

Government Personnel

Although they are less commonly involved than other actors considered here, government personnel provide a final set of participants who facilitate claims on the welfare system. Not surprisingly, the types of government personnel who help applicants tend to differ across the two groups of clients. While SSDI applicants are more likely to receive assistance from elected officials, AFDC applicants are more likely to be aided by street-level bureaucrats. Both elected officials and street-level bureaucrats tend to help with the task of gaining agency responsiveness. Street-level bureaucrats are also occasionally involved in earlier stages of the claiming process.

Like service professionals, street-level government workers are well positioned to accumulate knowledge about public programs and to develop a sense of commitment to clients' overall well-being. As Lipsky points out, "street-level bureaucrats are often . . . expected to be advocates, that is, to use their knowledge, skill, and position to secure for clients the best treatment or position consistent with the constraints of the service" (1980, 72). In a small number of cases, AFDC clients report that they received this sort of advocacy assistance from street-level bureaucrats. For example, when Alicia began to search for assistance for herself and her baby, she learned from friends and family that she was not old enough to be eligible for AFDC. Because of a long history of difficulties at home, however, she had a relationship with a caseworker in Child Protective Services (CPS). She turned to her CPS worker for help and received assistance that made it possible for her to win government benefits.

> Well, I knew I wasn't eligible because of my age. But then when he [the CPS worker] talked to them and told them the things I was going through, then that's when they applied me to go on. . . . I just went there and talked to that [CPS worker]. And he was real nice. He was cool. And he talked to me and he called down there. And the next day, I went down there and got an application and applied and got his consent when it was time for them to turn me on. And that's when it started coming.

In some cases, street-level workers may simply know a claimant as a member of the community and use their position to help the claimant along in the process. For example, Shelly received custody of her grandchildren when her son-in-law sexually abused them, with her daughter's knowledge. The detective who pursued the abuse charges had known Shelly for many years. He, along with the district attorney, told her she should apply for AFDC as a way to get the benefits she needed to cover her new responsibilities. He also assisted her at the agency itself. Shelly recalled,

> I didn't really want to go on welfare. But the district attorney told me if I needed help, to go for help. So the [detective] who was on the case took me down there and signed me up. I was out within, I would say, not even a half hour. I had everything arranged, the medical, the transportation. . . . I knew the detective who took me down there. I've known him my whole lifetime here. The caseworkers were good to me. They helped me. And the district attorney helped me.

SSDI clients were more likely to report that they received assistance from elected officials. Among the many reasons why constituents contact their elected representatives, dissatisfaction with administrative agencies ranks near the top (Moon, Serra, and West 1993). And elected officials, of course, have significant incentives to respond to these individual requests for casework (Cain, Ferejohn, and Fiorina 1987; Fenno 1978; Fiorina 1977, 42–49; Mayhew 1974, 108–10). Claimants who have had their applications rejected will frequently try to pressure an agency by mobilizing an elected representative. Mike compared this aspect of the claiming process to lobbying: "I wrote [my senator] and all of them, and I finally got it, a year and a half later. . . . It was kind of like I was lobbying them or something. I had to keep after them until I finally got my checks."

The political calculus that leads applicants to lobby their elected officials for assistance is simple: they expect members of Congress to be responsive to constituents who can vote them out of office, and they expect agency personnel to be responsive to the desires of elected officials. Dizzy summed it up this way:

> I was calling my congressman and [my senator]. They were checking on it. I explained it to them. I suppose the first thing they did was to look to see if I'm a registered voter, which I am. And [my senator] was very helpful. The people in his office always told me where my papers were and what was going on.

> *So, what led you to call a member of Congress to try to get into the program?*

> They have a name. I had been turned down once. And I figured it would be helpful if they had their name in there. And finally the judge advocate in Chicago OK'd it, and I was accepted.

Not surprisingly, clients who succeed after receiving this sort of assistance tend to see their experience as evidence that program access is achieved through political influence. Kitty recalled,

> Until there was some political clout involved [in my claim], I was some sort of piece of garbage. When [my representative's] office called and said, "You have to call this constituent," the person that called me I think would have washed my floors for me if I'd asked her to. But not until there was something from a U.S. congressperson. My logic was that it was a federal program. So I went to my federal representative. . . . I told [my representative's office] the situation, "These assholes have never called me." And they said, "OK." And the next thing I knew, somebody was on the phone.

As these examples suggest, clients tend to have considerable faith that claim outcomes are influenced by elected officials' efforts on constituents' behalf. Unfortunately, no research offers clear evidence indicating whether these contacts actually affect decisions to accept or reject applications. In one existing study by Johannes (1984, 56), however, agency personnel reported that while they would not break rules to fulfill elected officials' requests, they would handle cases more quickly, give them greater personal attention, and even stretch the rules a bit if plausible interpretation would allow it. Johannes (1984, 57) concludes that "pressure is occasionally applied (with success) and there is a degree of favoritism, at least with respect to the speed and diligence of replies to important members of Congress."

In sum then, government personnel are not as commonly cited as other actors in the claiming process. But like community organizations and service professionals, such officials have the capacity to recruit welfare claimants and to serve as a resource for individuals who are seeking benefits. For a relatively small group of applicants, government personnel can be an extremely important and effective source of assistance in the claiming process.

Conclusion

This chapter has presented an analysis of the welfare-claiming process that begins from the standpoint of the eligible citizen. While quantitative research offers a superior basis for estimating how frequently eligible people apply for welfare benefits (Blank and Ruggles 1993), it is less helpful for shedding light on how individuals move from a position of eligibility to a position of welfare receipt. The preceding analysis makes two general types of contributions to explanations of welfare claiming. First, it suggests a range of actors and contextual conditions that may be expected to influence the conversion of eligibility into demand making. For example, based on the analysis presented here, one would expect eligible people to claim welfare benefits at higher rates in places where they are able to derive greater amounts of assistance from local organizations. To test this hypothesis, Lael Keiser and I conducted a statistical analysis of variation in SSDI claiming rates across the fifty states. Consistent with our hypothesis, we found that after controlling for a variety of relevant contextual factors, rates of application in SSDI are significantly higher in states that have a higher density of nonprofit organizations (Soss and Keiser 1999).

Second, this analysis suggests explanations for patterns of welfare claiming that differ from common assumptions. Consider, for example, evidence that eligible people are more likely to claim AFDC if they come from families or neighborhoods where program participation is more common. Assuming that relevant individual characteristics are accounted for, it is plausible to interpret such a correlation in terms of value differences—that is, as evidence that AFDC participation has become normative in particular social groups. The analysis presented here, however, suggests an alternative explanation: people whose social networks include more AFDC recipients possess an information-rich social environment that is likely to hasten the conversion of eligibility into demand making. Unlike a culture-of-poverty explanation, this one assumes that context influences the actions of AFDC claimants in ways that are analogous to contextual effects in the SSDI program and in other modes of political action. The contributions of context described in this chapter provide good reasons to exercise caution in interpreting evidence that neighborhood and family traits correlate with claiming rates.

This chapter's third contribution is to provide a stronger empirical basis for theorizing about the politics of welfare claiming. Chapter 3 began with the premise that people who are eligible for welfare benefits occupy a political position that is analogous to registered voters: they are members of a group with the potential to articulate demands on government. In trying to explain why and how eligible people act on this potential, I have suggested that welfare claims have deep roots in the social and political relations of everyday life. At one level, welfare demands are instruments of survival politics, functioning as a means to achieve the basic preconditions of full membership within the day-to-day relationships that make up communities: autonomy, social dignity, self-respect, and the ability to fulfill duties to others. At a second level, welfare demands are products of survival politics, emerging through interpersonal processes of mobilization and assistance that are grounded in the same community relations. Thus, to understand either the production or the functions of welfare demands, one must look to citizens' activities within an informal politics of everyday life.

As an element of survival politics, welfare claiming may seem too tame to have much in common with the confrontational demands for relief mobilized by the NWRO in the 1960s. Although resistance to power can take many subtle forms (Scott 1990), there are important distinctions between the welfare claiming described by clients in this study and acts of welfare claiming that might be properly classified as expressions of defiance (Piven and Cloward 1993, 464). Nevertheless, I believe a close look reveals that survival politics and confrontational politics represent two modes of welfare claiming that lie on a shared continuum. When NWRO activists stepped in to mobilize welfare demands for disruptive purposes, they did not create a new political activity where none had existed before. Instead, their efforts at recruitment put greater muscle into informal political processes that already existed in poor communities; their goal of forcing major policy changes extended the political uses of welfare claiming that already existed for the poor.

Because poor people rarely wield organized influence in the representative branches of government, their political efforts are more likely to be found at the margins of the political system, especially in institutions that implement public policy at the community level. Welfare claiming plays a major role in these efforts, and like other forms of political action, it can be made to serve different political ends at different times. Survival politics and confrontational politics are, in a sense, two sides of the same coin. To be sure, there are critical differences between the two. When used as a tool of confrontation, welfare demands take on a far more organized form and are geared toward achieving broader changes in political institutions and policies.

As important as these differences are, however, they should not overshadow the elements that link the politics of survival to the politics of confrontation. The two sides of the coin are neither opposites nor mutually exclusive. Even at the height of disruptive NWRO demand-making, welfare claims continued to function as a tool of survival for applicants (Piven and Cloward

1977). The legal and administrative changes won during this era of confrontational politics produced more accessible and less discriminatory welfare institutions—institutions that served as more responsive targets for demands in the periods of survival politics that followed (Davis 1993; Rosenblatt 1982). Likewise, as an element of survival politics, welfare claims now serve to protect the autonomy and dignity that are necessary conditions for more confrontational political activism. In short, the two political modes of welfare claiming, survival and confrontation, are symbiotic elements that support one another in the political lives of the poor.

By comparing the NWRO's relief drive in the 1960s to the more quotidian efforts described in this chapter, it is possible to illuminate what is perhaps the most fundamental feature of welfare claiming as a political process. The conversion of needs and eligibility into demands on government is neither a natural nor an inevitable chain of events. It is a political outcome that hinges on the characteristics of an individual's social environment. Rates of welfare claiming do not simply reflect the traits of individuals and the economic incentives they confront. Claiming rates depend on the levels of recruitment, information, and support that surround individuals and on the interpretations of reality and suggestions for action that individuals receive from members of their communities.

CHAPTER 5

Evaluating the Application Encounter

The application encounter signifies a transition.[1] It is the culmination of the welfare-claiming process and, for those who succeed, it is the first experience of
welfare participation. Citizens enter the first encounter as claimants; they leave
as clients who have initiated an unusually direct relationship with government.
The application encounter is a moment of mutual evaluation. As agency workers inspect applicants for signs of eligibility and need, applicants take stock of
the bureaucracy and its personnel and draw conclusions about what becoming
a client will mean. This chapter explores three questions regarding clients' evaluations of application encounters: First, what criteria do applicants use to evaluate the first encounter, and what conclusions do they reach? Second, how do
experiences in this encounter affect applicants' beliefs about their political role
as clients of the welfare system? Third, how are clients' evaluations influenced
by differences in program design across the two tiers of the welfare system?

If welfare claiming is viewed as a mode of political action, the conditions
of the application encounter can be seen as a measure of the extent to which government institutions are open and responsive. Just as literacy tests, poll taxes,
and intimidation at a polling place can deter eligible voters (Lawson 1976), the
terms of the application encounter can dissuade welfare claimants (Bennett
1995; Lipsky 1984; Piven and Cloward 1993). Procedures that appear respectful, efficient, and responsive have the potential to encourage individuals to press
forward with their claims. But if would-be applicants find the first encounter too
arduous and degrading, if they surmise that their claims are unwanted and unlikely to succeed, if they are given reasons to believe that clients are routinely
abused and humiliated, they may retreat without claiming their entitlement.

Like other forms of political action, welfare claiming can also be viewed
as an educative activity (Pateman 1970). From this perspective, the political
significance of the application encounter lies in its potential to teach lessons
about authority, procedure, and behavior that set the tone for ongoing relationships between clients and agency personnel. During the first encounter, agency
workers try to teach newcomers the expectations and obligations that will make
up the "client role" (Alcabes and Jones 1985; Lipsky 1980, 61; Marziali 1988,
25). At the same time, applicants scour the agency and bureaucrats' actions for
clues about what to expect as a welfare client. Applicants gather first impres-

sions and make critical inferences about how the agency will treat them, how they will be expected to act, how much discretion is held by individual workers, and how much power these workers hold over clients.

Because the application encounter is the first step in a client's relationship with a welfare institution, it directs attention to a key insight of social citizenship theory described in chapter 1: the quality of social rights enjoyed by citizens hinges not only on the fact of benefit provision but equally on the institutional form of this provision (Marshall 1964). Social control theory extends this fact-form distinction to construct a broader political analysis of how welfare institutions may be designed to regulate work effort and other behaviors of the poor (Piven and Cloward 1993). The terms of relief, in this view, serve to regulate access to public benefits and express the social and political status of claimants. Differences in welfare institutions' designs can be used to limit access for some groups while granting it to others; such differences can define some recipients as deserving citizens while casting others as undeserving beggars.

Theories of dual social citizenship draw these two traditions together and apply them to the bifurcated structure of the U.S. welfare system. The heart of the argument is that the two tiers of the U.S. welfare system create a hierarchy of relationships to the state and function to reinforce social and political inequalities (Fraser and Gordon 1993; Gordon 1990, 1994; Jones 1990; Nelson 1984, 1990; Sapiro 1990). While social insurance programs position clients as "rights-bearing beneficiaries and purchasing consumers of services," the relatively disadvantaged clients in public assistance programs are positioned as degraded and dependent objects of social control (Fraser 1987, 113).

Client evaluations of application encounters provide an important subjective measure of the quality of social citizenship offered in each tier of the U.S. welfare system. A comparison of these evaluations in the AFDC and SSDI programs allows for an assessment of how each tier functions as a site of political action: the degree to which it is responsive to demand-making and the lessons it teaches through its response. The analysis that follows suggest that AFDC and SSDI applicants share a common set of criteria for judging the quality of their first encounters. The designs of these two programs, however, produce experiences that differ markedly. As a result, clients in AFDC and SSDI leave their application encounters with different assessments of the bureaucracy and different expectations for their relationship with government.

A Puzzle of Subordination and Satisfaction

Previous research offers some suggestive evidence regarding client responses to the application encounter. However, as Hasenfeld (1985, 623) notes, "There are two distinct theoretical and methodological approaches to the study of citizens' encounters with welfare state bureaucracies, each leading to diametrically opposed conclusions." Case studies relying on direct observation tend to focus on resource rationing and bureaucratic discretion in public assistance programs and usually conclude that applicants leave their first encounters feeling degraded and subordinated. These studies emphasize the callous and demeaning nature of standardized procedures, the discretionary power wielded by street-level bureaucrats, and the vulnerability of applicants who are left open to abuse by their need for agency services (Handler 1986, 1992; Hasenfeld 1985, 1987; Hasenfeld, Rafferty, and Zald 1987; Lipsky 1980; Prottas 1979).

Following the emphasis on "Durkheimian rituals" found in social control theory (Piven 1995), scholars in this tradition take a highly critical view of application encounters. Agency procedures are described as "public degradation rituals" (Prottas 1979, 24, 127), as "mortification rituals [that] reinforce subordination and individual isolation" (Edelman 1977, 135), and as "the ritual degradation of a pariah class that serves to mark the boundary between the appropriately motivated and the inappropriately motivated, between the virtuous and the defective" (Piven and Cloward 1993, 149). One recent review of this literature concludes that the "degradation of clients is endemic" (Rosenbloom and O'Leary 1997, 125).

Case studies can provide considerable insight into how institutional designs and worker discretion shape the conditions of the application encounter (Bennett 1995; Lipsky 1984). Researchers' direct observations, however, cannot identify which experiences are salient and meaningful to applicants, and one cannot be sure that researchers' negative appraisals correspond to the ways clients' evaluate their experiences. These limitations have been noted repeatedly by a second group of scholars who have relied instead on analyses of survey data. Goodsell (1985, 14), for example, argues that "ordinary citizens perceive bureaucracy differently from most professional students of the subject. The John Does and Mary Smiths of this land seem to know something about bureaucracy the experts do not."

When researchers ask clients to evaluate administrative agencies, the responses tend to be quite positive (Goodsell 1980; Daniel Katz et al. 1975; Martin 1986; Nelson 1981). Regardless of how they are conducted (for example, on the phone or face to face), surveys consistently show high levels of client satisfaction with bureaucratic performance (Goodsell 1985, chap. 2; Gutek 1992, 33). Clients in social insurance and public assistance programs routinely describe agency workers as courteous, considerate, prompt, efficient, helpful, and interested (Goodsell 1985, 17–29; Nelson 1981, 27–33). Indeed, the survey evidence suggests that "clients are quite satisfied on almost all dimensions. . . . Clients like the officials they meet and find the process and outcome of the encounter generally acceptable" (Nelson 1981, 27, 33). Goodsell interprets these findings as strong evidence against claims that bureaucratic encounters subordinate and degrade clients (1985, chaps. 1–3). He concludes, "the picture presented by citizens in their assessments of bureaucracy appears, in sum, as an almost complete contradiction of the hate image depicted in popular media and academic writing" (29).

The survey results seem to cast doubt on claims that first encounters are degradation rituals. For the questions pursued in this chapter, however, these results also have some important limitations. To begin with, they do not directly address how institutional differences affect clients' evaluations. In addition, global indicators of satisfaction do not offer much help in identifying which specific experiences shape client evaluations. Finally, the satisfaction questions in these surveys do not ask about power or status in welfare relationships. In fact, Nelson (1981, 37–38) ends one review of this literature by concluding that "many studies are essentially atheoretical, and few articulate their [political] reasons for investigating client satisfaction."

Thus, observation studies emphasize questions of power and subordination but rarely incorporate clients' perspectives. By contrast, evaluation surveys address the subjective views of clients but do not tie satisfaction to larger questions of status and citizenship. By showing how clients in AFDC and SSDI interpret application encounters as evidence of their own status, the analysis that follows brings these two streams of literature together and grounds them in political questions suggested by theories of dual social citizenship.

To find out which aspects of the first encounter were most meaningful to clients, I asked a very general "grand tour" question (Fetterman 1989, 51–52; Spradley 1979, 86–88): "Could you tell me a little about what it was like to go down and apply? What happened that day?"[2] Through follow-up questions, I then explored how clients evaluated specific experiences in the encounter and what these experiences led them to expect about life in the program. Clients in AFDC and SSDI tend to share a common set of criteria for evaluating their first encounters. These criteria can be organized into four broad categories: (1) access and waiting, (2) information gathering, (3) attempts to define applicants' circumstances, and (4) personal interaction with workers. Clients' evaluations of each of these aspects of the encounter varied considerably across the two programs.

To preview the findings, SSDI clients generally evaluate their application experiences in positive terms and rarely come away expecting to occupy a subordinate status as clients. These interviews support and elaborate on survey evidence that clients are satisfied with bureaucratic treatment. By contrast, AFDC clients are more likely to evaluate their encounters in negative terms and to view these experiences as degrading. AFDC program participants are also more likely to conclude that their positions as clients will be insecure, that they will experience poor treatment, and that they will not be permitted to exert much influence over the disposition of their cases. Surprisingly, these assessments are often accompanied by relatively positive evaluations of agency workers. To a significant degree, these results reproduce the puzzle found in the survey and case-study literature.

In the sections that follow, I explore each of the four types of experiences that underlie clients' evaluations of the application encounter, paying particular attention to differences between AFDC and SSDI. Following these four sections, I address the possibility that the disparity in client evaluations might reflect preexisting differences in the groups of people who enter the AFDC and SSDI programs. This chapter's conclusion offers some reflections on the concept of dual social citizenship and an attempt to reconcile the puzzle of satisfaction and subordination found in previous research.

Access and Waiting

The first aspect of the application encounter that shapes client evaluations is the experience of waiting for access to agency personnel. This waiting process tends to leave a lasting impression that clients view as evidence of their worth as program participants. Patterns of access and waiting can be important indicators of power and social status. Research in a variety of settings suggests that people with lower status tend to wait longer and that those who are forced to wait tend to feel mistreated and unimportant (Schwartz 1975). Left to stew in their own anxiety, applicants who wait for long periods may infer that their claims are unwelcome or that access to workers will be an uncertain privilege in the future (Lipsky 1980, 89; Sarat 1990, 360; Schwartz 1975, 30, 39).

Patterns of waiting in welfare agencies reflect broad policy decisions that may or may not be intended to shape access to program benefits. One of the most critical factors is funding. By cutting program expenditures, policymakers may hope to balance the budget, shrink the bureaucracy, or pressure bureaucrats to be more efficient. Regardless of their intent, such cutbacks limit the availability of administrators and the quality of agency facilities. Public assistance programs such as AFDC are particularly vulnerable to these problems because their funding is not protected by separate payroll contributions or a national tax base. Left to vary along with general tax revenues in the states and stigmatized as a handout to the poor, public assistance programs have always been more susceptible to cuts motivated by moral anxieties, economic fluctuations, business pressures regarding labor markets, and interstate competition (Noble 1997; Peterson 1995; Piven and Cloward 1997a, 71–72). For these and other reasons, AFDC administrators are less likely than their counterparts at the Social Security Administration (SSA) to have the resources needed to improve waiting rooms and intake procedures.

Patterns of waiting and access also reflect intentional policy decisions. Application procedures in SSDI, for example, are designed to accommodate claimants who might have difficulty getting to or waiting at a local agency. Applicants are allowed to file claims over a toll-free phone line and to send documents through the mail. By contrast, although AFDC claimants may also have difficulties getting to the agency (for example, they may lack transportation or child care), they are required in every case to file their claim in person, with no exceptions for good cause.

Approximately half of the SSDI clients in this study applied for benefits from their own homes, setting up appointments for phone interviews and exchanging documents with the agency through the mail. Clients typically see this procedure as a quicker and easier alternative to applying in person and express appreciation for the agency's accommodating policy. As Holly pointed out, "You don't even have to show up anywhere." SSDI clients also tend to value their freedom to choose how and when they want to apply for benefits. Kitty recalled, "I called the 800 number and I said I wanted to apply. And they set up an appointment by phone. They did give me an option. She said, 'Do you want to do this by phone, or do you want to come down?' And I said, 'No, I'm not going to come down.' And that was it."

Phone appointments allow administrators to set up interview times that are convenient for themselves and applicants. As a result, claimants rarely feel a sensation of waiting even if they are interviewed two or three days after their initial call. Instead, the act of being given an appointment strikes most applicants as professional and courteous. Dizzy, for example, was impressed by the efficiency of the phone procedure and felt that even the experience of waiting on hold showed that the SSA was on the ball: "When you call the 800 number, they put you on hold, but they tell you right away, 'Your call will be answered in seven minutes.' And then they go right down the line, five, four, three, two, one. And they're right on the button. How they do that is amazing."

About half of the SSDI clients applied in person at local SSA offices, usually for at least one of three reasons: they applied before the SSA adopted phone registration, they did not realize they had an option, or they hoped to expedite the process or reduce the possibility for error. Because the SSA does not require all applicants to apply in person, those who go to the local offices tend to experience relatively short waiting periods. Only three clients reported waiting spells they considered to be excessive, and no one recalled spending more than two hours in the waiting room. Joe gave a common description: "It was a short amount of time. In and out, shake hands."

Although most applicants do not view these relatively short waits as indications that they are highly valued, they do tend to come away feeling that clients can expect reasonably efficient responses from the agency. Expecting to find a stereotypically slow government bureaucracy, many clients express shock at how quickly their applications are handled. Francis recalled, "I was really surprised when I called up. It wasn't much of a hassle. I called up and the wheels got moving, and it happened. . . . I was surprised at how easy it was applying to SSDI. It wasn't a whole lot of hassle." Starr was one of the few applicants who felt she waited for too long (she estimated ninety minutes). Interestingly, her reaction to this waiting spell was more negative than the responses of AFDC clients who waited for comparable periods. She recalled, "You take a number, and you wait. And that's what you feel like. You feel like a number. I don't know that they can do it any other way, but it's pretty impersonal and humiliating in its own way."

AFDC clients reported waiting spells that were consistently higher than those reported in SSDI. Estimates ranged from about an hour to three days. My own observations were consistent with the middle range of these reports. When I accompanied women to the agency, we usually went at 8:00 A.M. and rarely left before noon. Before one trip, Alicia warned me, "You'll be down there at least three hours, and you sure enough better pack yourself a bag lunch!" Her three-hour estimate was about right, but in many cases the wait stretched to four or five. On one occasion, I spent an entire day, from opening to close, waiting at the agency with a client. Roughly two-thirds of the clients felt that they waited for excessive periods of time.

At the extreme, several clients reported waiting for more than one day to get through the application process. Alissa lost her AFDC benefits after she began working a minimum-wage job but decided to reapply when she discovered that her wages could not support her family. Alissa reported returning to the agency on three separate days (the longest wait in this study). Her account illustrates how a policy that requires a personal appearance at the agency can pose a barrier to welfare claiming for eligible people who are in a crisis situation and have no access to transportation.

> I went to apply at 7:30 in the morning, and I did the application and turned it in. And you sit for a while, and someone calls your name. And it's this whole system. And 3:00 comes around, and I'm still waiting—from 7:30 to 3:00. And someone finally comes up and says, "The offices are closed. Everyone else is going. Who are you waiting to see?" I said, "I don't know. I filled out this application." And she said, "If you can come back tomorrow morning at 8:30, we can help you." I didn't have any transportation, but of course I had to come back. So I walked from where I lived, thirty or forty blocks away, at 8:30 the next morning. And I sat there once again all day. And they still never got to me. I went to the windows and everything. And that day, I waited until 4:00, and they never got around to me. I never got to see everyone that I needed to see to start a case. Two days in a row! . . . On the third day, I walked down at 7:30 again because I had no money at this time. If it wasn't for my grandmother feeding us at this time, we wouldn't have even had food. There was no extra money for bus

tickets. So I walked because it was the only way to get there—the third day in a row.

Clients' interpretations of their application encounters largely corroborated scholarly claims that long waits convey low status and leave clients with the impression that "the Welfare Department assumes [they] have nothing else to do with their time" (Lipsky 1980, 95; Schwartz 1975, 30). Lynn captured a common sentiment when she said,

> It's pretty much like they're "up here" and you're "down there." And they let you know it every chance they get.

How do they let you know that?

> Just a blatant disregard for your time or your feelings. They act like because you're on welfare, you're not working a job, and so you must not have anything better to do. Well, just because I'm not working a job doesn't mean I don't have other important things to do. I do have a family, you know.

In addition to the length of waits, clients also tend to view the physical spaces that make up their waiting environments as evidence of their status (Lasswell 1979). Agency waiting rooms vary systematically according to their functions, their clientele, and their funding. They typically include physical symbols that can convey different orientations of authority or service to clients (Goodsell 1977). As Goodsell explains,

> Governmental waiting rooms of all kinds are important physical spaces because it is within them that we gain initial impressions of officialdom. The citizen is physically embraced, so to speak, by this physical setting during the often tense period after entering agency premises, but before receiving preliminary official processing. During this period the citizen receives cues which suggest accepted agency values, desired client comportment, and the organization's own image of its clientele. These cues and the impressions they generate are of vital normative importance in a democratic society. (1984, 467)

In SSDI, phone interviews allow applicants to wait in their own homes. Dizzy was typical in recalling that this option made the claiming process seem less intimidating: "You're anxious. You're nervous. But it was easier to do on the phone." Among those who went to the SSA offices, only a few found it to be an uninviting place. When I visited the agency, I found padded chairs, tables with program literature on them, and low open counters like one might see in the waiting room of a business or a law office (see Goodsell 1984). Moreover, and presumably because many people applied over the phone, the offices were relatively quiet and uncrowded.

It appeared that the waiting rooms had been improved in recent years. Several clients who had been in the program for longer spells described a waiting room that they found uncomfortable. Phil, who had applied ten years earlier, recalled, "It wasn't user-friendly at all. I mean you'd go into this waiting room, and the chairs were all hard metal chairs. And they were set up in rows, facing the door, so that everyone knew they were on their way out." Two clients who had applied during this earlier period (prior to the Americans with Disabilities Act) also described the SSA waiting room as inaccessible. Having turned to an agency designed to serve people with disabilities, they discovered that the office itself was poorly designed to accommodate their needs. Aside from these earlier experiences, however, SSDI clients had few complaints about the spaces provided for them. A majority did not mention the waiting rooms, and no one described them as threatening or degrading to clients.

The waiting area for AFDC clients differed considerably. The office I saw on most of my trips had a layout similar to what Goodsell (1984, 470–71) labels the "dog kennel" design, because it is authoritative and mazelike. Presumably for their own protection, workers stood behind high counters and were separated from clients by thick glass that stretched to the ceiling. Slots cut into the glass allowed clients to slide forms back and forth, and lines drawn on the floor indicated where to stand. Clients sat in rows of plastic and metal chairs bolted to the floor. Sheriffs circulated throughout the room, and a television monitor showed a picture of the U.S. flag. At a smaller office I visited on two occasions, there were no lines painted on the floor, and I did not see any armed security. Receptionists, however, were once again behind glass windows and high counters, and the hard chairs were fixed in rows. Both offices were clean and well lit.

Many AFDC claimants have to bring their children with them. With the limited resources at their disposal, however, neither AFDC office had provided child-care facilities, toys, children's books, or places to warm up bottles. Some parents tried to entertain their children on the floor. On one occasion, I accompanied a shelter resident seeking AFDC who gave up and left the agency because her young daughter continued to cry after several hours. Lynn remembered similar difficulties and interpreted the lack of help for parents as a sign that the agency was not responsive to clients' needs.[3]

> You've usually got your kids with you. And if they are at an age where they're running around, they're usually running around driving you nuts. If they're little, they're sitting there crying and bawling, wanting to be fed.

And you sit there all day. I don't understand why they can't schedule things. Everyone on AFDC is someone with kids, yet they act like you have all the time in the world to just sit around and shit. Kids don't like sitting in the fucking waiting rooms endlessly. Have you been into one of the welfare waiting rooms? Oh my God, you see a bunch of crazy moms. They don't know how to entertain their kids anymore in this stupid little waiting room. There's only so much you can do with your kids. And you keep saying, "Shhh, shhh."

Applicants tend to find AFDC waiting rooms directive and confusing. Because doors are marked only with letters of the alphabet, it is difficult for clients to negotiate the process on their own. In addition, the overburdened receptionists have little time to offer advice as they sit in front of long lines of impatient people. Clients typically wait for their names to be called over a loudspeaker, gather their belongings and children, and move quickly to wherever they are directed. Like other clients, Sandra felt confused by the process and feared that the agency would pass over people who could not keep up. "When your number is called, if you're not up there in a second, they just go on to somebody else. . . . They tell you to go to window A, B, C, or D. Why do they tell you that? . . . You don't know why you're going where you're going."

Waiting experiences allow AFDC applicants to make their first judgments about the agency. The length of waits, the uncomfortable setting, and the emphasis on security and authority seem to indicate that clients are considered unimportant or dangerous. A few clients compared the atmosphere to a prison setting, casting themselves in the role of prisoners.[4] After offering several analogies to illustrate the status she felt during the waiting stage, Alissa settled on a metaphor: "They're the cowboys, and you're a cow."

It's a big system. "Stand in this line." You feel like cattle or something being prodded. That's how I felt. You go all the way through this line to do this, and then this line to do that. It's like a cattle prod. It's like you're in a big mill. I felt like a number or like I was in a prison system. . . . It feels like you're in a cattle prod. They're the cowboys, and you're a cow. I feel like a cowboy would have more respect for the animals because he knows that the cattle are his livelihood. But these people are like, "I'm helping you. This is something I'm doing for you. So just be quiet and follow your line."

Alissa's vivid language highlights the disparity between experiences of access and waiting in AFDC and SSDI. People who claim SSDI benefits do not feel ennobled by the application process, but they do feel that agency procedures ease their efforts to claim benefits and involve applicants in the process.

They are allowed to exercise choice over how and when they apply for benefits, and accommodating policies suggest that administrators want to receive claims. Most applicants also leave feeling that the agency has been responsive. They tend not to feel that their waits are excessive or that waiting conditions are unwelcoming (at least recently). In short, most applicants come away feeling that as SSDI clients they can expect some accommodations for their needs as well as reasonably responsive and professional treatment.

In contrast, AFDC clients tend to recall that by the time they left the waiting room, they had already begun to feel degraded, frustrated, and angry at the agency. Rather than feeling involved in the process, applicants tend to feel herded. They typically view their waits as too long and their surroundings as uncomfortable and unwelcoming. They are keenly aware that the agency has failed to create a space that accommodates children or eases the burden of waiting to see caseworkers. As a result, AFDC applicants tend to see their waiting experiences as evidence that the agency does not highly value clients. Given these descriptions, it is hardly surprising that researchers find that some eligible people leave the agency without filing a formal application for AFDC benefits (Bennett 1995). Among those who successfully advance welfare claims, most leave the waiting room anticipating that as clients they will be expected to "follow their lines."

Information Gathering

The second theme clients emphasize in evaluating the application encounter concerns the types of questions they are asked. For agency personnel, the most basic task in the first encounter is information gathering. Information is needed to determine department jurisdiction, individual eligibility, and the amount of benefits that should be granted (Prottas 1979). For some applicants, however, the questioning process may prove to be embarrassing, frightening, or offensive (Gouldner 1952, 413; Marziali 1988, 23). The claimant's desire for privacy clashes with the bureaucracy's need for information to produce what Hasenfeld, Rafferty, and Zald (1987, 401) term a "paradox of the welfare state": "In order to exercise their social rights, citizens must disclose their private problems to officials. [But] to the extent that public disclosure is stigmatizing and the bureaucratic response demeaning, citizens will be reluctant to exercise their rights."

In addition to deterring eligible claimants, methods of information gathering can also shape expectations regarding welfare participation. Based on the scope of questions, applicants may draw conclusions about how much privacy or surveillance they can expect as clients. Moreover, they may view question-and-answer sessions as a form of interrogation demonstrating workers' power over clients. In social interaction, people who ask questions exert control over those who answer them (Scheff 1968). This inequality can translate into feelings of powerlessness and loss of control if applicants are repeatedly compelled to reveal information they do not want to share with others (Brodkin 1992, 63; Hasenfeld 1987; Kane 1987; Lipsky 1980, 84). Although all welfare bureaucracies must collect information, the specifics of this process are a matter of design rather than necessity. For example, procedures in both AFDC and SSDI have been designed to emphasize the goal of excluding fraudulent claims. Less emphasis has been placed on ensuring that all eligible citizens are admitted, securing a full account of why the applicant is claiming benefits, or asking what the applicant hopes to accomplish through the program (Piven and Cloward 1993, 160; Stone 1984). Despite this similarity, however, applicants encounter very different questions as they apply for AFDC and SSDI, in large part because these programs serve distinctive functions within the welfare system.

Because AFDC is a categorical program for poor families with dependent minors, street-level workers are directed to obtain information about applicants' family compositions, their assets, their living arrangements, and any relationships that might provide income. And because AFDC is designed to serve as temporary relief, caseworkers may use the first interview to seek out personal problems or find opportunities for reducing the need for benefits down the road. Finally, as a precondition for receiving AFDC, applicants must cooperate with child support enforcement. For all these reasons, questioning procedures in AFDC have considerable depth and breadth.

By contrast, SSDI provides extended aid to individuals with established work histories who have long-term disabilities. The official definition of *disability* used in SSDI was constructed to ensure that able-bodied people would be channeled into public assistance programs that, it was hoped, would encourage job searches through regular case reviews and lower benefits (Albrecht 1992, 33–90; Stone 1984, chaps. 2, 4). Information gathering in SSDI was designed almost solely to guard against fraudulent claims concerning employment and health (Stone 1984, chap. 4). Because of this focus, the questioning process today has considerable depth but limited breadth.

Compared to their positive experiences in gaining access, SSDI clients tend to express more concern about the SSA's attempts to collect information. To begin with, applicants usually find it difficult to document work and health histories. For many people, this problem is exacerbated by the fact that they apply during a period of personal crisis. Physical pain, psychological distress, and poverty make it difficult for many applicants to meet the agency's requests for information. In addition, approximately one-third of the SSDI clients in this study considered the questioning process invasive. Some did not want to contact past employers or reveal their psychological or medical histories. In two cases, applicants felt that their privacy was violated because they had to submit to a physical exam from an unfamiliar doctor picked by the agency. Marie recalled,

> They said that they had to do research on every job that I had had since I
> started a work history. But I had to do the research. And I had to write down
> and let them know what I earned on my first job, where it was, how long
> I worked there, what I did—the old application-type stuff, every job I had
> had from my first job up to that point. You have to keep in mind that I'm
> in the middle of an MS exacerbation. I'm not in the best of health, and I
> have to call . . . because, needless to say, I cannot remember what my first
> job was when I was fifteen years old. I remembered where it was, but not
> how much I earned. I remember now—it's etched in my memory. It was
> eighty-five cents an hour. . . . And to have to chronologically prove each
> job. . . . And I thought, "Wait a minute, I paid taxes on every one of those
> jobs. Shouldn't it be in my records somewhere?" But I still had to do all
> that. And I think that was the most difficult thing. And of course then you
> have to get all the records from your doctor. And then you have to go to
> their doctor, the doctor of their choice, which was very humiliating.

Requests for information lead many applicants to fear that their claims
might be viewed with suspicion. Starr recalled, "They talk to employers and
look at W-2 forms from years past, and I didn't like it." She remembered worrying at the time, "Maybe they think I'm faking, or maybe they think I didn't
try hard enough or that I made enough money before that I shouldn't be coming to this." The vast majority of SSDI clients also recall being anxious that
they would be denied assistance if they made a mistake or uncovered an unexpected piece of evidence. Sarah explained, "You have to go back to the company you worked for and get all this information. And you're kind of afraid you
might screw up."

Although concerned about the depth of the questioning process, most
SSDI claimants value its narrow scope. No one in this study reported being
asked about issues other than employment and disability, and nearly everyone
felt that these issues had legitimate links to their eligibility. Roughly two-thirds
of the applicants reported that they did not view any of the questions as overly
personal in nature. Bridget recalled, "I felt fine about the questions they asked.
They didn't ask me any questions I didn't want to answer." When I asked Kitty
whether she had to divulge much, she gave a typical answer and added an unsolicited comparison: "Yes, but just medical information. So that was fine. My
own business was left private, which I think is different from AFDC."

The limited scope of the SSA's questions serves to ease many applicants'
initial fears about government intervention. Marie, for example, worried that

the agency could "dig into all your personal life and your whole life if they want to." Many clients interpret the narrow range of questions in the application process as an encouraging sign that the SSA will not be interested in their personal lives in the future. Lee-Ann had a typical reaction: "It made me feel more at ease. It didn't make me feel better [about needing to apply], but it made me feel more at ease."

Information gathering in AFDC is broader and touches on more issues that clients consider private. Because means testing requires finding out whether applicants have untapped assets or sources of income, agency workers must collect a wider range of information.[5] As a result, AFDC applicants have to answer a variety of questions that are not asked in SSDI: Do you have access to a car, a boat, a stove, or a bank account? What are the names and incomes of all the people living in your home? Do you have a boyfriend? Does he stay with you? What is his income? How much are your rent and bill payments? Have you paid them all? Where do your children attend school? Do you buy your own food? Do you prepare your food alone?

All of these questions are designed to yield information needed for effective means testing. But when overburdened workers do not have time to explain the function of each question, applicants are left to draw their own conclusions. In most cases, clients' interpretations are shaped by the context of welfare stigma. Questions about men in the house and food preparation, for example, tend to be seen as attempts to monitor sexual behavior and as expressions of doubt about the applicant's competence as a mother. Here and in other instances, when workers do not explain how questions serve the purpose of means testing, applicants tend to view them as evidence of stereotypical assumptions and as an invasion of privacy. Thus, the messages taken away by clients depend not only on what is asked but also on how it is asked and how thoroughly it is explained.

Means testing also requires workers to identify relationships that might provide families with unreported income. Through "income deeming," the income of adult household members and support given to children in the family may be counted toward the income of the applicant (Hirsch 1988). As a result, AFDC claimants are asked to identify any friends, lovers, or family members who are living in the household and to provide information about their incomes. When applicants are not told how these questions relate to their own eligibility, they tend to view them as invasions of privacy. Lashell complained that workers asked

> personal questions that have nothing to do with AFDC. Questions like "Do you have elderly people living with you?" and "Joe, does your mother work? Does your sister get AFDC?" And those are questions that don't really have to do with you, Joe. They have to do with information that should

be personal about your family members. There really is no purpose for the personal questions about your family members.

If household members are reluctant to reveal personal information, this problem can stall an individual's efforts to claim benefits. For example, when Nancy ran out of money, her brother allowed her and her children to live with him until she could apply for AFDC. When she returned from the agency with a request for details about his wages and insurance, he became upset. She recalled him shouting, "Why am I giving you my personal work information? What has this got to do with me? These aren't my children!"

The questions that leave the deepest impression are those associated with child support enforcement, a program with which AFDC applicants are required to cooperate to receive benefits.[6] Although SSDI may offer aid when an absent parent has failed to pay child support, the SSA does not mandate cooperation with enforcement. For some SSDI clients, program participation would be unnecessary if full child support was collected.[7] Kitty, for example, recalled that "it was a choice between AFDC (which I didn't want), getting my ex-husband back into court (which would take an act of God), or apply[ing] to SSD[I]." Because cooperation with enforcement is not required in SSDI, claimants do not have to answer questions about paternity or sexuality as a precondition for aid. At a later point, they are free to choose whether to pursue child support on their own, and if they win support they can receive the money without a reduction in benefits.

Although child support bureaucracies may serve to promote gender equity in the broader population (Keiser 1996, chap. 2), AFDC clients tend to see more costs than benefits from enforcement as it is currently practiced (Harris 1988; Josephson 1997; Keiser and Soss 1998). With the exception of a monthly fifty-dollar pass-through, child support collections go entirely to the state as a "reimbursement" for AFDC payments. Moreover, because this fifty dollars is counted as income, it serves to reduce clients' food stamp payments (Roberts 1991).[8] None of the women I interviewed saw child support enforcement as a benefit to them. To see why such is the case, one must consider the broader context of social networks and survival politics in poor communities (Hardy-Fanta 1993). "Laying the law" on a father can jeopardize an individual's status within the cooperative community relationships that allow for day-to-day survival (Edin and Lein 1997; Stack 1974). As Stack explains, if a woman gives a father's name to the program, her

AFDC stipend remains the same while the father of her children has even less money to assist his mother and sisters' families, who depend on him. This loss of family resources diminishes what a woman can expect from her kin. In an environment where jobs are scarce, salaries are dismally low, and male unemployment is extremely high, . . . the decent, humane and collective spirit tells a mother it is simply wrong to 'lay the law' on the fathers. (1987, 144)

This dilemma was widespread among the women I interviewed and met at the shelter. Several clients also worried that child support enforcement might put them or their children in physical danger. Celina reported that she was not told about the possibility of a good-cause exemption for this risk even though she raised concerns about personal safety. "He was a drug dealer and . . . I thought that was dangerous and didn't want to be bothered with that. But still I have to go to court and see him and have him see me. . . . I think that is very dangerous."

Cooperation with efforts to establish paternity also requires claimants to divulge details about their sexual histories. These questions consistently strike applicants as the most degrading aspect of the first encounter. Kisha recalled, "They ask questions that are unbelievable. They want to know about your sex life and your sex partners and different places you had sex. It's terrible. When I went in there, I wanted to walk out at first because of those questions. But I needed the money, so I had to take it." Applicants felt exposed and humiliated by these questions and complained that their "business was out on the street."[9] Alissa summed up the experience in words that were milder than the norm:

> As I'm filling out this thing for paternity, they're asking me what days I had sex and how often I had sex and when and who. And I thought, "My goodness, this is awfully personal!" And I asked what would happen if I objected to this. And they said if I objected, I wouldn't be eligible. You have to answer every question. Later on, I felt like what if someone is sitting back there looking at my personal life and laughing. Are they sitting back there swapping stories about different people? They were just delving into something I didn't want to be exposed. And I shouldn't have to tell them.

In addition to leaving applicants feeling exposed and in some cases mortified, the experience of submitting to these sorts of questions also tends to leave applicants feeling powerless. As they answer questions that they see as objectionable and unnecessary, applicants are brought face to face with their inability to resist. Nancy recalled being furious about questions that she felt were designed "to make it as difficult for the recipients as possible so they will be disgusted and say 'forget it' and not bother." But when a worker informed her that she either had to provide the information or leave, she realized, "I couldn't [leave] because I had no money to live on."

In addition to their needs for resources, a second reason why applicants feel unable to object to sensitive questions is that the interview schedule appears predetermined. Application forms allow agency supervisors to standardize information collection while providing street-level workers with an important tool for controlling the agenda of the encounter (Hasenfeld and Steinmetz 1981, 90–91; Prottas 1979, 27). If applicants ask why particular questions are relevant or necessary, workers can truthfully respond that they are required to fill in answers for all of the questions. As one client put it, "They just say it's on every form."

Standard questionnaires also serve as a buffer between clients' harsh assessments of the questioning process and their evaluations of specific workers. These forms, along with verbal cues indicating that procedures are fixed by higher authorities, suggest to clients that individual workers are not to blame. As a result, clients rarely hold the messengers accountable for the message. Instead, they blame the institution. Several women commented that the workers who handled their cases seemed sympathetic or even apologetic as they asked for personal information. Most felt that asking the list of questions was simply the worker's job. For example, Tina complained, "[I felt] like I was under a spotlight, like they get to know everything about me. . . . So I was discouraged." But she also recalled, "I asked them why they needed to know certain questions. And they just said it's part of the application, and that I had to fill out the application. It was just their job to hand it out and say, 'You have to sign this.'" Tina later described the worker she met as "anxious to help me" and concluded by saying, "I give her a lot of credit."[10]

In sum, applicants rely heavily on information-gathering procedures as a basis for evaluating their first encounters and drawing inferences about their status as a client. SSA administrators conduct thorough investigations of a restricted number of issues, which leads some SSDI applicants to feel exposed, to believe that they are viewed with suspicion, and to worry that their applications might be denied. By a two-thirds majority, however, SSDI clients in this study did not feel that their privacy had been violated. Because the agency's questions seemed limited in scope and had clear ties to the determination of eligibility, clients tended to come away feeling reassured that the agency would not monitor or intervene in their personal matters in the future.

By contrast, the questioning process in AFDC extends to issues that clients consider private, such as personal relationships, household practices, and sexual histories. Applicants tend to come away feeling exposed and, in many cases, degraded. These feelings provide the basis for expectations about welfare relationships, in part because applicants are told during the first encounter that similar questions will be a part of regular case reviews and ongoing efforts to seek child support. To varying degrees, AFDC applicants leave the first encounter expecting that they will be vulnerable to agency scrutiny until they leave the program.

Defining Applicants' Circumstances

The third theme that clients stress in evaluating their application encounters concerns discussions about the nature of their circumstances. Specifically, clients focus on whether they are allowed to define their own situations and on the ways in which bureaucrats appear to categorize their situations. As described in the two preceding chapters, applicants usually go to the agency with stories that they and their significant others see as legitimating the act of welfare claiming. To applicants, these stories are extremely valuable: they explain the short- and long-term purposes of assistance, the sorts of aid that will be helpful, and why the individual's situation differs from the stereotypical welfare recipient. For these reasons, claimants are usually anxious to explain their side of the story to government officials. They want workers to understand, validate, and respond to their accounts (Prottas 1979, 104–5).

In the impersonal logic of administration, however, categories are more important than narratives. Life histories are far too complex for agencies to process in large numbers (Hummel 1977, 24–25). Administrators create "clients" by simplifying complicated lived realities and sorting them into generic taxonomies (Hasenfeld, Rafferty, and Zald 1987, 402; Loseke 1987; Prottas 1979, 3–4). Their job is to apply the agency's menu of preexisting categories to applicants' stories and to do so quickly (Lipsky 1980, 59; Prottas 1979). Agency workers are occasionally able to pursue longer conversations about personal hardships. However, in their own assessments of time pressures, and from the perspective of efficiency-minded supervisors, the less often they do so, the better.

Programs in both channels of the U.S. welfare system "require claimants to translate their experienced situations and life problems into administerable needs, to present the former as bona fide instances of generalized states of affairs that could in principle befall anyone" (Fraser 1987, 114). Several factors, however, lead to important differences across programs. In AFDC, the same problems of understaffing that lengthen waiting periods also limit the amount of time workers can spend with each client. In addition, the broader scope of information gathering means that more aspects of an individual's situation get discussed and categorized. Finally, the greater social stigma attached to AFDC receipt infuses a greater sense of urgency into applicants' desires to tell their own stories and heightens their sensitivity to others' interpretations.

With only a few exceptions, SSDI clients report that they were allowed to describe their own situations in the first encounter. Betty was typical in recalling that workers were "very receptive to our explaining everything that was going on." SSA workers ask applicants to describe their own abilities, problems they are having as a result of their disabilities, and their plans for work in the future. These openings allow clients to establish the initial definition of their own circumstances. Francis noted with approval, "I told them the situation, and they were very accommodating."

On application forms filled with closed-ended questions, claimants also find an open-ended item allowing them to write whatever they want in their own words.[11] Sarah recalled, "They had a last question asking did I have anything else to say. And I had a lot to say. . . . I didn't know exactly [what to write], but it was about a page or so. But that's where I put anything they didn't ask in a question. I was able to say what was going on."

Three SSDI clients reported that they had hoped for longer and more sympathetic hearings than they received. At some point in the interview, they were stopped and told that they had provided enough information. In addition, roughly half of the SSDI clients recalled being frustrated by their inability to find words that could adequately express their experiences to a stranger. Frank, for example, experienced recurring bouts of paranoia and schizophrenia. He sought SSDI for what he saw at the time as a physical disability: someone had stolen his eyes and hands.

> I only told him I was missing my hands. I didn't tell him anything else, about my eyes or any of that. I told him I couldn't work because my hand was missing all the time. People were taking my hand. And he walked out of the room, I think to think for a second. And he came back and said, "That's enough." And I said, "Well there's a lot of other things. I hear voices too!" He said, "No, that's enough for your Social Security." So, he let me go then. . . . What can you say when someone took your eye? Can you just say, "Someone took my eye?" People don't understand that kind of talk. It was hard to get across what was happening to me. . . . It was just hard to communicate with people that have never experienced that before.

Thus, some SSDI clients come away from the first encounter feeling that they wished they could express more. But with only two exceptions, SSDI clients in this study felt that the agency was open to their input and that they were allowed to play an active role in defining their situations. When I asked Dizzy, an SSDI client who had applied to AFDC several years earlier, if anything distinguished the two application experiences, he listed a number of differences, including, "In SSDI, I was more involved in the process. I got to explain more about the way things were."

SSDI applicants also tend to be reasonably satisfied with how administrators categorize applicants' stories. Clients recalled long lists of categories but did not find them objectionable. In a few cases, they reported feeling compelled to emphasize certain problems and downplay others in a strategic effort to identify themselves with conditions recognized by the agency.[12] Aside from this issue of prioritization, however, SSDI applicants tended to perceive the agency's categories as fair and appropriate, and most felt that workers avoided "unofficial categories" of moral judgment. Molly explained, "It was a pretty direct give-and-take sort of thing. It was a pretty straightforward process. I never had to defend the fact that I made the phone call. I explained the situation, and that was it." Similarly, Emerald recalled, "They have operating-procedure questions they have to ask. But I didn't feel like anybody was out to maliciously get me." These and other SSDI claimants felt that they played an active role in defining their own situations and that the agency used its categories in a responsive and respectful manner.

AFDC clients tend to come away with different impressions. Large caseloads and the need to gather extensive information leave AFDC workers with little time to listen to clients' personal stories. Moreover, processing a constant stream of applicants can be alienating work, further undermining tolerance for storytelling among street-level workers who feel they have heard it all and know the limits of what they can do to help (Lipsky 1980). Roughly two-thirds of AFDC clients felt that they were not given a chance to describe their needs and goals. Like others, Nancy interpreted her experience as evidence that the agency did not want input from clients about their problems, needs, or goals.

> No one asked what brought me there. . . . I wanted someone to help me transfer the seven years I spent in the army working in a hospital to something I could do out here and earn a living. . . . People come to AFDC knowing, in my opinion, that they can't find a job. They have already attempted to. [They come] knowing that they've been going out there and getting rejection after rejection. They already know that. Now, your job, in my opinion, is as an AFDC worker to help this person financially right now, to get them on their feet, but also help them find some other way to live their life. . . . AFDC should be trying, I think, to take the experience and education that people do have and to help them do something with it.

Unlike SSDI applicants, people who apply for AFDC benefits find that agency forms do not include an open-ended question after the closed-ended items. For applicants, the absence of any physical space to describe their situations is frequently seen as a symbol of the more general social process of being pigeonholed. Alissa recalled,

> They put [your situation] in their own categories that they have before you even get there. Even the application itself—certain circumstances are listed there. And if you're not one of those circumstances, you feel like you're not going to be eligible. There's no space that says "Tell us what happened." So, a lot of people just say "This isn't what happened. But it's the closest to what happened. So, I'll just mark that. I'll go along with

them." That's how it was for me originally. For two years, I just went along with whatever was said. And having to use their categories made me feel like maybe I was wrong. . . . They keep telling you, "This is what your situation is."

Relative to SSDI, AFDC applicants are far more likely to feel that they are judged according to unofficial categories. Their descriptions can be divided into roughly equal thirds. The first group comes away feeling they have not been allowed to give their own accounts, and although they do not hear explicit comments, they suspect that workers substitute stereotypes in place of their untold stories. Clients in this group sense a default welfare stereotype (made more salient by questions about sexuality and home life) and feel that they have been denied the opportunity to defend themselves against it. Renee, for example, applied to AFDC so that she could continue to pursue her schooling. Because she was not given a chance to explain this plan, she felt certain that she was viewed as just another lazy, promiscuous young welfare mother:

They've got their own categories. . . . You can't say "Well, me, I'm different from these other people. I'm not like these people. I want this welfare so I can get off welfare, so I can get a good education that's going to give me a job that can support me all the way." You can't say, "I'm different from this girl. I don't watch the soap operas. I don't have five kids, I only have one." You can't say that. You just need their taxpayers' money, and that's it. Period. . . . They don't see you as somebody trying to support yourself and the baby. They see you as just another welfare case. It's like a stereotype: "These people are lazy and don't want to work and just want to get free money." It's in the way they treat you and look at you when you're just trying to come and get help.

A second group also feels that they have not been allowed to explain their situations (making up the other half of the two-thirds majority). People in this group, however, cite explicit statements from workers that they see as expressions of moral judgments or stereotypes. Such comments typically concern efforts to find and keep jobs or sexual and reproductive behaviors. Hope, for example, reapplied to AFDC because of a pregnancy that resulted from one of the occasions when her abusive ex-husband raped her. When she went to the agency, she recalled that workers assumed she had returned because of her own promiscuity and a cycle of dependency.

They said, "Where's your husband? You know your husband isn't supposed to be living with you." And I tried to tell them that he comes to see the kids, and he rapes me. He forces himself upon me. And they were like,

"Yeah, right, uh-huh." I told them I called the police, and the police said he's got every right to be there. . . . [But the worker] said, "It's a cycle. Your kids will go on AFDC, and so will their kids. It's a cycle."

A final third of AFDC clients come away from the first encounter feeling that they were given a chance to present their situations and that they received support from administrators. Many clients in this group express strong feelings of gratitude. Their accounts resemble those of SSDI clients in some respects but place far more emphasis on compassion and sympathy offered by workers. Debber, for example, applied to AFDC as a way to escape her abusive husband. Unlike Hope, she described her worker as accepting and supportive. Like many in this group, Debber considered finding a helpful worker to be a rare piece of luck.

This woman, who was really nice, she sympathized with my situation. . . . I was lucky. I had a compassionate person to talk to. A lot of them aren't too compassionate. A lot of them don't care about your story, really. I was really lucky to have a nice person to talk to. She helped me out a lot.

The strength of AFDC applicants' reactions to whether they are allowed to tell their own stories flows, in part, from the fact that most feel they have been forced to answer invasive questions. Thus, in one-third of the AFDC sample, applicants who feel that they have already divulged personal details are extremely grateful to workers who allow them to provide a broader frame of reference. In the remaining two-thirds of the sample, applicants who feel that earlier questions have left them exposed and open to judgment grow even more frustrated when they are not allowed to defend themselves by telling their own stories.

In sum, clients in both programs place great value on being able to explain their situations and on the ways workers respond. The vast majority of SSDI clients come away from their first encounter feeling that they were (as Dizzy put it) "involved in the process" and allowed to tell their own stories. They generally find the agency's official categories to be satisfactory and rarely feel that workers recast their situations in unofficial ways by making moral judgments.

By contrast, a two-thirds majority in AFDC leave the first encounter feeling that they have not been allowed to define their own situations and that they have been judged according to stereotypes. These applicants usually conclude that the agency does not give much weight to clients' views or aspirations. Thus, despite the fact that AFDC is designed to place greater emphasis on individual casework and the goal of finding ways to reduce clients' future needs for assistance, AFDC clients are far less likely than SSDI clients to come away from the first encounter feeling that attention has been given to their personal situations.

Lynn recalled, "It made me hurt and angry when I left—not at myself, but at the system. This was the system that I had assumed was set up to help people. Silly me. [After the first day] I could tell that this was just a clearinghouse. There was no help."

Personal Interaction

The three evaluative dimensions discussed up to this point all involve contact with administrators. For applicants, however, interaction with individual workers also serves as an important evaluative criterion in its own right. In personal interaction, individuals pick up a variety of cues about how others view them and how they should present themselves in return (Blumer 1966, 1969; Goffman 1959, 1971). By communicating sympathy, offering advice, or adopting a condescending posture, a worker can confirm or change a client's emerging view of the agency and its personnel. This section focuses on three questions: (1) How do applicants evaluate the treatment they receive from agency workers? (2) How do they feel that they are expected to act as applicants? (3) What inferences do they make about how they will be expected to act as clients in the future?

In SSDI, clients' evaluations of administrators stick close to the middle range and show only slight variation. Like many of her fellow clients, Starr emphasized the detachment of workers: "I think Social Security employees are trained extensively on how not to get any personal contact or commitment." Several clients compared their application encounters to past experiences at private businesses. In doing so, they cast themselves in the role of a paying consumer and emphasized that workers seemed professional. Donna recalled, "I can't say they were rude. It was probably like being in any situation like that where you're like returning something to Target. [It's just] the process of what they have to do."

The central themes emphasized in evaluations of SSDI workers are distance and professionalism. Negative evaluations usually focus on a vague sensation of being processed rather than mistreated. For example, Phil recalled, "I remember thinking that [the worker] was very cold, because it was all business. There were no smiles. There was no 'Good day, how are you? My name is . . .' It was 'I'm Mr. So-and-so. We have to fill out these forms.'" In contrast to Phil, roughly three-quarters of SSDI clients gave favorable evaluations. The most positive clients sounded like Frank, who recalled, "They were courteous. They were nice to me. They treated me like an equal. And I felt like I was at home there. They had a nice system." Several clients reported being pleasantly surprised. Lee-Ann recalled, "It surprised me. I kept hearing so much about these people, they do this and they do that. But the ones I dealt with were real nice and real polite. And it was a nice experience, I guess. I don't know how else to put it." Francis captured the moderate tone of most evaluations: "They were nonchalant and matter of fact. It was the job they had to do."

On their own side of the encounter, SSDI claimants usually try to present themselves strategically, in ways that match their image of the ideal applicant (Goffman 1959). This image tends to be shaped almost completely by disability status. People with conditions that clearly qualify, such as blindness, feel most comfortable in the applicant role. Those with less apparent conditions tend to worry that they should seem more disabled or even helpless. When Emerald applied because of her rheumatoid arthritis, she felt uneasy because she was "someone with a nonvisible disease. My hands were still straight, and my body was still somewhat normal." Emerald felt unsure about the expectations of the applicant role and how to fulfill them: "What does somebody look like if they have a disability? How am I supposed to determine what I should look like if I have a disability? Am I supposed to look like I have Down syndrome or be in a wheelchair?"

Anxiety over the applicant role and subsequent attempts to engage in strategic impression management are most common among SSDI clients who apply in person. These applicants tend to worry that if they look too good, a worker might reject their application or think they are a welfare cheat. Marie felt sure that the worker at her interview must have seen her as "another faker. Basically, I looked pretty healthy. I mean, I wasn't crippled and drooling from my mouth and all that kind of stuff." To fulfill the applicant role, some claimants feel that they need to avoid putting on a good face. In fact, one piece of literature I received from the National Multiple Sclerosis Society advised applicants to dress and carry themselves in ways that would make their disabilities more apparent. Strategies for self-presentation were also a staple form of advice given in the disability support groups I attended.

Despite this strong sense of how applicants should appear, people in SSDI almost never recall coming away from the first encounter with a strong sense of how they will be expected to act as a client. When I asked Donna whether her contacts with agency workers left her with any ideas about how she should act in the future, she gave a typical response: "It was kind of nothing—no impression one way or the other." Similarly, Bridget recalled, "Basically, I didn't leave that first time with any impression." Thus, while many people in the SSDI program felt that they had to engage in impression management during their application encounters, they did not leave these encounters with a sense that they would have to conform to an ideal client role in the future.

Relative to SSDI, the design of the AFDC program provides a very different context for client-worker interaction. As the preceding sections have shown, personal interaction in AFDC is more likely to be conducted face to face, to occur after longer waits, to be colored by welfare stigma, and to address issues that applicants consider private. In addition, because the program includes case-work relationships, AFDC workers have stronger incentives to "teach the client role" during the first encounter (Alcabes and Jones 1985). To manage their time effectively and maintain some level of job satisfaction, AFDC workers have to construct relationships that will not routinely produce emotionally draining or time-consuming demands, questions, and confrontations. To do so, they must make sure that applicants quickly recognize some realities of bureaucratic life: the scarcity of time and resources for meeting client demands, the need for deference to worker decisions, the penalties for not following directions, the advantages of cooperation, and the costs of conflict (Lipsky 1980, 61–65; Prottas 1979, 115).

The AFDC clients in this study split evenly between positive and negative evaluations of administrators. But because of the greater intensity of interactions in AFDC, evaluations in both directions tend to be more personalized and more extreme. The most positive evaluations tend to be given by the same people who report that they were allowed to present their situations the way they saw them. Lisa recalled that she was surprised by the helpfulness of her worker: "I thought they'd be snobby, or turn me away. But they were real helpful. . . . She tried to be my friend and not just a worker." Similarly, Shelly reported, "The intake worker was fantastic. . . . She asked if we had more need, and I said, 'No, we're fine.' She suggested that we get food stamps, and I said, 'No, we don't need that.' She understands."

The other half of AFDC clients give administrators unfavorable evaluations. In this group, treatment from individual workers reinforced the impressions they had taken away from the rest of the first encounter. For example, Alicia complained, "They really put you down. . . . They don't have no kind of respect for you." Similarly, Renee recalled, "They had their attitudes. . . . They just treat you like shit. . . . They don't care. They don't give a damn." Nancy summarized the common sentiment by saying, "You go away with just the feeling that you're not a person."

Relative to their counterparts in SSDI, AFDC clients describe a broader variety of pressures influencing the ways they presented themselves during the first encounter. The first of these pressures resembles SSDI applicants' attempts to avoid looking too good. AFDC applicants tend to worry, for example, that wearing certain pieces of clothing might cause them to appear not needy enough. As Alissa put it, "They think if you're doing what you're supposed to be doing with your money, you're not supposed to have anything nice."

AFDC applicants also tend to believe that to succeed, they need to present themselves in ways that do not fit too closely with welfare stereotypes. Clients report feeling that workers expect deserving applicants to look morally virtuous (for example, by appearing to abstain from drugs, alcohol, and casual sex). According to clients, the ideal applicant appears intent on self-improvement and meets with administrators' standards of self-respect. Vanessa advised, "You [should not] present yourself like you're just on the streets, like you don't have anywhere to go, like you don't have no self-esteem about yourself." Noting the worn clothes she was wearing at our interview, she commented, "If I was to go down there looking like I'm looking, they would be like, 'Now, why is this girl coming down here looking like that?' You know what I mean? It's the way you present yourself." Shelly felt that the most successful strategy was to divert attention from yourself to forestall moral judgments: "You have to emphasize that you need help not for yourself but for your little kids that haven't done anything wrong."[13]

The final element of self-presentation concerns the need to convey deference (Lipsky 1980, 61–65). To win benefits, clients feel that it is helpful for applicants to appear appreciative, respectful, and nonassertive in dealing with workers. Clients who report more positive first encounters tend to cite these forms of impression management as key reasons for their good experiences. Clients who feel they received poor treatment emphasize the importance of accepting it in a deferential way. Like a number of her fellow recipients, Lashell saw deference as an integral part of the applicant role that could determine the outcome of the entire process.

> Just because you fill out an application doesn't mean you're going to get help. It depends on how your attitude appears to them, because they could so easily rip your application up and throw it away. You have to stay calm and kiss their ass. Because if you don't, then they will not help you. You have to show them that you can stay calm and answer all their questions: *whatever* they want to know. I had to do that because I needed not only financial help but also medical insurance and food stamps.

People who claim AFDC benefits tend to come away from the first encounter with a strong sense that as clients, they will be expected to accept decisions and procedures without protest and will not be asked for very much input. When I asked Renee if her first encounter left her with any impression of what her role would be as a client, she replied, "Yes, you know it. You know it! . . . They expect you to be submissive toward them or to act like they're your authority or something. And you are *expected* to act like that." When I asked Alissa how dealing with workers for the first time affected her expectations, she extended her earlier metaphor of cowboys and cows: "I was pretty sure I wouldn't be allowed to have much involvement, and that has proven to be pretty much right. We're like cattle. Of course you don't give the cows a choice about when they're going to do what they're going to do."

AFDC applicants typically assume that their roles during the first encounter will remain their future roles. For those who feel they have been treated poorly by workers, all of the various aspects of the first encounter seem to converge on a single troubling conclusion. Even applicants who have positive experiences with workers, however, tend to attribute this fact to their own willingness to go along with the process. And in light of the other aspects of the encounter, they still tend to arrive at pessimistic conclusions about the role that clients occupy in the program.

Tina, for example, felt that the worker who served her "was anxious to help me because she understood my predicament." However, she also reported that she sat with her mother for eight hours in the waiting room, that she felt "under the spotlight" because she was asked questions that were "really none of their business," and that she felt "discouraged" by the overall process. As a result, Tina came away feeling that her worker would do everything she could to help but that Tina herself would not have much say in the process. When I asked what expectations she took away from her first encounter, she replied, "I thought they would end up giving me the runaround, push me to do this, and push me to do that."

The Problem of Group Differences

The preceding analysis has suggested that program designs in the two tiers of the welfare system create unequal conditions for welfare demand-making. Citizens who act on their eligibility for benefits in the AFDC and SSDI programs experience distinctive patterns of access and waiting, information gathering, attempts to define their life conditions, and interaction with workers. As a result, their evaluations of the application encounter differ considerably, and the two groups leave this encounter with different expectations regarding their roles as welfare clients.

There may, however, be an alternative way to explain these differences across programs. Rather than being a product of unequal conditions in the two tiers of the welfare system, they might reflect differences in the groups of people who apply to the AFDC and SSDI programs. People who claim SSDI benefits, for example, might share characteristics that distinguish them from their AFDC counterparts and make them more likely to give positive evaluations. Clients' personal backgrounds undoubtedly influence their assessments of the application encounter to some degree. An analysis of the evidence, however, suggests that the disparity in client evaluations is not simply a reflection of preexisting differences between the two program populations.

Relative to AFDC clients, the SSDI clients in this study are older; they are more likely to be male and white; and they have a higher level of formal education (see appendix A). If these group characteristics account for the disparity across programs, two patterns should emerge in the interview data. First, there should be systematic differences in evaluations within each program: older SSDI clients should offer more positive evaluations than younger SSDI clients; men in SSDI should offer more positive evaluations than women in SSDI; evaluations of the AFDC encounter should be more positive among white clients than among people of color; and evaluations in each program should vary according to education levels. Second, the disparity between evaluations of AFDC and SSDI should disappear when similar subgroups from each program are isolated and compared: women should evaluate the SSDI and AFDC encounters in similar ways, white clients in the two programs should not differ in their evaluations, and so on. In a series of focused comparisons, neither of these telltale patterns emerges with any consistency across categories defined by race, gender, age, or education. Regardless of which groups are compared, evaluations tend to be consistent within each program and different across the programs.

Higher evaluations of the first encounter in SSDI might also reflect differences in class background. Relative to AFDC clients, people in SSDI are more likely to come from middle- or even upper-class families. If anything, however, there are good reasons to suspect that this higher status might produce lower evaluations in SSDI. People tend to evaluate bureaucratic encounters against a baseline of what they expect to receive, and this standard is strongly influenced by the types of treatment to which they have grown accustomed in the past (Martin 1986, 190; Rees and Wallace 1982). From this perspective, it seems likely that the same treatment might be judged more harshly by people with higher socioeconomic status. Although it is hard to discern a clear pattern of this sort because of the link between past income and program usage, the interviews do offer some suggestive evidence.

For example, all three SSDI clients who complained about excessive waits reported times that were shorter than those recalled by any AFDC client who lodged a similar complaint, and a number of AFDC applicants who waited for longer periods did not consider them excessive. In addition, the small number of AFDC applicants who came from middle-class backgrounds were among those who expressed the strongest sense of outrage in recalling their first encounters. Lynn offered some self-reflection on this point:

> I don't know, maybe it's because I came from an upper-middle-class background—a lot of people would think I was snobby to say this—but I'm used to being treated with a certain degree of respect. . . . So I thought that I could go in there and at least be treated like a human being. And I found that that was not at all the case.

Nancy, a thirty-seven-year-old client who grew up in a poor family, agreed with this argument linking class background, expectations, and evaluations:

> I grew up knowing that poor people didn't get treated right. So I kind of expected that [treatment] when I went down there. . . . I certainly can't

imagine someone who had a middle-class childhood, who never signed up for social-welfare programs in their life, and all of a sudden they're thirty or thirty-five years old and have to apply for welfare. I can't imagine what that would be like. I think it would be devastating. It would be like being raped, I think. Of course, that doesn't really say much about the fact that many of us were raised on it and come to expect that kind of behavior, being treated that way. I can't imagine what it would be like because I know what it felt like for me, even having been used to it and expecting it. For someone who has no idea what they're getting into, it's got to be difficult.

Thus, if one considers the potential bias introduced by prior expectations, the consistently higher evaluations in SSDI seem all the more impressive. Indeed, one might go farther and suggest that favorable evaluations of the AFDC encounter may partly reflect the low expectations held by poor people who have heard stories that leave them afraid to apply for benefits (see chapter 3).

Finally, in assessing whether the disparity in evaluations reflects prior group differences or institutional differences, it is worth paying special attention to the evaluations of two SSDI clients who had applied to AFDC earlier in their lives. By looking at a single individual's reaction to two different application encounters, it is possible to control almost entirely for background differences (with the exception of the period between the two experiences). Dizzy was among the group of clients who had some complaints about applying to SSDI. However, his evaluation of this experience was far superior to his view of the application encounter in AFDC.

[AFDC] is terrible. . . . Their whole attitude is like they don't want to be doing this job and like they think you're trying to get over on them. It's like you're trying to do something illegal just to get free money. . . . It was very hard with SSDI, but they were not rude. [The difference] was like night and day. [SSDI] treated me with respect, which is something I demand. And in SSDI, I was more involved in the process. I got to explain more about the way things were. [The people in SSDI] were kind and understanding, I must say, and they listened, unlike the people in the AFDC program. I really feel for [AFDC clients]. Until I had gone down there, I didn't know what it was like to sit down there and to not be treated like a human being when you see a caseworker. I mean, I wanted to hit the son of a bitch. If I'd have been younger, I would have—back when I was strong enough. And I probably would have went to jail for disorderly conduct. That would have been fine with me, because I sure wanted to hit him.

Dizzy's claim that the difference "was like night and day" was supported by Joy, an SSDI client who had participated in AFDC earlier in her life.

[SSA personnel] were very nice. They were very helpful.

Was that similar to AFDC?

No. It was totally different than the way I thought it would be based on AFDC. They were very [informative]. They let me know what my rights were. So, it wasn't as bad as I thought. Compared with AFDC, it was like I moved from a two to a seven on that one-to-ten [scale]. When I went to AFDC, they told me I was too fat to work in [this state], that I would be too risky to hire. I told them what I wanted from them and that I just needed medical, food stamps, and help getting a job. I had all my papers saying my skills and experience. And the woman from job services just said, "I'm sorry, you have to just go on AFDC." So can you imagine how far down you can go at the welfare office? It's like they're saying, "Just get your ass downstairs, apply for welfare, and then go home and take care of your kids and forget about it."

Did you feel like you were able to present your situation to the people at Social Security?

They were very understanding. They were very pleasant. They encouraged me and they let me know that if there were any changes, it wouldn't be a problem. They said I would be able to go to work if I could. And that made me feel good. They listened to what I said I wanted. That's not like AFDC. There, it's like it's automated for you to be on this track. Boing! You go to door A or B. It don't matter who you are or what. I don't care for it.

In sum, although there are good reasons to suspect that individual characteristics have some effect on client evaluations, the evidence from this study points to real differences across the two tiers of the welfare system. The disparity between evaluations of the first encounter in AFDC and SSDI cannot be accounted for on the basis of age, race, gender, formal education levels, or class background. Moreover, the differences in evaluations expressed by clients in AFDC and SSDI are strongly corroborated by individuals who have applied to both programs.

The First Encounter: Puzzle and Politics

Clients' evaluations of their application encounters provide an important measure of how welfare institutions function as sites of political action, a subjective indicator of the quality of social citizenship offered in each tier of the U.S.

welfare system (Hasenfeld 1985, 623). The terms of the application encounter are constructed through institutional design. As a necessary step in the welfare-claiming process, this encounter can serve to deter or facilitate demands on government. And as the first step in the process of welfare participation, it can shape clients' expectations regarding authority, procedure, and behavior in welfare programs.

The evidence presented here supports claims that the two-tier welfare system institutionalizes a hierarchy of social citizenship. Critics have charged that clients in public assistance programs endure "administrative humiliation," while social insurance recipients are positioned as "paying consumers" and hence "qualify as social citizens in virtually the fullest sense the term can acquire within the framework of a male-dominated capitalist society" (Fraser 1987, 111). Applied as a blanket description of clients' accounts, this summary would overstate the case. Even the most upbeat SSDI clients do not describe an unequivocal affirmation of citizenship, and AFDC clients do not paint a seamless portrait of degradation. Nevertheless, their evaluations suggest the existence of significant inequalities. People who seek AFDC benefits are far more likely than their counterparts in SSDI to feel that they receive repellent treatment from the agency and to come away believing that clients occupy a low status in their relationships with the agency.

SSDI clients generally evaluate their first encounters in positive terms. Most come away expecting the agency to be responsive to and respectful of clients in the future. Although many are anxious about applying at first, they typically find the application process reassuring. They generally feel that procedures are set up to accommodate their needs and facilitate their claims. They are pleasantly surprised to find that they can choose their own appointment times, apply from home, and initiate their claims in an efficient manner. Some applicants see agency questions as intimidating and difficult to answer but are typically relieved to find that they are not required to divulge information that they consider especially private. Because most SSDI clients feel able to define their own situations during the first encounter, they tend to come away feeling that they have played an active role in the process. While they rarely express strong sentiments about individual workers, most clients believe that administrators have handled cases in a professional manner. And even though applicants experience pressure to "look disabled" during the first encounter, they do not leave with a sense that they will have to display deference or live up to any other behavioral expectations as clients.

In short, client evaluations in SSDI conform to both the findings of survey research and theories of dual social citizenship. Clients who apply for social insurance do not come away feeling subordinated or objectified. Some even echo the literature by making analogies to being treated as a paying consumer. In contrast to the metaphors used in AFDC (being run through the mill, being a prisoner, being a cow), dealing with the SSA is described as "like returning something to Target." Consistent with the findings of survey research, most SSDI applicants leave with positive evaluations of the services they receive. And like some survey researchers, a number of these clients offer their evaluations as refutations of "hateful" stereotypes of bureaucracies (Goodsell 1985).

AFDC applicants are far more likely to leave their first encounters feeling that they have been mistreated and demeaned. They tend to feel herded as they wait for long spells in rooms that they sometimes compare to prisons. They see little effort to ease the claiming process by addressing their travel difficulties or their needs as parents. Most feel that they are forced to answer objectionable questions about their personal lives yet also feel that they are prevented from explaining their own situations or goals. They perceive pressures to be deferential to workers and fit into workers' images of the deserving poor. And while SSDI applicants come away with little sense of a clearly defined client role, AFDC applicants tend to feel that they have taken on a dependent status that entails vulnerability but does not promise active involvement.

In the midst of their negative reactions to this application process, however, half of AFDC clients arrive at positive evaluations of the workers who carry it out. In this regard, AFDC clients reproduce the puzzle described at the beginning of this chapter. Their accounts clearly support the claims of social control theorists and participant observers who suggest that applicants are degraded in the public assistance tier of the welfare system (Lipsky 1980, 1984; Piven and Cloward 1993; Prottas 1979). At the same time, though, clients report a level of satisfaction with workers that is comparable to what researchers have found using closed-ended survey items. Half of the clients in this study gave positive evaluations of their workers, only slightly less than the two-thirds majority that found their workers to be courteous and helpful in Goodsell's exit poll of clients (1985, 31).

Researchers have usually assumed that survey evidence of satisfaction and observation studies showing subordination point to "diametrically opposed conclusions" (Hasenfeld 1985, 623). To resolve these contradictory findings, one could appeal to concepts such as false consciousness or self-deprecation. Perhaps benevolent images of charity cloud the dynamics of power, leaving applicants so grateful for assistance that they do not recognize what outside observers consider to be mistreatment. Alternatively, perhaps AFDC clients lack the self-esteem needed to believe that they deserve respectful treatment and hence consider poor treatment to be an appropriate response from the agency. The interview evidence presented here casts doubt on each of these explanations. AFDC clients in this study clearly perceived mistreatment in their first encounters and overwhelmingly believed that it was undeserved.

To solve the puzzle of satisfaction and subordination, it is more helpful to begin by accepting the seemingly contradictory responses of clients as real and meaningful. In-depth interviews routinely reveal ambivalence and disjunction when citizens are asked to speak about deeply felt political experiences or issues (Chong 1993; Hochschild 1981, 1993; Lane 1962). In light of this research, it is not surprising that the first encounter produces mixed emotions for clients. Despite feeling degraded by elements of the encounter, clients' expressions of satisfaction reflect a real sense of relief that their worst fears have not been realized. Such is the case in two respects. First, because the application encounter involves such high stakes, successful applicants tend to enter with a great deal of anxiety and leave with intense feelings of relief. Second, because most clients assume that good caseworkers are an exception to the rule, their assessments of their own workers reflect a genuine belief that things could easily have been worse.

Beyond these two sources of satisfaction, the ambivalence expressed by AFDC clients can be made more interpretable by making two analytic distinctions. First, the agency and the individual worker make up separate objects of evaluation for clients. AFDC applicants tend to feel demeaned by an agency that they perceive as a hostile institution. If anyone is responsible for long waiting spells in intimidating rooms, it is surely higher officialdom at the agency. The invasive questions asked by workers are required by these same authorities; workers simply fill out the forms. Workers who end interviews without letting applicants explain themselves mention the heavy caseloads and time pressures as justifications. Like congressional candidates who vilify Congress to show they are on the same side as their constituents (Hibbing and Theiss-Morse 1995), caseworkers use these sorts of comments to deflect blame toward an amorphous bureaucracy and establish trust with clients (Prottas 1979). In fact, given clients' negative views of agency procedures, a sympathetic worker may seem like a prized advocate in an uncaring institution (Lipsky 1980, 72).

Street-level workers' attempts to deflect blame are generally reinforced by clients' perceptions that the agency is a difficult work environment. Lynn was among the strongest critics of how the agency treated applicants, but she paused to distinguish her evaluation of the agency from her view of its employees: "I wouldn't want to be one of the workers either. . . . I'm criticizing the system more than I'm criticizing the workers." Lynn's distinction is crucial: clients tend to blame government institutions (the "system") more than individual bureaucrats. Even in the half of the sample that gave negative evaluations of their workers, clients occasionally tempered their criticisms based on the difficulty of working at the welfare agency. Renee complained that "they just treat you like shit" but later explained,

> Most of them don't like the job. They feel like they've asked and answered the same questions over and over again. They feel like it must be the same person asking the same question again. They get very irritated. They don't

like to answer a lot of questions, period. I know they're in a rush. And I know they deal with a lot of ignorant people. I deal with the public, too [as a grocery cashier], so I can understand. But they're real irritated and rushed. You can't ask a single question.

The second important distinction is that there is a difference between clients' evaluations of workers as individuals and their evaluations of the client-worker relationship. There are important links between perceptions of the worker and perceptions of the relationship, but the two should not be conflated. A subject standing before a benevolent monarch can recognize with a sigh of relief that the king is kind yet still despise the inequality of power. Likewise, a client who senses that her worker controls her fate and has access to her private life is all the more grateful if this worker appears to be caring and sympathetic. The easy coexistence of satisfaction and subordination was well captured by Shelly, who told me, "I've got a real nice worker" but later cautioned, "You can't be assertive. You can't."

By taking these two distinctions into account, it is possible to see how clients might simultaneously feel degraded by agency procedures, subordinated in their casework relationships, and satisfied with the helpful and supportive demeanor of specific workers. Evidence of satisfaction and subordination only point toward diametrically opposed conclusions if one assumes that clients arrive at a single global evaluation of the application encounter. Instead, clients typically have at least three targets of evaluation: the agency, the worker, and the relationship they will enter as a client. Satisfaction and subordination intersect to reveal the political complexity of bureaucratic encounters.

CHAPTER 6

Welfare Participation and the Client's Dilemma of Action

As public welfare provision has grown in the United States, the quality of citizenship has come to depend more heavily on the ways in which individuals are positioned as clients of the welfare state. As welfare clients, citizens confront fundamental questions of right and duty and difficult dilemmas of action and quiescence. This chapter explores political dimensions of the client role, concentrating on how institutional designs in each tier of the welfare system shape citizens' abilities to act as vocal subjects in their welfare relationships. Welfare agencies are political institutions. Their designs establish decision-making and dispute processes, distribute authority and power in welfare relationships, and structure interaction between citizens and government personnel. These designs can encourage clients to participate actively in the decisions that shape their life conditions or position clients in a manner that leaves them feeling silenced and unable to challenge decisions they find objectionable.

The political significance of client assertiveness flows from a number of sources. Rights-based grievances, for example, are essential for the effective operation of due-process mechanisms that protect citizens from abuse at the hands of agency officials. Formal rights in welfare relationships are only meaningful to the extent that clients can and do invoke them to dispute rule violations or complain when entitlements are withheld (Handler 1986; White 1990). Beyond this defensive function, client assertiveness is also a precondition for welfare agencies that are responsive to citizens' needs and interests. If clients are silenced in agency decision-making processes, they are in effect denied the political right to self-government, the right to participate in the exercise of political power as it shapes their life conditions (Marshall 1964, 72).

Political rights to participate in the exercise of power take on particular significance in the welfare context for three reasons. First, the issues at stake in agency decision making are far more personal and consequential for the client than most decisions made by government. When clients become unable or unwilling to speak, they are reduced to spectators in the determination of their individual fates. Second, welfare clients, especially those in public assistance programs, are unlikely to exert much influence in other branches of government (Verba, Schlozman, and Brady 1995). Thus, if clients are excluded from decision making at the welfare agency, they are silenced in the government institution that provides them with their most direct connection to the policy process (Nelson 1984). Third, when clients dispute agency decisions, they not only help themselves but also reshape the government institutions their fellow citizens encounter. As Gutek has argued, client quiescence is a political problem in part because a public agency's responsiveness depends on its clientele's assertiveness:

> Disputes can serve as catalysts for change within organizations. They expose problems within organizations and serve as a feedback mechanism regarding the organization's performance, broadly defined. In short, disputes have some positive effects on organizations. Therefore, it is important to understand if and when a dispute fails to arise, that is, when conditions of inequity, discrimination, or injustice exist and the "victims" fail to dispute those conditions. (1992, 39)

To understand why clients become more or less willing to speak up for themselves in welfare programs, it is necessary to build on two themes developed in the preceding chapter. The first, drawn from participatory-democratic theory, suggests that participation is educative: it teaches lessons that influence individuals' orientations toward political action, and these lessons depend on the nature of institutional designs (Bachrach 1967; Pateman 1970; Schneider and Ingram 1997). The second, drawn from theories of social control and dual social citizenship, suggests that the two tiers of the U.S. welfare system provide citizens with an unequal framework of institutional settings for welfare participation (Gordon 1994; Nelson 1984, 1990; Piven and Cloward 1993). Taken together, these theories point to a political-learning explanation for client assertiveness and predict disparities in client assertiveness across the two tiers of the welfare system.

In what follows, I show how the policy designs of the AFDC and SSDI programs position clients in ways that produce systematic inequalities in the political dimensions of welfare participation. As clients participate in these two programs, they learn different kinds of lessons about how the agency works as an institution, how agency personnel make decisions, how clients are expected to act, and how clients are likely to be treated if they assert their rights or interests. These lessons, in turn, shape individuals' responses to the dilemmas of action they confront as clients of the welfare state.

The Client's Dilemma of Action

Like the applicant's dilemma of action (see chap. 3), the client's dilemma of action focuses on decisions about whether to make oneself heard by government. As clients in welfare relationships, citizens must decide whether to express needs that might be met by agency resources, whether to voice interests regarding bureaucratic decisions, and whether to file grievances when rules have been violated or entitlements have been denied. In some cases, of course, clients do not assert themselves for reasons that have little to do with decision making: they may fail to perceive the existence of an injury or problem, they may not hold the agency responsible for providing a remedy for this problem, or they may be unaware that an administrative remedy is available (Handler 1986, chap. 2). The question pursued in this chapter, however, concerns clients' conscious decisions about whether to speak up in situations where they believe they have legitimate problems that the agency should address. Although clients in these situations have formal rights to challenge workers or to request fair hearings, in practice they confront the client's dilemma of action:

> Should I wait my turn and submit to the procedures of the agency, despite reservations? I risk being unable to gain attention to my particular needs and concerns. Should I speak out forcefully and demand my rights? I risk the antagonism of the workers by disrupting office procedures. (Lipsky 1980, xiv)

As this description implies, the client's dilemma is shaped by two structural characteristics of welfare participation. First, welfare clients occupy a dependent position in relation to the welfare agency and its workers (Handler 1992, 335–44; Hasenfeld 1987). Agency workers control critical resources and usually possess levels of experience, expertise, and legitimacy that exceed those of clients (Hasenfeld 1987; Hasenfeld and Steinmetz 1981). Clients depend on the agency for support and can rarely afford to lose assistance even for a short period of time. As a result, they may be afraid to risk conflict by speaking up for themselves (Handler 1986; Hasenfeld 1987; Lipsky 1980).

Clients generally recognize these disparities in power, but this recognition does not lead inevitably to silent compliance. Despite being unequal, some welfare relationships allow clients to participate actively in decision making, and in some cases, of course, dependent clients do not hesitate to initiate open conflict with agency workers (Prottas 1979; Sarat 1990, 377). Thus, to explain why clients do or do not speak up for themselves, it is not enough to cite the objective existence of power disparities. The more critical task is to illuminate the perceptions of power and vulnerability that provide a subjective frame of reference for clients (Simon 1985). That is, to understand patterns of client assertiveness, one must identify what clients believe about power in welfare relationships and explain why they believe it.

The client's dilemma of action is also shaped by a second structural feature of welfare participation: interactions with agency personnel occur within an ongoing relationship, what some might call a repeated game. As a result, clients have to assess possibilities for action today "with a keen sense of the importance of tomorrow" (Handler 1986, 29). Success in a small dispute with a worker might easily prove to be a hollow victory if it leads to punishment, exclusion, or a negative decision in the future.

Thus, in deciding whether it is better to opt for speech or silence, clients have to rely on their beliefs about how agency decision making works over the long haul. Two considerations are primary. First, clients assess the extent to which administrative decision making and action are open to influence: If I speak up, if I complain or file a grievance, can I expect to be effective? Second, clients evaluate their own security in the welfare relationship and the vulnerability that might result from expressing their needs or asserting their interests. If I speak up now, is it possible that I might lose benefits, suffer indignities, or be denied opportunities down the line?

Clients in AFDC and SSDI differ sharply in their willingness to raise questions or grievances with welfare bureaucrats, and the direction of this difference is consistent with theories of social control and dual social citizenship (Fraser 1987; Gordon 1994). Out of twenty-five SSDI clients, only one (4 percent) reported that she would not speak up if she had a major problem. By contrast, a significantly larger majority of AFDC clients, seventeen of twenty-five (68 percent), said that they would be unwilling to raise a grievance under almost any condition ($p = .001$).[1] Eight AFDC clients were more willing to speak up (32 percent), but even individuals in this group said that they would do so only in very particular situations.

The high levels of reticence found among AFDC clients in interviews were corroborated by my observations at the shelter for homeless families, where difficulties with the AFDC program were common. In some cases, a late welfare check had caused a family to be evicted from its home. More often, homelessness itself led to problems: families were left without an address for the agency to use; women were unable to get to agency appointments; families who fled from abuse or lost their homes to fire could not locate their identification and medical cards. When I suggested dealing with these sorts of problems by contacting a caseworker, I typically encountered resistance from residents. Women in the shelter were usually quick to question the wisdom of making any waves that might draw attention from agency workers.

Circumstantial evidence of this dynamic can also be found in previous research. In an exit poll of AFDC clients, for example, Goodsell (1980) found that only 6.7 percent reported arguing with agency personnel. Although this low percentage might be viewed as evidence of satisfied clients and smooth welfare relationships, it is also consistent with the possibility that "clients wanted to argue with personnel but decided against it" (Nelson 1981, 31). An earlier study by Handler and Hollingsworth (1971) suggests even more strongly that silence in AFDC relationships is a learned response: the authors report that the rate of client-initiated contacts with AFDC workers decreases over time, with more experienced clients less likely to make themselves visible than people who are new to the program (see also Prottas 1979, 129).

The fact that clients in SSDI and AFDC differ in their willingness to speak up for themselves might be explained, in part, by differences in the background characteristics of the two client populations. The disparity across programs, however, remains clear in analyses that control for demographic differences by isolating similar subgroups in the program samples. With only one SSDI client reporting that she would hesitate to raise questions or grievances, the gap between SSDI and AFDC does not fade in comparisons that include only white clients, only female clients, or clients with similar ages or education levels. In addition, as I discuss later in this chapter, the AFDC clients who express a greater willingness to speak up are not concentrated in particular demographic groups.

If recipients in both programs were reluctant to express themselves, one might suggest that welfare benefits provide relief and reassurance in a way that functions to quell disruptiveness, that dependence on aid for basic necessities leaves recipients too vulnerable to risk speaking up, or that this dependence cultivates passivity and undermines self-esteem in a way that leaves clients unable to assert themselves. But because each argument locates the roots of quiescence in the fact of welfare provision itself, none can explain the disparity across programs. Clients in both AFDC and SSDI depend on government benefits for survival. In fact, the group that is more willing to speak up receives higher levels of assistance.

To explain AFDC and SSDI clients' different responses, it is necessary to investigate how differences in the form of provision across the two tiers of the welfare system shape clients' beliefs. Following participatory theory, one must ask how institutional designs shape the experience of participation and, in so doing, leave their imprint on individuals' orientations toward action. Client statements make it clear that welfare institutions are sites of political learning and that welfare participation has educative effects. Consider, for example, the explanation offered by Joy, the only person who reported being reluctant to speak up in SSDI. By her own account, Joy did not make waves in SSDI because of lessons she learned earlier in life as an AFDC client.

So, have you ever challenged anyone at the agency [SSA] about anything?

No, because even after knowing it's a different program, I still know from [AFDC] that you've got to let the system be. I don't want to challenge anything and have the problems that will make my blood pressure go up. I take it as it is and go from there.

If you felt like you did have a grievance or a complaint, would you feel OK to bring it up?

Any problem I have with money or food, I would tend to manage it on my own, as opposed to saying I deserved this or that. . . . It's just that I want to make it on my own. Plus, I've seen other instances [in AFDC]. And I'm not going to subject myself to it.

In what follows, I argue that SSDI clients are less reticent than AFDC clients because of the different ways policy designs position clients in the two programs and the lessons clients learn as they occupy these positions.

Lessons of AFDC Participation

For AFDC clients, silence in the face of consequential decision-making processes appears rational for two reasons. First, clients come to expect that their efforts will be futile. As Anna put it, "No matter what I say, they'll do it the way they want to do it." Second, clients come to believe that if they make waves, they may provoke some form of punishment. Common fears range from losing access to a case worker to losing income and health benefits to having the police or Child Protective Services visit their homes and remove their children. Alicia offered clear statements of each of these two themes as she explained why she did not raise questions or grievances at the agency.

Futility: You just have to wait and see what they do to you. That's how I feel. Sometimes I do want to say something, but I just leave it at that because I feel like I'll get treated the way I've been getting treated anyway, so it wouldn't matter if I said something or not. Whatever they want to do, they're going to do regardless, whether I say something or not. They've got the power, so you have to listen to what they say.

Vulnerability: I figure if I say something back, they know a way of getting me cut off of AFDC. And then I wouldn't have anything for me and my kids, just because I said something. That's their power, right there. That's the power. That's why nobody complains.

Under most circumstances, women in AFDC believe that challenging the agency is simply too ineffective and risky to be worthwhile. Such is especially the case on minor decisions, when it appears safer to endure a small hardship than to risk retribution down the line. But even under a threat of termination, most clients argue that there is little to be gained by speaking up. Clients believe that challenging a termination decision will be emotionally difficult and time-consuming, and they expect the agency to be unresponsive. With a variety of other pressing responsibilities at hand, most surmise that there is little reason to waste the effort. It is, in a sense, easier to find some other way to make it through the crisis and then reapply later. As Hope explained, "You know you're going to lose. There's no way you can fight. So you just go down anchor and all."[2]

In explaining the basis for these expectations, clients emphasize their experiences in the AFDC program. In fact, many clients explicitly adopt a language of education and point to the chilling effects of the lessons they have learned as clients. Nancy explained,

> I think it's that you learn not to [say anything], because you learn that if you upset this woman or make her angry (or this man, but it's mostly women that work there), that if you upset this person in any way, you're going to pay for it. And so you don't do that. You learn to be quiet and just take whatever is dished out.

Through experience, AFDC clients develop a characteristic set of beliefs about their own status and the agency's power in relation to them. First, a substantial majority of AFDC recipients report feeling humiliated, exposed, and vulnerable in their encounters with the welfare agency. Second, they come to see the agency as a pervasive threat in their lives, as a potent force whose limits are unclear. Third, they perceive their welfare relationships as one-way transactions in which the agency has the authority to issue directives and client status limits options to compliance or exit. Fourth, their view of agency decision making emphasizes the unopposable personal discretion of individual workers rather than institutional rules. Fifth, clients come to understand the agency's capacity for action as an autonomous power over them rather than as the power to act on their behalf. Celina offered a typical example of how AFDC clients describe power in their welfare relationships:

> They are all in your business. They can cut you off at any time for anything that they see wrong with you. You are always under their thumb. And I don't want anybody having that much control over my life, that much power. . . . They leave you with a feeling that you are totally powerless. You have to totally succumb to them.

The origins of these beliefs can be traced to the design of the AFDC program. Unlike people in SSDI, AFDC clients are subject to casework relationships, regular case reviews, and an ongoing need to prove their means-tested eligibility. In addition, street-level bureaucrats in AFDC tend to hold more power over clients and possess greater discretion to use it (Handler 1992; Lipsky 1980, 6). Thus, AFDC participation is designed to include regular interaction under conditions defined by individualized administrative control. Each of these design elements contributes to the likelihood that AFDC clients will come to see themselves as ineffective and vulnerable in their relationship with the agency.

To begin with, AFDC program rules require clients to deal with the agency on a relatively frequent basis. In addition to coming in for case reviews at regular intervals, many clients are also required to attend educational classes or job training programs. And because cooperation with child support enforcement is mandatory, some clients also have to appear at an agency or court every six months until the state establishes paternity and begins receiving reimbursements. These frequent contacts serve as a constant reminder of the agency's presence and of the individual's status as a welfare client. Moreover, the notices that announce these routine meetings include a statement that benefits can be terminated if the client does not appear. As a result, AFDC clients receive a virtually continuous stream of evidence that they occupy a precarious position.

From the standpoint of administrators, these regular contacts may appear to be necessary instruments for achieving specific program goals. To clients, however, the most important feature of these regular meetings is the threat of termination. Few believe that the meetings are designed in any way to address their needs or goals. Clients complain that money obtained through child support hearings goes to the state rather than to their children; case reviews involve long waits followed by a perfunctory survey of the usual bills and receipts; even job training programs seem like empty symbolism that offers clients no real help in attaining the economic security for which they hope. Penny explained,

> It's not job training or anything like that. They just sit you in a room with the current newspaper want ads, a telephone, and a phone book. And they say, "Find a job." And if you don't go, your benefits may be cut. . . . It does nothing for you. I can go out and get a newspaper. I have a telephone. I have a yellow pages. It doesn't do anything. . . . I'm pretty sure they want all AFDC recipients working. But I need child care. It's not like I'm not working because I don't want to. I'm not working because I need someone to keep my child. And that's what they don't understand.

Thus, routine reviews and other appearances do not appear to serve clients' interests, needs, or plans but do pose bureaucratic hurdles that can lead to termination. These contacts also shape clients' perceptions of their welfare relationships for a third reason: the meetings are almost always initiated by the agency. Typically, clients receive a letter in the mail that lists a date, time, and place for them to show up. They are summoned, and they appear. There is little, if anything, about these routine interactions that suggests to clients that they can be effective initiators or that the agency can act in a responsive manner. As Nona Mae put it, "They make an appointment. They tell you what time to be there. And you be there or be square."[3]

For all of these reasons, the regular review comes to be seen as a sort of cat-and-mouse game in which the agency lays traps and clients try to negotiate them. The game holds no promise for clients but does pose risks. On several occasions at the shelter, residents mentioned that they were "beating the system" in AFDC. At first, I mistakenly thought they were referring to unreported income or other undetected violations of program rules. In fact, they meant that they were winning the cat-and-mouse game. Despite being homeless, they were reporting to the right places at the right times; they were "crossing all the *T*s and dotting all the *I*s" needed to prevent termination. Regardless of whether these residents may also have been violating program rules in some way, their statements are a telling indication that the welfare agency does not appear to clients as a neutral and responsive government institution. Its role is perceived as adversarial to such an extent that eligible clients believe they are beating the system simply by avoiding being forced off the rolls.

The difficulty of complying with AFDC program requirements varies but should not be underestimated. Just as clients have to appear in person to apply for AFDC benefits, they also have to find a way to the agency for regular reviews and hearings. Thus, the same transportation problems that pose a barrier to claiming benefits persist as a barrier to maintaining benefits. In addition, each time clients are called in for a review, they revisit the waiting conditions they experienced in their first encounter (see chap. 5). Lynn described her activities on a typical review day:

> My day starts before I even get there, with anxiety over having to go. And usually I have it set up three days in advance that someone is coming with me. I have to prepare to go to the welfare building. Once I get there, it's just a matter of going upstairs to the office and checking in with the receptionist—usually you have to stand in line to check in. They tell you to have a seat, and then you just sit there and sit there and sit there. About every forty-five minutes, you look up at the clock and think "Well, gee . . ." So you go back up to the reception desk and say "Excuse me, I was just wondering if . . . " [They say,] "We'll get to you! Just go sit down!" You get scolded for asking a question—really. It's like you're not an adult. From the minute you walk in the door, it's like they're principals or nuns or something and you're the underling. You get scolded. . . . It's like trying to deal with a priest, or something that doesn't like you, or a cop.

Clients' perceptions that the agency has set up a game designed to trap them in a violation are reinforced by rules that require clients to continually reproduce information to maintain their eligibility. Some of this information is obviously necessary for ongoing means testing. But because clients provide a good bit of this information when they apply for benefits, they tend to interpret these recurring procedures as evidence that the agency is looking for technical reasons to terminate their cases. Mary explained, "I can see the rent receipt, the gas, electric, and the report card since kids can change schools from year to year. But to bring your birth certificates and Social Security cards down there every month? They've got copies of them. What do they need them for?"

The agency's requests for information also reinforce clients' fears that they may be vulnerable to surveillance. At each meeting, clients see that caseworkers have lengthy files and computer databases at their disposal. Clients tend to be unsure about the extent of information possessed by the bureaucracy and in some cases fear that it might extend to the most private details of their lives. Celina expressed a suspicion held by many recipients when she confided, "It makes me feel scared about what they might know about me. But that's the way it is. They *know.*"

The focal point of AFDC participation is the casework relationship. Clients are virtually unanimous in saying that this relationship determines the difficulty or ease of program participation. As a result, they tend to attach great symbolic importance to the fact that they are not given a say in the process that assigns them to a caseworker. Some clients hope to find a specific worker who has helped a relative in the past or to avoid one who is infamous among their associates. Others do not enter with preferences but still would like to receive information that would allow them to choose among potential caseworkers (just as patients with low levels of information prefer to exercise some degree of choice over their primary physicians in health care organizations). The fact that clients have no say in selecting the person who will have the most direct control over their case reinforces their perceptions that they play no effective role in agency decision making. Nona Mae complained, "You don't get a choice [over] who you want to be your worker. They just give you somebody who you don't have any say-so over. . . . They are in control of whoever I have to deal with. They *tell* me."

After establishing a relationship with one caseworker, clients may be notified that their cases have been shifted to someone else. An unexpected transfer of this sort generally makes the agency's decision-making processes appear mysterious, capricious, and beyond client control. For clients who have established a comfortable working relationship with a worker whom they like as an individual, a transfer to a new worker also raises new fears of abuse and concerns about privacy. Lashell explained this experience:

> They change case managers on you just when you're getting used to some person. Everything tied up with your case is really personal to you, so you want to keep one person. But when they keep changing case managers on

you, it's like everybody knows your business. They can just change them on you without asking. They don't call you and say, "Do you mind if we change your case manager?" Welfare doesn't care what you feel. They don't discuss with you "What are your feelings about this?" They just do what they do.

A casework format leads to relationships with agency workers that are both more personal and more discretionary (Handler 1992; Lipsky 1980; Prottas 1979). Relative to "mass contact" agencies in which clients deal with different workers in each successive encounter, one might expect stable "individualized" relationships to appear more responsive and hence to facilitate "people's willingness to express grievances and press their claims for justice" (Gutek 1992, 48). But in the AFDC program, the casework format has quite the opposite effect.

It is important to reiterate here a conclusion from chapter 5: AFDC clients are split on their sentiments toward agency workers as individuals, but they consistently fear caseworkers' power in welfare relationships. The casework design in AFDC focuses clients' attention on the discretionary power held by a single worker. Clients' contacts with the agency are almost always mediated by their caseworkers, who make critical decisions and decide what information will be entered into bureaucratic records. From the clients' perspective, caseworkers appear to hold nearly complete power to assist or punish. Nona Mae painted a common portrait of the caseworker as the ultimate master of a client's fate:

> Your life is in their hands. Your kid's life is in that worker's hands. If that worker don't like you, if you don't smile at that worker, she'll make your check late or whatever. She can do anything she wants to. She can send you your check, or she can't. If your information is not all there, and she thinks you're supposed to have it all there, then she can not send you a check. But if it's a good worker, she understands that you might have lost something or you can't find your Social Security card. She'll give you a couple weeks to get it. They're all in power. You feel like nothing when you go down there. . . . We all fear our caseworkers. Caseworkers are feared because they have control over our financial abilities.

Because clients depend so heavily on their caseworkers, they tend to develop extremely positive or extremely negative evaluations of them as individuals. The clients in this study who approved of their current workers were not always the same as the ones who said they liked their workers during the first encounter, yet the overall proportion of positive evaluations remained about the same. Roughly a quarter of the sample expressed both fear and hatred in describing their caseworkers. Another quarter reported having several workers during their time in the program, including some they liked and some they disliked. Half of the clients in AFDC gave their workers positive evaluations but nevertheless felt vulnerable in their casework relationship.

Not surprisingly, clients usually express strong feelings of gratitude for favors provided by their caseworkers, but the gratitude is laced with anxiety. Most recipients surmise that if caseworkers have the power to help out, they can also make a client's life more difficult. As a result, clients tend to appreciate their caseworker's efforts while still believing that they occupy a vulnerable position. Clients who believe they depend on individual kindness tend to enter each review fearing that they or someone else might do something to upset their worker. They are grateful for benevolent treatment in the past but not feel they occupy a position of security or power in their relationship. Many clients express sentiments like those of Tina: "[My caseworker] is nice to me, and if she feels she can help me out, my caseworker will try her hardest. But I don't have any power."

By focusing client attention on a personal relationship, the casework design obscures the role that agency rules and supervisory structures play in determining specific decisions. Caseworkers occasionally cite agency rules as a way to deflect the blame for unpopular actions, but over time, small favors and quick decisions reinforce clients' perceptions that workers have significant discretion. Most clients do not see agency regulations as fixed laws binding both sides of the welfare relationship. Instead, they view the rules as tools wielded by street-level bureaucrats. Karla, for example, told me, "I know the clients don't really have a say-so over anything. The workers, they have all the power." When I asked her where that power came from, she responded, "That's the way the state wants it. They've got the laws, and we don't."

This perception of rules as tools controlled by agency personnel fosters the expectations of futility and vulnerability that lead clients to shy away from voicing grievances. Penny, for example, believed that it was futile to challenge her worker because "they just use the rules to do whatever they want to do anyway." During the year prior to our interview, Penny discovered that her caseworker had failed to tell her she was eligible for food stamps and that (as an employed client) she was eligible to seek child care benefits. When I asked her if she felt she had a legitimate grievance, she replied, "I did. But I didn't feel like my worker would listen to me." In addition, Penny believed that if she made a formal request to be assigned to a new caseworker, she would have little chance of winning and might earn herself a reputation as a troublemaker. To get a new caseworker assignment, Penny intentionally provoked a case termination (by withholding a monthly wage report) and reapplied to the program the following month. Compared to initiating a formal challenge to her worker, it struck Penny as more effective to go through the application process a second time (and suffer the economic losses).

Because clients do not feel protected by binding rules, they also tend to feel vulnerable to retribution. Josephine explained, "They're using the system to their advantage, especially the law and justice part. They will use that to their advantage to get what they want. . . . Not just to get another recipient off [the rolls], but, [also to save] a little money gained or to discipline you or to show others what will happen." This feeling of insecurity leads many clients to avoid making even small requests out of fear that they will irritate their workers. Renee complained,

> When I do want to ask stuff, I'll be holding back so bad. And there's stuff I need to know. And I hate to call her on the phone. But then I feel like I let her get me. I should get to ask her any questions whether she sounds irritated or not. And if she hangs up, I should call back. I should say, "Look, I've got the right to have my questions answered!" But then I don't want to pressure her. I don't too much want to bother her.

Thus, the high salience of worker discretion and the low salience of agency rules combine to leave AFDC clients feeling dependent on their worker's good graces. Clients worry that direct requests or assertive behavior might alienate a helpful worker or make an unhelpful one angry. They consider it more effective and safe to present themselves as grateful, cooperative, and worthy of assistance. When I asked Nona Mae if she had ever challenged her caseworker, we had the following exchange:

> No, you kiss ass all day. Point blank: you kiss ass, whatever they say. Even though we only see them every six months, whatever they say, whatever they want, however they want you to act, however they talk to you, whew, however they look at you, *you kiss ass.*

> *So, if someone challenged a worker . . .*

> Then they're stupid!

> *And how do you think it would turn out?*

> They'll get a notice of decision. And the notice of decision will say, "You are currently cut off from your AFDC benefits. You have to come in and have a fair hearing."—if you don't kiss that worker's ass.

> *So, have you actually had complaints or grievances that you have not brought up because of that fact?*

Yeah, because I know my worker has control of my life and my benefits. . . . I don't talk about how I really feel about the system to her.

Just the system in general, or are there specific things you might have brought up if you felt more comfortable?

Yeah, about my food stamps, about how they dropped me off and everything. I don't go and have any sort of negative input on the system to my caseworker.

In sum, then, the tendency toward reticence in the AFDC program can be traced to a chain of factors. The design of the AFDC program shapes clients' participation experiences, these experiences give rise to characteristic sets of beliefs about welfare relationships, and these beliefs in turn guide clients' responses to dilemmas of action. AFDC clients exercise very little effective control over the timing, location, and subject matter of their contacts with the agency. They tend to leave these interactions feeling that their goals and needs have not been addressed and that they have had to jump through a series of administrative hoops to beat a system designed to push them off the rolls. In addition, clients' perceptions of how the agency works are filtered through the prism of an individualized casework relationship. As a result, clients tend to develop a keen awareness of worker discretion while losing sight of institutional rules and supervisory structures. For all of these reasons, AFDC clients tend to feel vulnerable to retribution and see agency decision making as an autonomous process that lies beyond their reach. More than two-thirds of the AFDC clients in this study felt that it would be too futile and too risky to pursue a grievance that they considered legitimate.

Explaining the Exceptions

AFDC offices are not silent spaces lined with docile clients. With some regularity, clients register complaints, request fair hearings, and challenge their workers' decisions. Clients invoke the agency's formal mechanisms of due process or assert themselves in disruptive confrontations with workers. Some of these confrontations are merely unplanned expressions of anger—spontaneous reactions to the frustrations and feelings of powerlessness described in the preceding section. In other cases, however, open conflict indicates that a client is willing to create a scene, if necessary, to claim what she considers to be her right. Client choices to assert themselves through formal or informal means stand out as important exceptions to the general pattern I have described so far.

Almost one-third of AFDC clients in this study (eight of twenty-five) reported that if the stakes were high enough and if they had a legitimate grievance, they would be willing to speak up for themselves when dealing with the agency and its workers.[4] In explaining their responses, women in this group tended to cite three kinds of reasons. First, they did not want to suffer a perceived injustice in silence and hence saw an expressive value in challenging the agency. Like the Latina women in Hardy-Fanta's (1993, 45) study of survival politics, these clients saw a political and personal value in "taking a stand" in dealing with those who exercised control over their lives. Second, despite their doubts about influencing the agency, they hoped for success and hence saw an instrumental value in speaking up. Third, all eight women described taking a stand as a duty growing out of the obligation to protect their children. Kisha, for example, successfully appealed to a supervisor when her case was about to be terminated. Despite believing she had "no say-so," Kisha felt that she had to say something because "they're messing with my kids."

Lynn provided a good example of the ambivalent mixture of doubt and resolve expressed by this group of clients. Despite feeling that workers "can do whatever they want to you, and you just have to take their abuse," Lynn challenged several notices of termination she received in the mail. When I asked if she would challenge an agency decision again in the future, she told me,

> You kind of have a catch-22 where, yeah, [challenging them is] the right thing to do and it will probably get you more. You know what they say, the squeaky wheel gets the oil. But at the same time, there's such a fear that it's going to adversely affect you. And you're in such a shitty position as it is. If your check is already a week late, you're afraid to call your worker and piss him off because what if the check comes in, and they say, "Ha ha ha, I'll show her. I'm going to file this away until next week's mail." You know what I mean, and there's nothing you can do about it. So there is an absolute fear that by speaking up you're going to be really making your child's welfare real bad. . . . [But] I would challenge them again in the future just because my income, my child support, depends on it. I have to have that in order to support my children, so I would have no choice but to challenge them. Certainly, my feelings about having to do that would be affected by [the earlier experience fighting a notice of termination] because I would go into it very cynically.

These more vocal clients provide a counterpoint to the dominant pattern in AFDC, underscoring that the process I have been describing is not deterministic. The AFDC program's design does not impose a rigid code of silence on clients. Rather, the design shapes clients' experiences and perceptions in ways that lower the overall probability that they will assert themselves when they have legitimate grievances. Still, it is worth asking whether there might be a more systematic explanation for why some clients appear less reticent than others. Two facts provide important starting points for such an explanation. First, this subgroup does not appear to have social or demographic characteristics that set it apart from the rest of the AFDC sample.[5] Second, clients in this group generally share key beliefs about welfare relationships expressed by their fellow recipients: caseworkers have large amounts of discretionary power; clients have little or no say in decisions; clients should not expect to be effective in challenging the agency; and troublemakers risk provoking retribution. What, then, accounts for their different response to the client's dilemma of action?

A key part of the answer appears to lie in the same process that accounts for quiescence in the AFDC program: the capacity for participation experiences to teach lessons that influence citizens' orientations toward political action. The AFDC sample was not a homogeneous group. Thirteen clients were enrolled only in the AFDC program, but another twelve had additional experience with organizations that explicitly encourage involvement. In this latter group, eight clients had children enrolled in Head Start, three were involved in activist organizations, and one participated in both. These types of organizations allow clients to experience the benefits of engagement and the efficacy of asserting themselves. Positive lessons learned through participation in these organizations tend to spill over into AFDC and encourage clients to be more assertive in their welfare relationships. Consequently, these twelve clients were significantly more willing to voice grievances in AFDC than were the thirteen clients who had no outside organizational involvement (67 percent vs. none, $p = .001$).[6]

Of the four activists in the AFDC sample, three could be found among the minority who were more willing to speak up in the AFDC program. This pattern is consistent with historical evidence that the level of client assertiveness is influenced by a broader political context. Just as welfare rights organizations may encourage welfare claiming (see chap. 4), they may also foster a deeper commitment to pursuing disputes in welfare programs. As long ago as the 1930s, Almond and Lasswell (1934) found that more "aggressive" client behavior was not a product of psychological pathology, as was often suspected. Instead, such behavior reflected stronger feelings of entitlement largely produced by contemporary New Deal social movements (see Gordon 1994, 241–51). Likewise, in the 1960s, the NWRO worked diligently to encourage clients to assert themselves through disruptive demand-making and formal grievance procedures (Davis 1993; Patterson 1986; Piven and Cloward 1977; West 1981). Although group mobilization was certainly at a lower point during the period of my interviews, political activism continued to make clients more effective agents in relation to the welfare state. As Handler explains, on the question of client involvement, it would seem that social-movement groups are crucial. Groups provide solidarity, encouragement and information. They show clients that they are not alone, that others share their burdens; they can collectivize grievances. Groups can provide training and experts. Clients need groups in order to be able to participate. . . . This means that the bureaucracy also needs the groups if it is to get . . . client participation. (1992, 360)

Involvement with Head Start programs appears to have similar effects. Head Start parents are required to participate in policy councils and local decision-making processes (see Head Start Bureau 1992, §§1304.5-1–5, appendix B). These requirements reflect the goal of "maximum feasible participation" that served as a cornerstone of programs initiated during the Johnson administration's War on Poverty in the 1960s (M. Katz 1989, 95–101).

Of the eight AFDC clients who participated in Head Start (excluding the Head Start client who was also an activist), five were among the group willing to voice grievances at the welfare agency. Their accounts suggest that Head Start programs can provide a critical venue for poor parents to engage in collective decision making and learn countervailing lessons about the importance of involvement. Kisha explained, "Head Start gives you an opportunity, by volunteering, to get the feel of doing different things. [Head Start] makes me feel needed." Likewise, Karla emphasized how the Head Start design differed from AFDC and encouraged her commitment to speaking up:

AFDC makes you want to shy away and hold back. Head Start, they work with you. You can see the progress you're making. Me, myself, I've made a lot of improvement in the last two or three years. I went into the citywide policy meetings as a shy, quiet person, and now I've begun to open up a lot more. I talk a lot. I participate in everything they have available.

For two reasons, it is also instructive to consider the responses of the three clients who were active in Head Start yet remained reluctant to assert themselves in AFDC. First, these clients underscore that lessons learned through participation in one context do not automatically spill over to shape an individual's orientations in a different institutional setting. Second, the contrast between AFDC and Head Start described by these three clients helps to bring the importance of policy design into sharper focus. If clients' orientations toward involvement flow solely from preexisting characteristics (in other words, if policy design has no effect), one would expect clients to hold a single orientation toward involvement across different program contexts (AFDC versus Head Start). These three clients shared their fellow recipients' fears and doubts about speaking up in AFDC yet felt quite opposite sentiments about client involvement in Head Start. The excerpts that follow offer a powerful illustration of how a more participatory program design (Head Start) can foster engagement for individuals who are quiescent in the context of a more directive design (AFDC).

CHERYL: It would be great if I could have a say in AFDC like I can in Head Start. . . . I get to go to the meetings, and I know the laws of Head Start. And [at Head Start] it's different. You have to have parents' say-so. You have to have a majority of parents present to vote for certain things and certain people. AFDC is not like that at all. I've never seen or heard about it being that I could have a say-so, so why even think about it? But here, I know it. I know I can have input, so why not get involved? Now, if there was someplace in AFDC where I could go say how I feel and what welfare mothers need, then I'm sure I would have done it by now. But that's not the way it is.

LISA: Being involved with Head Start now, they give me a lot of options. It's helpful for giving you some insight into AFDC and your caseworker. Like they have a lot of parent involvement, and right now I'm on the policy council. And on the policy council they have components set up on health care, social work, disability plans, and all that. . . . You get to be more involved with Head Start. They don't tell you that you have to do it. They just give you the opportunity to get involved. So I feel like I'm wanted, like I'm needed to do something. A lot of people are depending on me to do this, and that's great. . . . With Head Start, they'll say, "Just bring [your kids] to the meeting, and let them play off to the side." And then I can still get my business taken care of, even with my kids. That's how you know they want you there. And then afterward, you feel like you accomplished something.

NANCY: I have watched parents blossom in Head Start, parents who never said a word. They never talked because they had just been beaten down. They don't feel like they have anything to contribute. I've watched them get some empowerment from Head Start and in two years become leaders of this whole citywide group of people. Two years ago, they wouldn't even open their mouths at meetings. [The people at Head Start] value your opinion. I guess that's the first thing, is when someone all of the sudden starts valuing what you have to say. That right there is the start. And that's probably the first thing that happened to me. I was impressed that when you go to orientation, they say, "We need you to help." And then they give you an opportunity to help. They not only give you the opportunity to help with little stuff in the classroom, they give you the opportunity to go to a meeting where *you* are making decisions. You are actually involved in the hiring. No one can get hired for this program unless they're interviewed by a group of parents. And that in itself is like, "Wow, really? I can do that?" It gives you control over the education your child is getting, the kind of food your child is getting to eat, the kind of curriculum in the classroom, the people that are actually working with your child. That sense of empowerment starts there. But if you get involved in the program, it just keeps growing more and more. Now, not everyone is going to take advantage of it. And I understand that. But if people want to, they can do it.

Clients tended to express a strong belief that Head Start's design positioned them in a way that differed from AFDC's design. In discussing this contrast, clients routinely expressed a desire to be equally involved in AFDC. For example, when I asked Cheryl if the kind of involvement she had in Head Start would make a difference in AFDC, she replied, "Would the program be any better? Hell yes. Hell yes—if all of us mothers got to have a say." Contact with the Head Start program created a tangible contrast that heightened the injustice clients associated with their subordinate role in the AFDC program. Less intense versions of this sentiment, however, could be found throughout the AFDC sample. To varying degrees, clients harbored a desire for more active involvement yet saw no outlet for this desire in the AFDC program.

Most AFDC clients have preferences about their own cases and claim that they would like to have more say-so in the program. In fact, when I asked clients how, if at all, they would like to see the program changed, they almost always listed greater client input among their suggestions. At a minimum, clients usually wanted to be more involved in decisions affecting their own cases. For example, they wanted to select the types of job training that would best suit their talents and needs. They also wanted to discuss the mix of resources that would fit best with their economic and familial goals (for example, education, job training, child care, or transportation subsidies). And of course, most clients wanted to be more involved in decisions that might end their eligibility. Many clients cited specific occasions when they wanted and, in their eyes, deserved to have a greater voice. For example, when her son suffered a burn on his foot, Sandra lost her benefits while the agency investigated her for child abuse. Although she could not pay her rent or bills until after she was cleared of the charge, Sandra's biggest complaint was that she was not allowed to speak on her own behalf.

They just had these people come in, and they did what they did. And I asked, "Why can't I say something?" . . . I felt like I didn't get to know nothing about it. It made me worry about what could happen. And they just told me, "You'll get something in the mail." I said, "Well, can I talk to my worker?" And they said, "No, it will come in the mail." And my worker told me later that it comes to her, and then they revise it and it goes to a board, and if they think everything's OK they reopen your case. If not, *then* you get to come in front of everybody and give your part of the story. And I said, "But that should have been done in the first place, instead of these people coming in trying to make me look like an abuser." I mean, what's going to happen if someone just calls and says you're selling dope or something? Are they going to just bang down my door and take everything away? I mean, I didn't even get to have a say-so that time. My worker told me, "No, there's no need for you to speak. They look into everything before they close it up."

Not surprisingly, the focal point of clients' desires for more input is the case review. Clients regularly express a desire to have more say-so in these meetings and, in a smaller number of cases, suggest that they would like to play a role in redesigning their format. Alissa explained,

OK, with the review, I think their whole intent was to get people down there to have some input into their own case. But when you go down for a review, all you do is answer the same old questions you answered when you first applied. And in twenty minutes, you'll go over your bill status, and you'll be gone. You haven't addressed any issues. You haven't changed anything. It will be the same exact system for the next person applying; and it will be the same for you at your next review. Nothing changes. The people who should have input are the people who are experiencing it. Those are the people who know. Those are the people who know what needs to be done, what things need to be improved.

Thus, it would be a mistake to view the tendency toward reticence in the AFDC program as evidence that clients prefer to receive their benefits in silence. Instead, this reticence is a product of lessons learned through participation under the AFDC design. Evidence from Head Start and welfare rights groups suggests that contacts with community organizations that encourage involvement can make poor citizens into more effective political agents in the welfare system. But the majority of AFDC clients have had few, if any, supportive participation experiences of this sort. For these clients, participation experiences in the AFDC program offer a variety of reasons to resist the urge to speak up.

Lessons of SSDI Participation

Like AFDC recipients, SSDI clients occupy a position of resource dependency. Most cannot afford to lose benefits supplied by the SSA, and the ongoing nature of this relationship encourages clients to consider the long-term consequences of their actions. Despite these structural similarities, interviews with SSDI clients yield very different images of agency power and client expression. Benefits in the social insurance tier of the welfare system are provided through institutions that encourage clients to feel more secure and allow them to see the potential for agency responsiveness. Out of twenty-five SSDI clients, twenty-four reported that they would not hesitate to raise legitimate questions or grievances. Their responses strongly suggest that the relationship between resource dependence and quiescence hinges on how policy designs position clients.

Relative to AFDC, programs in the social insurance tier of the welfare system are designed to provide citizens with welfare relationships that are less invasive and directive. From its inception, the "social insurance orientation was not paternalist. It broke away from the personal, caretaking dimension of social work and moved [administrators] toward a structural relation of social control between themselves and the poor—one that was distant, not individually supervisory" (Gordon 1994, 162). Clients in the SSDI program, for example, do not have caseworkers, are not required to attend mandatory reviews, and are not forced to cooperate with child support enforcement or other programs. Although SSDI clients depend on the SSA for benefits, these benefits are not tied to directive and supervisory institutional requirements.

The gap between policy designs in AFDC and SSDI was especially apparent in my interview with Joy. Joy repeatedly contrasted her experience in SSDI with her earlier feelings of powerlessness and vulnerability as an AFDC client. Imitating her caseworker in AFDC, Joy said in a scolding tone, "You can only do this, you can only do that. You can't do this, you can't do that. . . . Did you make an extra dollar so you can buy grass seed? You have a dog?!" Joy summed up the contrast: "In Social Security, it's pretty tolerable. I feel pretty lucky to have it. In AFDC, it was just constantly the pits."

Most SSDI clients do not know much about the SSA at the time they apply for benefits (see chap. 4). Through participation in the program, however, they develop a characteristic set of beliefs that almost completely inverts AFDC recipients' beliefs. First, SSDI clients rarely feel denigrated or placed in a vulnerable position in their encounters with the SSA. Second, they tend to view the SSA as a distant and constrained presence in their lives. Third, they perceive their welfare relationships as two-way transactions in which both clients and administrators have standing to make requests. Fourth, their view of agency decision making emphasizes the rules of the institution rather than the personal discretion of individual workers. Fifth, they believe that the agency's power over them is complemented by a power to act on their behalf.

As part of a two-way relationship based on rules, SSDI clients tend to expect that they can effectively raise questions or grievances. Kitty explained, "You have some control over the program as well as the program controlling you. Control works in both directions in SSDI." Most clients express an awareness that there are obstacles to gaining a response from the SSA and that the agency holds some power over them, but they consistently believe that clients hold the capacity to influence agency decisions. Sarah concluded, "Well, if there is any power, I guess they have more than I do. But I haven't come into a situation where I've seen it. . . . I always feel like I have some say-so in the process." In the end, most clients believe that the SSA can be counted on to offer a reasonably fair and prompt response to client requests. Darryl's expectation was typical: "If I ever need anything, I know that's their job. They'll be there."

In addition to having stronger expectations of effectiveness, clients in SSDI also feel far less vulnerable than their AFDC counterparts. Most SSDI clients find it hard to imagine how raising a problem or questioning a decision might open them up to retribution. In fact, many seem confused when asked about this possibility and respond by expressing a sense of security that, to them, seems entirely natural. For example, while talking with Molly about decisions to raise grievances, I asked her whether she would worry that her actions might be seen as causing problems or provoke a response. She replied, "No. Why would I be worried about that? I feel secure enough with them that I could bring [a grievance] up." Likewise, Bridget commented, "I would feel comfortable bringing anything up with them. Why not? What could the problem be?"

To SSDI clients, the SSA and its workers appear to be constrained and distant actors who operate according to rules and share power with clients in a two-way relationship. The origins of these perceptions can be traced directly to the SSDI program's design. Because SSDI's design does not include mandatory reviews, clients initiate most of their dealings with the agency instead of responding to directives backed up by threats of termination.[7] With only occasional exceptions, SSDI generally provides clients with an unobtrusive source of income that does not require much personal involvement. Marie described her seventeen years of welfare participation as follows: "I didn't even think about receiving that check every month. It was like my salary for the month. So I didn't even think about it because I was just going along."

This aspect of the SSDI design not only allows clients to feel more secure but also gives them control over the timing and subject matter of interactions with the agency. The SSA may occasionally notify clients of changes in policy or adjustments in benefit levels. But over the long haul, SSDI clients tend to initiate the vast majority of nontrivial contacts with the agency. Communication from the SSA tends either to require no response from the client or to be a direct reply to a client request. As a result, the experience of SSDI participation offers clients evidence over time that they can act as initiators, that the bureaucracy can be a responsive institution, and that they are free to go about their lives without fear of surveillance or punishment. Molly noted, "I don't have to deal with anyone. I don't have to talk with anyone over the phone unless I want to know a certain thing." Kitty elaborated on this point:

> [Being the initiator] gives me a greater sense of control as far as who is doing what. . . . Usually if you have something to do with any federal agency, when they contact you, they're telling you they are going to do whatever. They're going to cut that or increase that—whatever. When you call them, it's because you want something done. And it either gets done or it doesn't. If it doesn't, you go to the next step. And so you feel like it's under your control.

Other elements of SSDI's policy design reinforce clients' feelings of control. Because of federal administration, the SSA appears to be a remote operation that is unlikely to keep tabs on individual clients throughout the nation. In addition, SSDI clients do not routinely have to produce new information for the agency, and they do not have a specific caseworker assigned to them. These features, combined with the rarity of agency directives, suggest to clients that the SSA pays very limited attention to individual cases. As a result, clients come to view themselves as somewhat anonymous beneficiaries. Donna, for example, suspected that the SSA granted her initial application "and that's the end, as far as they're concerned, of Donna." Darryl echoed a large number of clients when he observed, "I'm just one person out of millions."

To SSDI clients, this perceived anonymity is not an unmitigated good. In some cases, clients describe the SSA as cold or uncaring and express a desire for more personalized attention. The feeling of being lost in the administrative haystack, however, permits clients to breathe a bit more easily, confident that they are unlikely to be targeted for scrutiny or punishment. Clients use a variety of different metaphors to convey this feeling, one of which allows for a telling comparison with AFDC.

Clients in both SSDI and AFDC made frequent reference to feeling like they were "just another number" or "just a statistic." When AFDC recipients used this image, it almost always referred to their impression that the agency viewed them as expendable objects. To be a number meant being less than a full and equal human being, occupying a degraded and precarious position. Anna commented, "You're like a number, and they can treat you however they want." Similarly, Tina observed, "They really don't give a crap about you. You're getting the money, so you're lower than them. So they don't have pity for you or anything. You're just like a number." By contrast, SSDI clients rarely used this phrase to signify a degraded status. Instead, being a number meant that they were not likely to be singled out from others in the program. It referred to a sense of anonymity that was compatible with feelings of security. Sarah and I had the following exchange after she said that as an SSDI client, "you're on their rolls, and you're just a number."

What do you mean when you say you're a number?

Well, a lot of people say, "I feel like a number." Well, you feel like one of millions getting SSDI, so that means you don't feel like they're watching over you. They can't watch over every single person.

So when you say that you feel like a number, are you saying that you feel like less of a person, or are you just saying you feel like they don't single you out or watch you?

Like they don't single me out. I don't feel like less of a person. I know if I had questions, I can call them on the hot line. And actually those people are very nice.

In addition to fostering a sense of anonymity, the lack of an ongoing case-work component in SSDI also serves to dampen the salience and intensity of clients' perceptions of agency workers. Unlike their AFDC counterparts, SSDI clients' evaluations of workers rarely change after the relatively intense experience of the first encounter and rarely include strong personal feelings. Roughly three-quarters of SSDI clients held moderately positive views of SSA workers, describing them as considerate, efficient, fair, and competent. Dizzy echoed the assessments of most clients: "They are very professional. They are not rude. They are very businesslike. Some of them are actually nice and try to be helpful, and then some are just like it's their job. But they're not rude."

Because their relationship with the SSA is not mediated by a caseworker, SSDI clients also tend to develop perceptions of their welfare relationships that have an institutional rather than personal focus. When they contemplate whether to pursue a question or grievance, they focus very little on the individual workers who blend together over time as impersonal but reliable cogs in the administrative machine. Instead, SSDI clients pay greater attention to institutional features of the SSA, specifically its size and complexity and its elaborate system of binding rules.

The need to decipher agency rules without the aid of a caseworker can leave clients feeling frustrated. Recalling her experience trying find out if she could work part time without losing benefits, Marie commented, "If you talked to one person, you heard one thing. And if you talked to somebody else, you heard something else. . . . It was very very confusing." Without a caseworker to act as a simplifying filter, the agency seems less comprehensible and hence harder to negotiate. Starr commented,

I wish I had someone to talk with about [the program]. I don't know how it works. And I personally would like to know how things work. When I go on an airplane, I can't believe there are two hundred people in this big piece of metal gliding through the air. How does it work? Well, Social Security is not unlike that. How do all these people get in this one program and have it work? How does it work?

A heightened awareness of rules also leads clients to develop a somewhat rigid view of the SSA that suggests little room for individual influence. Donna explained, "It's more or less black and white. And you fit into a category. And maybe there are one, two, or three categories. But whatever I was requesting, I would either fit or not. So nobody would really have influence over anybody. They have to follow the rules, and so do I." Patty offered a similar assessment: "They have their set ways, which they are required to do them that way under the law. I'm sure they don't have any choice on how they do it. At times, you get very irritated with the fact that it's this way. But you know it's this way. They can't do anything about it, and you can't do anything about it." These and other SSDI clients develop an almost Weberian view of the agency in which administrators act solely on the basis of "calculable rules" and "without regard for persons" (Weber 1946). The result is that they tend to doubt that agency workers have flexibility needed to respond to clients' special requests. Holly explained, "They're set by their standards and rules, so they can't really help the little person."

Thus, the tendency for clients to focus on the SSA's elaborate system of binding rules leads to two reasons why clients suspect that it might be difficult to achieve a desired response from the agency: complexity and rigidity. At the same time, however, the binding nature of these rules also makes clients less fearful of arbitrary uses of authority and more confident that the agency will not ignore legitimate requests. As Betty put it, "I think the rules are so rigid and the program is so big that you can't really have influence, but in some ways I guess I'm glad the rules are there."

Binding rules suggest to clients that valid claims will be granted, agency responses will be predictable rather than capricious, and workers who violate regulations can be held accountable. Darryl explained, "They've got to follow those rules, too. It's all equal like that. I don't bend them, and they don't bend them." Thus, just as SSDI clients learn that special favors are unlikely, they also learn that if their claims are legitimate and if they are willing to work their way through a confusing institution, they can be effective. Francis captured the typical view succinctly: "I can ask questions and get answers, if I struggle."

Faith in binding rules also helps account for why SSDI clients find the idea of personal retribution hard to imagine. Clients tend to assume that workers who cannot grant favors also cannot dole out punishments. As a result, clients rarely worry about making waves and rarely feel that they have to ingratiate themselves to administrators to get their due. The following exchange with Starr provides a representative example.

> There are rules. It either is, or it isn't. I didn't have to be especially nice to the intake person so they would write one thing instead of another. I never got the impression that speaking up would make things difficult for you. You know it will either work or not based on the formula.

> *Do you think there is anyone that holds the power to do what they want?*

> No, not at all . . . which is that impersonal feeling you get when you call. No, I don't. There are some places you call, and it probably wouldn't be good if you were screaming and crying. But I've never gotten the sense you could be blackballed for that.

In sum, SSDI clients are more willing to voice complaints because they believe doing so will be effective and will not put them in jeopardy. In their encounters with the agency, clients are rarely summoned or threatened with having their cases terminated. Instead, they are positioned as initiators seeking a government response. Left to navigate the SSA on their own, many clients learn that it is hard to get results from a large, complex bureaucracy. But the SSDI program's design also encourages a sense of anonymity and a faith in binding rules that leaves clients feeling safe from retribution. Most importantly, SSDI recipients develop a sense that as clients, they occupy an institutional position that entitles them to an impartial, rule-driven response. As a result, clients expect to be effective if they persevere in advancing a legitimate claim.

Points of Contrast

In the SSDI sample, there is little need to account for exceptional cases. The only client who reported that she would not raise complaints, Joy, attributed her reticence to lessons she had learned participating in AFDC. Her desire to avoid the agency can be brought under the same explanation that accounted for exceptional cases in the AFDC half of the sample: in her current client role, she applied lessons learned through participation in a different context.

The task for this section, rather, is to show that the patterns described in this chapter reflect more than just differences in the characteristics of the two program populations. There are a number of reasons to conclude that policy designs have effects on client assertiveness that exist apart from any traits that might predispose SSDI clients to be more vocal than their AFDC counterparts.

First, as the preceding sections have shown, AFDC and SSDI clients volunteer specific program experiences to explain why they would or would not contact the agency with a legitimate problem or grievance. They ground their responses not in global beliefs (for example, that it is always best to avoid trouble) but rather in their experiences as clients. Moreover, the experiences they describe match up well, on their face, with the lessons clients claim to have drawn from them.

Second, attempts to control for social group influences do little to erode the large gap in assertiveness across programs. With only a single SSDI client reporting that she would not contact the SSA with a legitimate problem, the disparity between programs hardly fades at all in comparisons that isolate groups based on gender, race, age, or education. In addition, if social traits were the key factor, one would expect to find meaningful group differences within each program. As noted earlier, however, the more vocal minority of AFDC clients do not appear to have any social characteristics that set them apart from other AFDC clients or make them more likely to behave like SSDI clients.

Third, when single individuals participate under different policy designs, they develop different types of beliefs and evaluations. Joy's contrasting assessments of SSDI as "pretty tolerable" and AFDC as "the pits" offer one example of this sort, and clearly corroborate the pattern found in the whole sample. A second example is provided by the group of clients who felt silenced and degraded in AFDC but relished their more participatory role in Head Start. An equally telling piece of evidence can be found in the different ways SSDI and AFDC clients respond when they encounter a single design in the Supplemental Security Income program (SSI).

SSI is a means-tested supplement available to people with disabilities if they do not qualify for SSDI or if they still meet the needs-based cutoff after receiving their SSDI benefits. Because it is means tested, SSI entails broader information gathering than SSDI and more documentation when clients combine program benefits and work. Its design, however, does not include some of the key elements found in AFDC. For example, SSI recipients do not have to appear for regular reviews or participate in child support enforcement, and they do not have caseworkers.

For these and other reasons, AFDC clients usually consider SSI to be a superior program.[8] By contrast, SSDI clients tend to view SSI as an inferior program and cite its poor conditions as a way to accent the merits of SSDI. Kitty, for example, brought up her experience with SSI as a point of contrast that, in her eyes, helped to explain why she felt a sense of privacy, security, and control in SSDI. To underscore the contrast, she compared treatment in SSI to the conditions she believed could be found in AFDC, a program in which her daughter had participated for two years.

SSI is a substitute AFDC. If you get SSI, it's like you're really getting welfare, and they treat you about as low as whale shit. You don't exist for them as a human being. There is a huge difference between [SSI and SSDI]. If it was possible, I'd like to just have SSDI.... The assumption [SSDI makes] is that, in order to get on, your disability has to be proven permanent. [So] the assumption is that they'll leave you alone and let you live your life. And actually they have. The only problem I've ever had is with SSI.... The disability is still permanent with them, but their objectives show the way they look at it like AFDC in a sense. Their goals are similar in AFDC and SSI: "We want to get you off as soon as we can." [In SSDI] you have some, to use a very trite expression, safety net. Whereas, with SSI or AFDC, you don't.

The following exchange with Francis offers a similar assessment. In describing problems with SSDI, Francis expressed the common theme of trying to negotiate a complex system without a caseworker but said he would feel comfortable raising a complaint. When he shifted to SSI, however, his description sounded more like those expressed by AFDC clients, including the conclusion: "You don't want to raise questions, because it's not worth the hassle."

I think it's beaten me down to where I don't even try anymore. I think, especially with all my involvement with SSI, "I can't fight the system, so why try?"

Do you feel beaten down in both SSI and SSDI?

It's much more SSI. With SSDI, my frustration is not knowing all the information about what is out there. You're left to go along in the process. You don't get beaten down by them so much. You just feel frustrated by not knowing what's out there and by them not doing stuff. In SSI, they hassle you and beat you down. In SSDI, it's the information flow. SSI is more beating you down to the point where you don't want to work, and you don't want to raise questions, because it's not worth the hassle.

In SSDI, if you had a complaint, do you think you would feel comfortable raising it?

I would feel comfortable. It's getting information that's harder.

Finally, in addition to these comparisons across programs, it is also helpful to consider a historical contrast within the SSDI program itself. The SSA has always conducted a small number of investigations to insure that clients continue to meet eligibility requirements. Prior to the 1980s, very few clients were selected for review—less than 4 percent per year in the 1970s—and the reviews themselves were often cursory (Derthick 1990, 34; Weatherford 1984, 49). In 1980, however, Congress responded to rising program costs by passing legislation that called for more regular investigations of clients whose conditions might show improvement.[9] Picking up on this initiative in 1981, the Reagan administration charged that fraudulent claims had bloated the agency's benefit rolls and began pressuring the SSA to pursue investigations more vigorously than it had in the past (Derthick 1990, chap. 3; Weatherford 1984).

In doing so, Deborah Stone argues (1984, 12), "the Reagan administration [subjected clients in SSDI] to much the same treatment as that given to AFDC mothers in the 1970s." Indeed, the SSA quickly moved toward a more hands-on style of welfare administration that shared some characteristics with the AFDC program. The agency initiated a larger number of contacts with clients, stepped up the number of case investigations, and raised the percentage of cases terminated through this process. In 1976 the SSA investigated 152,323 cases, terminating benefits for 33,664 clients (Weatherford 1984, 54). Between March 1981 and April 1982, the number of reviews skyrocketed to around 405,000, and the agency terminated the cases of roughly 191,000 clients (Derthick 1990, 42). Derthick (1990, 36) describes the magnitude of this transition as follows: "What had been conceived in Congress in 1980 was deliberate invigoration of a review procedure that had been too feeble to have much effect. What was set in motion in 1981 was more like a purge." By 1983 national media were running what were commonly called horror stories about people who obviously lived with disabilities yet were hastily tossed from the program (Derthick 1990, 36). The period of intensive review ended under virtually unanimous criticism in the spring of 1984.

Without interview evidence from the 1980s, it is difficult to know whether the SSA's more supervisory style of administration had a chilling effect on client assertiveness in the SSDI program. The "horror stories" of this era, however, were mentioned by clients both in the disability support groups I attended and in interviews. Clients described a climate of fear that resulted as individuals saw their friends receive unexpected notices of termination in the mail—a pervasive sense of vulnerability similar to what AFDC clients describe. Like other SSDI clients, Starr recalled the era of horror stories as a point of contrast that helped to explain her feelings of security in the contemporary period.

> I know there were people who were actually cut, so there were people actually in a crisis situation. Letters were going out. . . . It was a scary time. It was real scary. It was unlike right now. Right now on SSDI, I for sure know, and most of us on SSDI know, that our money is pretty secure. At least that's the feeling we are getting from the government.

My evidence concerning this earlier period is not at all systematic, but it suggests that when the SSA changed its approach, clients lost some of the beliefs that encouraged them to pursue legitimate problems and grievances. They felt more vulnerable to scrutiny and punishment, more like objects in a one-way transaction in which the agency exercised power over them. By contrast, the program's format in the 1990s led clients to feel more secure and in control: the agency appeared to respect and respond to them. Thus, while most SSDI clients did not feel that they needed to make demands on the agency, they also did not feel too vulnerable to do so. When I asked Donna if it bothered her to feel "like a statistic," as she described herself, she replied, "I guess I feel OK about it. I don't need anything more from them. And I'm glad they kind of leave me alone. . . . At least this way I don't have any horror stories."

Conclusion

The quality of social citizenship offered by the U.S. welfare system must be measured not only by its benefits but also by the state-citizen relationships it constructs for clients. Through welfare participation, individuals enter a relationship with government that may be designed in a variety of ways. From the standpoint of political analysis, it is essential to ask how particular welfare institutions position citizens in relation to government and how experiences in these institutions shape individuals' beliefs, decisions, and actions. The evidence presented here suggests that the potential for citizens to act as engaged and effective participants in relation to the welfare system can be either cultivated or suppressed through policy design. As participatory theory suggests, "political action depends largely on the sort of institutions within which the individual has, politically, to act" (Pateman 1970, 29).

Policy designs structure welfare participation experiences. In so doing, they provide clients with raw materials needed to construct beliefs about how government bureaucracies operate and how one should act in relation to them. In this sense, welfare participation is educative: it teaches citizens lessons about whether they can be effective in petitioning government and whether they have standing to act without fear of retribution. In this manner, policy designs structure and condition responses to the client's dilemma of action. They can supply reassuring evidence of client security and agency responsiveness, or they can cultivate a paralyzing sense of futility and vulnerability.

Interviews with AFDC clients offer support for key claims found in social control theory. Although AFDC benefits may enhance recipients' security in their daily lives, these benefits are provided in a manner that is "discretionary, subject to the successful hurdling of bureaucratic inquisitions and runarounds and continuing bureaucratic surveillance, all of which shapes the understandings of . . . the people who endure this treatment" (Piven 1995, xiv). As social control theory predicts, AFDC clients frequently report feeling demeaned, exposed, and vulnerable in their welfare relationships. Through experiences under AFDC's supervisory and directive design, clients come to believe that they are vulnerable and that the agency is unresponsive. In the eyes of the majority, it is ineffective and unwise to pursue legitimate questions and grievances.

The more vocal minority of AFDC clients suggest two additional conclusions regarding the political dimensions of welfare participation. First, client assertiveness is not solely a product of policy design but also depends on a broader political climate. Organizations and government programs that bring clients together, affirm their full and equal standing, and encourage involvement make welfare clients into more effective advocates on their own behalf. This dynamic is easiest to see in periods such as the 1930s or 1960s, when social movements challenge welfare stigma and encourage a sense of entitlement (Gordon 1994; Piven and Cloward 1977). But it is equally important when the general political climate is hostile to welfare participation and clients are likely to feel that they occupy a precarious position.

Second, the vocal minority in AFDC also suggests that the educative effects of participation in one setting can spill over to affect citizens' behaviors in other political domains. In particular, the greater willingness of Head Start parents to assert themselves serves to underscore a major claim of participatory theory: experiences that affirm the value of participation in one context also encourage a desire for involvement in others. This potential for positive spillover effects, however, is matched by an equal potential for the lessons of participation to dissuade future political action. In the SSDI program, for example, Joy felt that conditions were far better than in AFDC, yet she remained reluctant to assert herself because, in her words, "I still know from [AFDC] that you've got to let the system be." The consequences of these sorts of spillover effects for broader political orientations and patterns of political action will serve as the focal point for analysis in chapter 7.

A comparison of client experiences and beliefs in AFDC with those found in SSDI yields striking evidence of a hierarchy of social citizenship in the U.S. welfare system. Relative to their AFDC counterparts, citizens who enter SSDI occupy a client role that is, from a political standpoint, superior. SSDI clients enjoy more autonomy, more anonymity, and a greater sense of entitlement. Their contacts with the SSA are not initiated by a summons backed up by a threat of termination; their interactions with the agency are not mediated by a single individual who controls their access to benefits, information, and program opportunities. Instead, SSDI clients are usually positioned as initiators in their interactions with the agency. The SSA may be judged as efficient or intransigent in meeting client requests, but in either case, it is perceived and evaluated in terms of responsiveness, not as a hostile and directive arm of the state.

Unlike AFDC clients, SSDI clients develop a feeling of security in their welfare relationships and come to expect that, if they persevere, they can gain action from the agency. As a result, SSDI clients are far more willing to pursue legitimate questions and grievances.

Policy designs shape patterns of client involvement in at least three ways. First, they establish formal rules that forbid, permit, or mandate client input. Unlike AFDC or SSDI, for example, Head Start requires its adult clients to participate in policy councils. Second, policy designs define the terms of interaction in welfare relationships. They set the frequency and scope of decision making, bestow formal authority to make binding decisions, and distribute resources, information, and legitimacy. In these ways, policy designs can structure welfare participation as a two-way transaction or as a unilateral relationship of power and dependency in which clients are made objects of direction and supervision. Clients in AFDC and SSDI do not merely have different beliefs about how they are positioned; they are, in fact, positioned differently.

Third, program designs affect client involvement by influencing individuals' perceptions of their welfare relationships. Given that the SSA is one of the largest government bureaucracies in the United States (Derthick 1990, 4), it is not surprising that SSDI clients come to see it as a big and complicated place. What makes their descriptions noteworthy is the contrast between programs. AFDC clients also engage bureaucracies that are (by most standards) large and complex, yet these qualities are almost never mentioned when AFDC clients describe their participation experiences. Similarly, although SSA administrators undoubtedly exercise a degree of choice in how they interpret agency rules (Kerwin 1994; Meier 1993), it is the rule and not the room for discretion that is salient for clients. By contrast, while AFDC caseworkers also exercise discretion within limits set by rules and supervisory structures, client attention is directed toward individual workers' capacity to dole out punishments and rewards.

Thus, policy designs not only shape the objective conditions clients encounter but also focus clients' attention on some agency characteristics while obscuring others. Because SSDI clients have a welfare relationship that is not mediated through a single caseworker, they are more likely to perceive the immensity, complexity, and rule-driven nature of the organization in which they are embedded. AFDC clients are positioned in a manner that makes these institutional features less salient than the discretion of a single worker. Although agency regulations may exist on the books, they do not appear to have a fixed existence that can be counted on to protect clients, guarantee entitlements, or enforce agency responsiveness. In the perceptions that provide AFDC clients with a subjective frame of reference for action, rules do not bind both sides of the welfare relationship; they are tools invoked and wielded by caseworkers when it suits their interests.

Based on the preceding analysis, it may be tempting to conclude that the casework format and caseworker discretion inevitably function to marginalize clients. Such a conclusion, however, would fail to recognize the political significance of discretionary casework relations for clients who have little access to influence elsewhere in government. Welfare participation allows citizens to influence policy implementation only to the extent that they can insert themselves into a decision-making process. When the discretion of frontline workers is curtailed, power to make decisions is retained at higher levels of authority, levels that lie at a greater distance from clients. In this sense, street-level discretion is a necessary but not sufficient condition for client involvement. Caseworker discretion undermines client assertiveness when it is embedded in a broader policy design that does not foster trust or give clients countervailing sources of power in dealing with bureaucrats (Handler 1992). Its effects depend on whether clients are positioned in a way that allows and encourages them to advocate on their own behalf.

Policy designs may be viewed as a bureaucratic form of what Goffman (1959) called the "presentation of self." In everyday life, people communicate who they are to one another through the informal gestures and cues that make up personal interaction. We do not have complete control over how other people view us, and we may not intend many of the impressions we leave behind. Nevertheless, the images we convey systematically influence the evaluations, expectations, and responses of the people we encounter (Goffman 1959, 1974). In much the same way, policy designs deliver both intended and unintended cues that shape the ways citizens perceive and act in relation to government (Schneider and Ingram 1997). In welfare programs, policy designs function as a bureaucratic presentation of self that systematically influences citizens' beliefs about how the agency works and how they should respond to the client's dilemma of action.

CHAPTER 7

Policy Design, Political Learning, and Political Action

A central task for political research on welfare participation is to explain how this activity relates to other dimensions of citizens' political lives. Theories of social citizenship and social control suggest that welfare participation has the potential to strengthen or weaken citizens' attachments to the polity (Marshall 1964; Piven and Cloward 1993). In chapter 3, I suggested that benefits offered by the U.S. welfare system serve important positive political functions for citizens: through welfare claiming, individuals protect their political autonomy, status, and capacities against the corrosive effects of poverty. By contrast, this chapter investigates how differences in the form of provision across the two tiers of the U.S. welfare system affect broader patterns of political thought and action. Specifically, I ask how experiences of participation in AFDC and SSDI influence citizens' beliefs about government and orientations toward political participation.

Welfare recipients have an unusually visible material stake in government policies. Their immediate fates depend on the actions of public officials, and this fact is routinely underscored by speeches delivered in electoral campaigns and legislative debates. As Dizzy put it, "Whether we get that welfare that keeps us alive depends on who's in office." In light of such strong personal incentives, one might expect welfare recipients to be more politically active than other citizens (Olson 1965). Research on political action, however, suggests that public assistance recipients are an especially quiescent group (Verba, Schlozman, and Brady 1995). Indeed, the pattern is so striking that some scholars have suggested that the United States is characterized by a "bifurcated politics" in which "those most dependent on government are counterpoised against a more educated and affluent portion of the population who, though they do not rely on the government as much for basic needs, are the more politically involved" (Verba 1978, 26; Nelson 1984).

Why are public assistance recipients an especially quiescent segment of the citizenry? The most widely accepted reason, which I will call the preexisting characteristics explanation, is simply that members of this group tend to come from segments of the population with less abundant political resources and skills (Verba and Nie 1972; Verba, Schlozman, and Brady 1995). As Verba,

Schlozman, and Brady (1995, 411) explain, "Recipients of means-tested benefits are, not unexpectedly, less well educated and less well off financially. . . .
The lift given to their participation by their [greater] interest in issues of basic
human needs is insufficient to overcome their other resource deficits."

A second possibility, which I will call the passivity explanation, is suggested by conservative critics who argue that welfare benefits discourage political involvement by cultivating personal traits of dependence. Few themes in
welfare politics have endured as well as the idea that poor relief undermines the
motivation to work (Handler and Hasenfeld 1991). Over the past two decades,
critics have extended this image of dependent passivity to the realm of politics.
Fullinwider (1988, 262), for example, suggests that welfare receipt is associated with a tendency to be less "law-abiding, civil, and politically active." Similarly, as part of his argument for a "new paternalism" in welfare policy, Mead
(1985, 1992, 1997b) suggests that welfare recipients are less than competent or
functioning citizens: "Most of them are too withdrawn and dependent to shoul-
der the burdens of political activism. Elites must then take the lead" (1992, 227).

A third possible explanation can be gleaned from arguments that welfare
provision can divert or temper political demand-making. Piven and Cloward
(1993), for example, argue that even though welfare benefits empower workers,
extensions of poor relief also serve to blunt popular demands during times of
unrest. Edelman offers related arguments suggesting that welfare benefits supply a pacifying reassurance to poor people (1964) and that "helping" images of
public assistance obscure the need for political demand-making (1977). By ex-
tending these analyses to the individual level, one might suggest a co-optation
explanation—that is, benefit provision itself produces demobilizing effects.

In one way or another, each explanation bypasses the experience of welfare participation itself.[1] By contrast, a fourth possibility is suggested by the
combination of theories employed in the preceding chapter. Participatory democratic theory highlights the educative effects of participation and the ways in
which institutional arrangements leave their imprints on citizens (Pateman
1970). Social control theory points to differences in institutional design across
the U.S. welfare system and suggests that these designs may shape clients' behaviors both within and beyond the welfare agency (Piven and Cloward 1993).
Taken together, these theories suggest that the lessons of welfare participation
described in chapter 6 may have broad political consequences. Perhaps the
clearest statement of this political learning explanation can be found in Schneider and Ingram's (1993, 1995, 1997) work on policy design, democracy, and
the social construction of target populations.

> In our theory of causation, motivations of elected officials are linked to the
> types of policy designs they construct, which affect people's experiences
> with the policy and the lessons and messages they take from it. These, in

turn, influence people's values and attitudes (including their group identities), their orientations toward government, and their political participation patterns. . . . The welfare policy case nicely illustrates one of the central lessons of our work for improving policy design for democracy. The delineation of targets in Social Security . . . was the better design for democracy. . . . In contrast, AFDC, targeted to match economic and later racial and social classes, disempowered its intended targets. (1995, 442, 445)

This chapter presents evidence that welfare programs are important sites of adult political learning (Sapiro 1994). As described in the preceding chapter, policy designs structure program experiences in ways that shape clients' beliefs about both the nature of the welfare agency and the effectiveness of asserting themselves. These lessons spill over to influence broader orientations toward government and political action for two reasons. First, clients tend to view their experiences with welfare institutions as evidence of what can be expected from government as a whole. Second, a broader political discourse suggests to clients that elected officials are responsible for the conditions experienced in welfare programs and that client status is as meaningful to these officials as it is to agency workers.

The political learning explanation leads to empirical expectations that distinguish it from the other accounts described so far. First, unlike the passivity and co-optation explanations, it suggests that receipt of social welfare benefits should not, by itself, dampen political engagement. Rather, the relationship between welfare receipt and political engagement should vary across policy designs: only experiences in AFDC should foster lower levels of participation. Second, the political learning explanation predicts that participation differences between AFDC and SSDI will exist even after one accounts for the influence of preexisting characteristics. Third, it suggests that AFDC and SSDI recipients should express general views of government and political action that mirror their perceptions of the welfare agency and beliefs about client demand-making.

It is important to point out that these four explanations are not mutually exclusive. While I do not find much support for the passivity explanation, the political learning argument should be seen as a complement to the other two. For recipients of public assistance, the demobilizing effects of resource scarcity are exacerbated by lessons learned through welfare participation. These influences reinforce rather than displace one another. Similarly, an emphasis on the educative effects of welfare participation does not deny that the material or symbolic value of poor relief can serve to divert political demand-making. On the contrary, the political learning approach taken here elaborates on arguments regarding institutional design that are a central component of social control theory (Piven and Cloward 1993).

The chapter is organized to present a chain of evidence that links welfare program designs to patterns of political action. The first section presents evidence that AFDC clients are less politically active than SSDI recipients and that this disparity remains after accounting for other characteristics that distinguish the two groups. The remaining sections reconstruct the links that connect this outcome to the lessons of welfare participation described in chapter 6. The second section explains why beliefs developed in welfare programs have a spillover effect on broader orientations toward politics. The third section provides a detailed analysis of how clients view government and political action, paying particular attention to how these descriptions fit with their earlier accounts of welfare programs. In the fourth section, I show how program experiences also explain what at first appear to be exceptions to dominant patterns in the evidence. Finally, I explore the link between program experiences and internal political efficacy, arguing that low participation rates among AFDC recipients do not flow from a sense of political incapacity.

Patterns of Political Action

Do clients of the U.S. welfare system engage in political action as often as other citizens? If lessons learned through welfare participation influence political involvement, then the answer to this question should vary across programs. This is precisely the pattern reported by Verba, Schlozman, and Brady in their comprehensive study of political action, *Voice and Equality*.

> The receipt of benefits per se does not imply a low level of activity. Those who receive non-means-tested benefits such as . . . Social Security are at least as active as the public as a whole. In contrast, those who receive means-tested benefits such as AFDC . . . are substantially less active than the public as a whole. The differences imply that those who would be most in need of government response . . . are the least likely to make themselves visible to the government as a whole. (1995, 210)

Unlike social insurance recipients, public assistance clients are underrepresented in every political activity measured by Verba and his colleagues. The fact that social insurance recipients are "at least as active as the public as a whole" belies the charge that government assistance, by itself, undermines political involvement. But because these results do not control for differences between the program populations, it is possible that they might be explained by clients' preexisting characteristics. Although Verba, Schlozman, and Brady (1995, 219–20) do not identify a specific trait that can account for participation differences across programs, they conclude that the gap probably results from background characteristics rather than program participation itself.

Table 1, which presents a logistic regression analysis of turnout in the 1992 national elections, helps distinguish program effects from demographic differences (on logistic regression, see Aldrich and Nelson 1986, 115–55; for variable descriptions, see appendix B). Relative to SSDI recipients, AFDC clients are more likely to have low levels of education and low family incomes; they are more likely to be women, to be younger, and to be people of color; they are also more likely to live in the South and (outside the South) in central cities (U.S. House of Representatives 1998). To control for these demographic differences, the model includes the following variables: *Woman, Black, South, Education, Age, Income,* and *Urban.* The model also controls for respondents' strength of *Partisanship.* The results suggest that the odds of going to the polls are significantly higher for women, older people, people who feel stronger partisan ties, people who have more income and education, and people who live outside the South. By contrast, all else equal, African Americans and people who live in central cities appear no less likely to vote than other citizens.[2]

The first two lines in table 1 address the relationship between program participation and voting. The first line indicates that the odds of an SSDI recipient voting are not statistically different from those of a nonrecipient who shares

TABLE 1. Electoral Participation by Program Participation and Control Variables (logistic regression)

Independent Variables	Coefficient	Standard Error	Probability Level
Program Participation			
SSDI	−.328	.247	.184
AFDC	−.831	.267	.001
Demographics and Partisanship			
Woman	.271	.131	.039
Black	.191	.185	.301
South	−.619	.131	.001
Education	.573	.051	.001
Age	.026	.004	.001
Income	.037	.011	.001
Urban	−.022	.144	.878
Partisanship	.409	.061	.001
Constant	−3.330	.318	.001

Overall model LR χ^2 = 414.86, 10 df, $p < .001$
$N = 1998$
$N_{AFDC} = 82$
$N_{SSDI} = 101$

Note: Coefficients are from the logistic regression procedure in SPSS; one-tailed test for AFDC, two-tailed tests otherwise. Data are from the 1992 NES (Miller, Kinder, and Rosenstone 1993).

similar background traits. By contrast, all else equal, participation in AFDC has a significant negative effect on the likelihood that an individual will vote ($b = -.831, p < .001$). By exponentiating this coefficient ($e^b = .435$), it is possible to estimate that, even after controlling for demographic variables, being an AFDC recipient reduces the odds that a person will vote to slightly less than half of what it would have been otherwise.[3]

When combined with the broader study by Verba, Schlozman, and Brady (1995), this analysis suggests the following starting points for investigation: (1) AFDC clients are less likely to engage in political action than are SSDI recipients; (2) this disparity partly reflects differences in such traits as education and income; (3) the disparity remains even after controlling for key demographic differences and hence cannot be dismissed on the basis of prior characteristics; (4) AFDC clients are less likely to be politically active than are nonrecipients who share salient demographic characteristics, which suggests that their quiescence may be traceable to some factor associated with welfare participation itself; (5) SSDI clients are just as politically active as the rest of the citizenry, suggesting that whatever this welfare-related factor might be, it is not simply the receipt of cash benefits.

The gap in political engagement that separates SSDI and AFDC clients was equally apparent in my field research, as illustrated by the different ways each client group responded when policymakers threatened to cut off important program benefits. During the year of my fieldwork, state officials decided to terminate existing programs providing AFDC benefits and home health care (a service that allows many SSDI clients to live in their homes rather than health care institutions). Activists in the disability community immediately began working to organize a protest around the home health care issue. Less than two weeks after the organizing began, a large group met for a confrontational rally at the state legislature. Aided by statewide media coverage, the effort pressured lawmakers into continuing the program. Merton, an SSDI client who was not at the rally, recalled this victory two months later when I asked him if a movement of SSDI recipients could be effective in seeking political change.

> The recipients of SSDI, they can fight. With the advocacy groups getting behind it, I think we've made some significant changes. We stopped personal care from being cut. The finance committee in [the capital] wanted to abolish Title XIX payment for personal care. Well, they went to [the capital] and protested. And then they changed their minds on that. All these legislators and people voting for it had to change their minds.

Welfare rights activists made equally determined efforts to mobilize AFDC clients. Despite having few resources, organizers managed to transport a group of protesters to the capital, where they shut down the street in front of the governor's house. In the end, however, these activists were unable to bring out a large group on a sustained basis and never gained attention from the press or policymakers. The disparity in outcomes across the two programs reflected a variety of factors. The disability community had a much stronger organizational base in the form of independent living centers and support groups. They also had more resources to spend on recruitment and transportation as well as sympathetic media coverage that mobilized bystanders inside and outside the disability community. In addition to these group differences, however, two individual-level factors also made AFDC clients an especially difficult target for mobilization, and each of these barriers can be traced, at least in part, to the AFDC program.

First, relative to their counterparts in SSDI, AFDC clients were harder to mobilize because they were more likely to be poor. This difference reflects not only the higher level of poverty among those who apply to public assistance programs but also the fact that public assistance programs are less effective at lifting clients out of poverty (Danziger and Weinberg 1994). Here, one encounters an important way in which the hierarchy of social citizenship found in the two-tier welfare system supports political inequality (Gordon 1994). Relative to poor people who enter social insurance programs, public assistance recipients are far more likely to remain in an economic position that forces them to struggle daily just to fend off crises and make ends meet (Edin and Lein 1997). These continual efforts at triage sap the time and energy citizens need to attend to the activities of elite policymakers.

> People who are completely unsure about food and shelter in the coming days for themselves and their families will be worried sick and, as it were, understandably obsessed with this issue all the time, in a way which leaves little room, very little mental space, for any general and long-term reflection on issues that go very far beyond their present predicament. . . . Need, then, and the urgency of demands that it generates, can radically undermine the possibility of civic politics and distort the contribution that an individual participator can make. (D. King and Waldron 1988, 425–26, 428)

Thus, relative to the aid supplied by the SSDI program, the meager benefits offered by the AFDC program are less successful at realizing a central goal set forth in social citizenship theory: to protect the political equality and engagement of citizens against the marginalizing effects of poverty (D. King and Waldron 1988; Marshall 1964). In discussing the failed attempt to mobilize AFDC recipients around the threat of benefit cuts, Lynn, one of the four activists in the AFDC sample, explained,

I think part of the problem . . . is that when you're talking about poor people, you're talking about people who don't really have the time, re-sources, or energy to get organized or be organized. Most of them are wor-ried about day-to-day living. . . . If you were living on General Assistance and didn't know how you were going to eat every day, you wouldn't have a lot of time to go to protests or pickets or meetings. . . . There's a lot of barriers in organizing the poor.

In addition to the problem of poverty, AFDC clients were also especially difficult to mobilize for a second reason: they did not believe their demands could be effective in influencing policymakers. Lynn explained, "There's . . . a lot of us who don't get into politics. And I don't think it's because we don't care at all. I think it's because we feel it doesn't make a difference." When I asked AFDC clients why they did not protest the proposed cuts, they typically em-phasized the same themes of futility and vulnerability found in their explana-tions for why they did not raise grievances at the welfare agency (see chap. 6). If clients could not influence small and immediate decisions about their own cases, what hope could they have of influencing decisions about the shape of the whole program? Like decisions in the casework relationships, clients ex-pected decisions about the AFDC program as a whole to be made in an au-tonomous manner, without input from clients, and worried that they could make things worse for themselves if they adopted a confrontational posture. Anna's comments captured both of these themes:

[Policymakers] just act in their own way. It's like they're in their own little world. They don't think about the people in need out there or what we want. To me, it's like the welfare office. It's just a big runaround, a big game. They say what they want and then do what they want. And if it does get done for us, it's just another waiting process. You have to sit and wait for them to do it. . . . Too many people are too scared [to organize]. [AFDC clients] think that the government is going to throw them away if they try to have a say-so in it. But everybody should have a right.

In what follows, I argue that AFDC clients' beliefs about policy-making point toward a second way in which policy designs in the two-tier welfare sys-tem reinforce political inequality. The AFDC program not only leaves recipi-ents in poverty conditions that undermine political engagement, it also supplies them with firsthand experiences that leave them pessimistic about govern-ment's responsiveness and the efficacy of political action. AFDC recipients are less politically active than SSDI recipients and less active than others who share salient demographics, at least in part because of the lessons they learn about government and demand-making as they participate in the welfare system.

Bridges to Broader Politics

I haven't been to most of the government, but I'll bet they just treat you the way the welfare office does. That's my fear. They'll treat you the same way. (Hope, an AFDC client)

When they start talking about voting, I turn the TV [off]. I do. It's no guarantee. This person can make all these promises, but that don't mean they're going to do it. The rest of the government mostly works like the AFDC office. I mean, I don't deal with the government when I can [avoid it]. (Vanessa, an AFDC client)

By shaping participation experiences, program designs influence welfare recipients' views of client status and agency decision making. Thus, as described in the preceding chapter, clients in the AFDC program come to believe that they occupy a degraded status and that the agency is directive rather than responsive, while SSDI clients come to perceive the agency as large and complicated but expect that it will respond to demands that are within the rules. It is not surprising that these divergent expectations would lead AFDC clients to be less assertive than their SSDI counterparts when they deal with the welfare agency. But why would these program-specific perceptions spill over into broader beliefs about government and political action?

A group discussion I observed in November 1994 at the shelter for homeless families suggested an important clue to this puzzle. Twice each week, the shelter held support group meetings where residents, more than 80 percent of whom were in AFDC, could talk with one another about personal problems. Although the subject of AFDC came up frequently at these meetings, broader political issues usually did not. On the night after the 1994 midterm elections, however, there was a welfare rights activist staying in the shelter, whom I will call Carol. At the meeting, Carol chastised the other women for not voting in the election and for (in her opinion) allowing the Republican victory to happen. In the ensuing argument, the almost unanimous response was that voting would have made no difference. Moreover, residents defended their response by arguing that Carol was naive if she did not realize that the rest of government "does what it wants, just like the welfare."

There may be many reasons why residents did not vote that day. For example, most were busy trying to find housing, since they soon would have to leave the temporary shelter. But the repeated claim in the meeting was that government, like the welfare agency, was going to do whatever it wanted, and it was useless to get in the way. Over the following year, I found the same theme articulated on many occasions when residents discussed the subject of politics or welfare reform. In a number of cases, the phrase *just like the welfare* was also used by residents as a shorthand for decisions that were made on their behalf without their input. Sometimes the term referred to decisions made by shelter staff, but the comparison to welfare was particularly likely when the discussion turned to government.

Perceptions of specific welfare bureaucracies persist and get applied to other government institutions because, in clients' eyes, government is a single system. In interviews, clients from both programs tended to identify welfare bureaucracies as institutions of government. Participants rarely sorted these institutions into neat administrative and political categories. For example, when I asked Dizzy about the SSDI application process, he said, "Well, it's political. Isn't anything with the government political? Everything with the government is political." Clients did not simply view the welfare agency as a part of government; they saw it as a microcosm of government. Like others, Mary felt that "in politics, welfare, SSI, it's all the same." Another AFDC client, Nancy, stated this view in greater detail.

> I don't know if people in the government would be responsive to me. If it's anything like trying to deal with the AFDC system, I don't see how. And to me, AFDC, the Department of Social Services, Department of Child Protection, Juvenile Court, those are all the same system. They're just different departments in the same system. And I have not had luck with any of those systems. . . . I would expect the same sorts of treatment in Congress or wherever. . . . That's why I say the government is all just one and the same program with different departments.

These statements bear a striking resemblance to those recorded by Austin Sarat (1990) when he interviewed welfare clients about their attempts to obtain legal services. Sarat writes, "Just as Spencer portrayed himself as 'caught' in the web of legal rules, he saw the legal services office caught within the welfare bureaucracy. . . . Legal services . . . was not only inseparable from but was identical with welfare" (1990, 352). One client told Sarat (1990, 352) that lawyers and caseworkers "are both part of government," and another said, "Doesn't matter whether they call it welfare or legal services. It's the same shit." In this unified view, images of the welfare bureaucracy become, in effect, images of government, and lessons learned about speaking up at the agency spill over into other forms of political demand-making.

There are many reasons why clients may see welfare institutions as part of "one big system" of government. For example, when elected officials help applicants gain program benefits or solve problems with the agency, their actions (and credit claiming) suggest that agency responses are influenced by actors in other branches of government. Also, many clients are aware that agency workers consult with, and occasionally influence, personnel in other parts of government, such as Child Protective Services or the courts. As Lynn put it, welfare workers are "part of the clique . . . only a phone call away from Child Protective Services."

The primary reason for the spillover effect, however, is simply that welfare participation provides so many clients with their most direct connection to a government institution. In these cases, the welfare agency serves as clients' most proximate and reliable source of information about how government works. To most of my informants, welfare bureaucracies offer a salient representation of government as a whole. The spillover effect occurs not because they think their perceptions of the agency transfer to government but because they recognize that they have been dealing with the government all along.

For many clients, media stories about welfare policy debates or electoral campaigns reinforce this unified view of government. Not surprisingly, news stories that refer to welfare programs have a special salience for people who depend on them for benefits. These stories frequently present elected officials as policymakers who are responsible for the current or future shape of welfare programs. As candidates and legislators outline their plans for Medicare, Social Security, or AFDC, they appear as a group to be the "executive directors" of welfare agencies. At a minimum, clients tend to infer that program conditions reflect the desires of elected representatives, and in some cases, clients perceive welfare bureaucrats and legislators as occupants of a single institution. Holly complained, "They don't seem to care at Social Security, and they don't seem to care nowhere else in the Congress. That's the way the government is."

For AFDC recipients, news stories dealing with welfare also tend to have a second effect. When legislators and candidates give speeches about welfare reform, they often make generalizations about "welfare mothers." To clients, these descriptions often seem degrading and unfair. On several occasions, women recalled turning off the television because they did not want their children to hear what was being said about them. To many clients, news stories on welfare suggest that the degraded position they occupy in the program carries over to the rest of the polity. The stigmatizing discourse on welfare creates a bridge between their status as clients and their status as citizens.[4] Celina described this bridge:

> You hear about yourself on TV. They're stereotyping you all the time. And I'm tired of it. . . . The rest of the government is just like AFDC: You're a number to both, and neither of them care. The government looks at me as someone on AFDC, one of the statistics. I had my kids when I was young. So that's all they figure they need to know about me. So the whole government sees me the way the AFDC office does, except for they don't get to swear at me.

Thus, a variety of factors combine to forge a connection between welfare experiences and beliefs about other political institutions. This connection is stronger for some clients than for others. As research on adult political learning leads one to expect (Sapiro 1994), clients assimilate the lessons of welfare participation into what their life history has already taught them about politics. Consequently, beliefs about agencies do not always extend to the rest of government. This point is well illustrated by a focused comparison of two SSDI clients.

Darryl is a forty-four-year-old African American man with a high school diploma. He has been homeless many times and has been in prison. Mark is a thirty-six-year-old Native American man with a ninth-grade education. Like Darryl, he has experienced periods of homelessness and incarceration. One might expect these two men to share uniformly pessimistic views of public institutions, but their attitudes toward government diverge in significant respects. When I asked Mark about government, he referred to experiences in SSDI that he considered to be direct evidence of government responsiveness. By contrast, although Darryl similarly considered the SSA to be very helpful and responsive, when it came time to discuss government as a whole his program experiences were eclipsed by his lifetime of marginality. He never mentioned SSDI as he told me about government, and his description of politics emphasized his own powerlessness.

DARRYL: [Public officials] make decisions that influence or govern the
    smaller people in the world, people who don't have no say-so or noth-
    ing. . . . I'm what you call the "little man." I'll always be the small man.
    I don't have any power. I don't have any say-so. . . . Power is . . . I don't
    know what word I'm looking for. It's a dominating type of thing. You
    can move people around like puppets just by making laws and having
    the police enforce those laws. If you do something that the people with
    power don't like, they'll have you arrested, and there's nothing you can
    do about it.

MARK: The government is so big, they probably wouldn't have time to listen
    to our particular stories about what the government ought to do. . . .
    When you talk about government, I keep thinking about my dad. He's
    complaining about the government, that it's corrupt. But yes, I think
    they're listening to me. I mean, I got SSD[I]. They knew I needed some
    kind of income, and they were there to listen and do something. So I fig-
    ure if they're doing right by me in SSD[I], they must care about me in
    the rest of government.

Mark's and Darryl's divergent responses serve as an important reminder that the spillover effects of program experiences vary across individuals. For most recipients, however, there seems to be at least some connection between program experiences and general political orientation.

To summarize, clients draw political lessons from their program experiences because welfare agencies are usually the most accessible and consequential government institution in their life. Welfare agencies are easily recognized as a part of government and have clear links to its other branches. For many clients, welfare agencies serve as the most direct source of information about how government works. For people in AFDC, program experiences also are linked to the rest of political life by news stories that seem to imply that the status of "welfare recipient" is as relevant in other government institutions as it is at the agency.

All this suggests that the same experiences that make AFDC clients less willing to challenge the agency may also contribute to their lower levels of political involvement. To make this explanation compelling, however, we must consider the content of clients' views of political action and its relation to their views of demand-making in welfare programs.

External Efficacy: Views of Government and Political Action

Views of political action flow partly from one's perceptions of government. Political participation seems less worthwhile if policy making appears to be a directive rather than responsive activity. Even if government officials seem to pay attention to some citizens' preferences, specific individuals or groups may not expect to receive equal treatment. These sorts of beliefs are a critical element of political efficacy, the feeling that one's activities can influence the political process and that it is worth the effort to get involved (see Campbell, Gurin, and Miller 1954, 181–94). Students of political behavior usually distinguish between external efficacy (beliefs about governmental responsiveness) and internal efficacy (perceptions of one's own ability to understand and participate in political life) (Niemi, Craig, and Mattei 1991). Both forms of efficacy have been shown to be strong predictors of political participation (Abramson 1983, chap. 8), and I will argue that the internal/external distinction is critical for understanding how welfare participation relates to political involvement. In this section, I analyze the effects of program experiences on external efficacy. In a later section, I will suggest that the same experiences have very different effects on feelings of internal efficacy.

To understand clients' beliefs about political action, it is necessary to begin with their more general conceptions of the political system. In interviews, I asked clients to tell me about politics and government—who and what can influence policy decisions, why political outcomes turn out the way they do, and whether government does what citizens want. From their responses, I derived a large number of common themes, which I then reduced to four broad views of government. I allowed for ambivalence by treating these views as complementary rather than mutually exclusive. In prototypical form, the four views are as follows:

Democratic: Government is open and responsive to the preferences of citizens, who are in meaningful respects politically equal. An established political process governed by laws allows citizens to have influence and hold public officials accountable.

Capitalist: Government exists to serve rich people and corporations. While it may not literally be the executive committee of the ruling class, government is primarily influenced by economic inequalities. The political process is governed by money and the people who have it.

Complicated: Government is too large and has too many complicated systems and laws. As a result, one public official does not know what another is doing. Officials cannot pay attention to citizens' real needs, do not respond in a timely manner, and are difficult to influence.

Autonomous: Government officials do whatever they want, whenever they want. They can evade or change laws if their goals require it. They have to confront one another when they disagree, but important decisions are not swayed by popular actions.

Figure 1 shows how frequently clients in each program expressed each of these views. Virtually equal majorities from both programs raised the capitalist theme (56 percent in AFDC, 60 percent in SSDI, not significant). Francis, an SSDI client, said, "In the big scheme, it's the haves and the have-nots. It's who has the money and the power and who doesn't. That's all it boils down to." Like a majority of AFDC clients, Debber concurred:

> The rich have greater influence. If you have no money, you're nobody, you're nothing. That's the way it is in the United States. The hardworking man, the blue-collar man . . . if you ask me, their opinions and their beliefs don't mean nothing. If you've got money, then you can talk. . . . If you have money, then you can do something to change the system, the government. But the poor can't. What can the poor do?

Because clients in AFDC and SSDI emphasized the political importance of material inequality to a virtually equal degree, this belief cannot by itself ac-

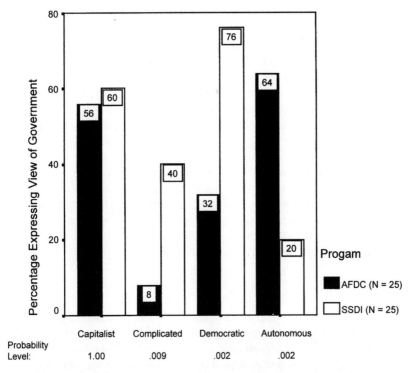

Fig. 1.   Views of government by program. (Probability levels are based on Fisher's exact tests.)

count for differences in political engagement across the programs. Instead, the two groups must be distinguished by the additional themes.

An autonomous view of government was significantly more common among AFDC recipients (64 percent versus 20 percent in SSDI, $p = .002$). As described in chapter 6, caseworker autonomy was a prevailing theme in clients' descriptions of AFDC decision making. Alissa gave a typical description: "Whatever [agency workers] want to do, they're going to do regardless, whether I say something or not." Likewise, after noting the influence of wealth in politics, Debber asserted, "There's nothing I can do because the government is going to do what they want to do regardless of what us people say." In a manner similar to Debber, most AFDC recipients see government decision making as a directive rather than responsive process. They expect that if public officials do listen to citizen preferences, these preferences will be the opinions of rich people.

SSDI clients are more likely to emphasize the two themes that distinguish their descriptions of the SSA. While only 8 percent of AFDC recipients mentioned government's size and complexity, this theme cropped up in 40 percent of SSDI clients' accounts ($p = .009$). Betty commented, "Government has gotten so big and has so many rules that it can't be influenced. . . . The government is very large, and whenever anything is large, it starts getting hard to run or affect." Francis was even more explicit in linking this inference about government to his SSDI experience: "In SSDI and SSI, you really learn something about how the system creates itself. [Government] is such a huge organization that A doesn't know what B is doing. They're too big to know what they're doing." Patty agreed:

> Social Security is no different from the rest of the government. It's a lot of paperwork and a lot of Mickey Mouse stuff. When you're in something like Social Security, you learn a lot about the way the government does things. There's a lot of paper, and nothing moves very fast. Everything goes slowly. . . . Government has just gotten so big and so removed from the individual. They don't see it. They don't see the problems we have all the time.

SSDI recipients are also significantly more likely than AFDC recipients to view the government as open and democratic (76 percent versus 32 percent, $p = .002$). Like the SSA, government as a whole appears to be responsive to persistent efforts to obtain action, and this responsiveness is guaranteed by a system of laws. Bridget, for example, argued that "in politics, the squeaky wheels get what they want. You have to make noise to get a big government to do anything." Likewise, Phil believed that citizens can "initiate change" if they "use the process" and that "it comes down to the old thing of one person, one vote. You want to vote out an incumbent, you get to do that. You get to vote against an incumbent." By a three-quarters majority, SSDI clients believe that citizens can bring about change, as Starr put it, "within the letter of the law." Starr observed, "I know it's a very grueling process, but yes, I think locally we are heard."

For most people in SSDI, then, the government appears to be open and responsive to citizens. This point should not be overstated. Few people in SSDI consider government officials as responsive as they should be, and SSDI clients were more likely than AFDC recipients to believe that the government's ability to act on popular desires is limited by its size and its complicated system of laws. People in SSDI shared the expectation that public officials would be more responsive to people with money, but these doubts did not alter their fundamental expectation that even if the government is slow to act, it eventually will respond to citizens who vote, organize, and lobby public officials.

In addition to soliciting clients' general images of the political system, I asked them several direct questions related to political efficacy. As figure 2 shows, their answers were consistent with what one would expect based on their

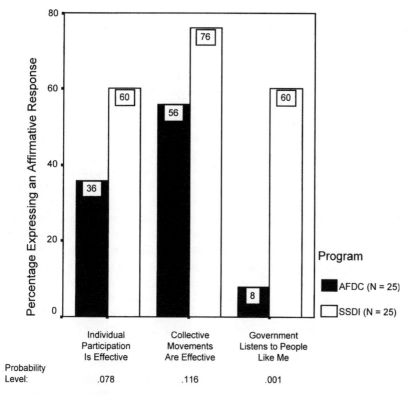

Fig. 2. Feelings of external political efficacy by program. (Probability levels are based on Fisher's exact tests.)

views of government. SSDI recipients are more likely to believe that their individual actions can affect government decisions (60 percent versus 36 percent in AFDC, $p = .078$) and that a collective movement of people in the program can influence government actions (76 percent versus 56 percent in AFDC, $p = .116$). The most dramatic differences emerged when I asked individuals whether government officials listen to people like them. While 60 percent of SSDI participants believe that officials listen, only 8 percent of the AFDC clients agree ($p = .001$). In sum, the disparity in political efficacy suggested by clients' general views of government shows up consistently across these three more specific questions.

Looking beneath these numbers, it becomes clear that even responses that were coded the same way across the two programs often had different rationales and that these differences echoed program experiences. For example, most SSDI clients expect that collective action will be effective because the system is open to interest groups. Bridget explained, "I would favor some sort of political organization with all of us in it. That kind of organization could make a real difference. We wouldn't have the money to be as effective as the cigarette companies or anything, but [the government] would still have to listen to us because that's the way it works." A majority of AFDC recipients also believe that a mass movement could be effective, but often because they view such a movement as the only way to force action from an essentially unresponsive government. According to Renee, "They haven't been listening. They never had to. So why would they listen now? What's going to make them listen now?" A typical answer was given by Vanessa, who surmised that if all of the AFDC recipients joined together, "it would be too many people not to listen."

Similar differences in meaning occurred when clients talked about whether government officials listen to people like them. The minority of SSDI clients who gave negative responses to this question usually explained their answer by saying that government officials simply do not listen or are out of touch. By contrast, the large majority of AFDC recipients who gave negative responses tended to link their answers to their own client status. In some cases, they used welfare politics itself as an example. Penny complained, "They listen to welfare advocates but not [clients]." In most cases, AFDC clients feel that they will not be heard because, as welfare recipients, they occupy a degraded status. Alissa explained,

> I feel like [public officials] would listen even less because I'm in this group of people that they're trying to—that they have these stereotypes against. [Public officials] say, "She's lazy, she's black, she's sitting there, she's received AFDC for all these years. Why can't she work, what's wrong with her?" . . . I'm looked at totally differently because of the fact that I am a recipient. Everyone in that category is a lazy person who doesn't know what she's talking about. [Imitating a public official,] "So, shut up, I'm trying to hear this man here who went to Harvard. He knows what he's talking about. I'm going to listen to him." That's how I feel it is, based on what's been said.

In sum, clients in both programs made explicit statements indicating that they draw inferences about government from their experiences with welfare institutions. In addition, participants tend to have views of government that mirror the perceptions they developed in their respective programs. Finally, just as AFDC clients are more likely to believe that challenging the agency will be futile, they are also more likely to expect other forms of political action to be ineffective. All of these pieces of evidence point toward the conclusion that program experiences affect beliefs about the efficacy of political action.

Again, however, these differences across programs might simply reflect differences in preexisting characteristics. To address this possibility, I first looked for patterns within each program. I did not find systematic relationships for some group differences (e.g., sex and race), but exposure to college education was strongly associated with more efficacious views in both programs. This suggests that one reason SSDI recipients had more optimistic expectations is that they were more likely to have had experience with college (60 percent versus 20 percent in AFDC).

A multivariate analysis of NES data offers an opportunity to control for a wider range of background factors and to test the interview findings with a larger sample drawn from a national population. Table 2 presents an OLS regression analysis in which the dependent variable is a scale measuring external political efficacy (see appendix B). Like the interview data, the results of this analysis indicate that education level has a significant positive influence on levels of external efficacy. Higher income and stronger feelings of partisanship are also associated with significant positive effects. In accord with the interview data, this analysis of survey data also shows no significant relationship associated with race or sex. Most importantly, the estimates indicating how program participants differ from the rest of the population show the expected relationships. The responses given by SSDI clients are indistinguishable from those given by the rest of the population. By contrast, after controlling for demo-

TABLE 2.   External Political Efficacy by Program Participation and Control Variables (OLS regression)

Independent Variables	Coefficient	Standard Error	Probability Level
Program Participation			
SSDI	−.330	.235	.160
AFDC	−.525	.265	.024
Demographics and Partisanship			
Woman	.167	.111	.132
Black	−.076	.164	.642
South	.006	.117	.957
Education	.297	.035	.001
Age	−.004	.003	.155
Income	.022	.010	.019
Urban	.214	.121	.077
Partisanship	.188	.053	.001
Constant	−7.628	.253	.001

Overall model $F = 17.39;\ p < .0001$
$R^2 = .08$
$N = 1981$
$N_{AFDC} = 85$
$N_{SSDI} = 110$

Note: Coefficients are unstandardized and are from the OLS regression procedure in SPSS; one-tailed test for AFDC, two-tailed tests otherwise. Data are from the 1992 NES (Miller, Kinder, and Rosenstone 1993).

graphic characteristics, AFDC participation is associated with a significantly lower level of external efficacy ($b = -.525, p < .024$). Interestingly, tests for interaction with the other variables in the model turned out negative, which suggests that the effects of AFDC participation on external efficacy are relatively constant across these demographic groups.

The NES evidence corroborates my analysis of in-depth interviews. Background differences in the client populations, particularly education level, do contribute to the disparity in feelings of political efficacy. Still, the political views of people in welfare programs differ from those expressed by people with similar backgrounds. The same themes of size, complexity, and responsiveness that filled SSDI clients' descriptions of the SSA can also be found in their views of government and the political process. Likewise, AFDC participants think that other citizens may have opportunities to influence government, but most do not expect this privilege to be extended to people who occupy the degraded status of welfare recipient.

To connect welfare program experiences to broader patterns of political action, one link still remains to be added to this chain. To play the mediating role I have assigned it, feelings of external political efficacy not only must be influenced by program experiences but also must affect political actions. The evidence so far shows a disparity in external efficacy that is consistent with the disparity in political participation. But is there a connection between the two? There are good reasons to question this linkage. Many observers have pointed out that attitudes can be very poor predictors of political behavior (Luttbeg 1991). Because political actions always occur under concrete circumstances, the influence of any general attitude can be blunted by a variety of situational factors and contextual cues (Fishbein and Ajzen 1975, 351–81).

Nevertheless, three observations suggest that clients' feelings of external efficacy affect levels of political involvement. First, the link between external efficacy and political participation has been demonstrated repeatedly in political behavior research. Rosenstone and Hansen (1993, 141–45) are typical in confidently asserting that this connection is supported by "a mountain of empirical evidence." Second, as the women in the shelter demonstrated when they responded to Carol's charge that they had stood by and let the Republicans win, clients themselves tend to offer these sentiments as explanations for their actions. Third, research in social psychology indicates that attitudes predict behaviors more accurately when such attitudes have been developed through direct experience with an "attitude object" (Eagly and Chaiken 1993, 193–202). Attitudes arising from direct experience tend to have greater clarity and are held with greater confidence. They also tend to be more stable, more readily accessible from memory, and more likely to be activated without conscious effort. Thus, if clients' attitudes toward government come from their direct experiences with government (and clients believe that their attitudes do), there is little reason to expect the normal relationship between external efficacy and political action to be attenuated for welfare recipients.

Explaining Exceptions in AFDC: The Effects of Head Start

If experiences in AFDC appear to discourage political involvement, then it is worth taking a closer look at this group. In the preceding chapter, I noted that while thirteen of these clients were enrolled only in the AFDC program, twelve had additional experience with organizations that explicitly encourage involvement. In this latter group, eight had children enrolled in Head Start, three were involved in activist organizations, and one participated in both. These additional participation experiences produced countervailing lessons about demand-making that spilled over to increase some clients' willingness to voice grievances in the AFDC program. Do these same experiences also help to identify a subgroup of AFDC recipients with a higher level of political efficacy and stronger commitment to participation? If lessons learned in AFDC undermine beliefs in government responsiveness, they should have their greatest effects on clients who have no countervailing experiences. Clients who participate in additional organizations that encourage involvement should have more positive orientations toward political action.

In exploring this possibility, it is most illuminating to focus on the effects of involvement with the Head Start program.[5] As described in the preceding chapter, Head Start parents are required to participate in policy councils and local decision-making processes (see Head Start Bureau 1992, §§1304.5-1–5, appendix B). Many critics have deemed this requirement of "maximum feasible participation," initiated by the Johnson administration's War on Poverty, an unmitigated failure: maximum feasible participation did not reduce poverty and did not enhance poor people's political involvement (Banfield 1974; Moynihan 1969). In some respects, this conclusion is warranted. The initiative certainly failed to overcome a variety of factors that contribute to poverty and powerlessness. Nevertheless, some case studies have suggested that this design feature can bolster poor people's involvement in some arenas of local politics by giving the "participatory ideal . . . widespread currency" (Marston 1993, 126, 132).

Does Head Start's "maximum feasible participation" affect broader orientations toward political action? This question can be addressed by comparing the eight AFDC clients who participated in Head Start to the thirteen AFDC clients with no other group participation. Such a comparison is aided by an accident of sampling that makes it possible to distinguish the effects of education and program experience. The eight Head Start participants in this study had relatively little formal education: only one of the eight obtained a high school diploma. By contrast, although the comparison group of thirteen clients with no additional group involvement includes five who did not complete high school, the group also has eight people who did receive their high school diplomas. Thus, the latter group has more formal education overall than those who participated in Head Start.

Excluding the four political activists, a comparison of the eight AFDC clients in Head Start to the thirteen in AFDC alone yields the following contrasts.[6] Whereas 63 percent of Head Start participants consider the political system open and democratic, only 8 percent of those in AFDC alone hold this view ($p = .014$). Also, whereas 77 percent of clients participating in AFDC alone see government as autonomous, this view is held by only 50 percent of the Head Start participants ($p = .213$).

Similar patterns emerge in responses to the three political efficacy questions. Despite a higher average level of education, clients in AFDC alone are far more likely to believe that their participation would be ineffective (92 percent versus 50 percent of the Head Start group, $p = .047$), that government does not listen to people like them (100 percent versus 50 percent of the Head Start group, $p = .012$), and that a movement of people in the program would be ineffective (39 percent versus none of the Head Start group, $p = .063$). Regarding all three questions, Head Start participants are more likely to have the sorts of expectations that support political involvement. The reasons for this pattern are not hard to discern from the transcripts. Just as clients made inferences from their experiences in SSDI and AFDC, they also drew lessons from experiences in Head Start.

The existence of (and the term) *policy councils* facilitates a connection between Head Start experiences and broader beliefs about politics. Lisa volunteered this explanation of what happens at a Head Start meeting: "It's like politics. We have different views, say, about a disability plan for Head Start. We're like a decision-making body. And it feels good because it's like you're deciding Head Start's policies throughout the city and in our own centers." These experiences leave an imprint on general beliefs about political involvement.

In sum, the evidence indicates that Head Start experiences consistently mitigate or supersede the demobilizing effects of AFDC. This finding suggests a revised view of maximum feasible participation. Like many programs in the War on Poverty, this initiative was judged a failure because it did not live up to the unrealistic standard of total victory promised by an "unconditional declaration of war" (M. Katz 1989, 88). Indeed, it remains important to recognize the limitations of this policy. Insofar as consensus may often result from the exclusion of difficult issues or competing views (Bachrach and Baratz 1962), we should not be surprised if the addition of clients' perspectives produces misunderstanding, conflict, and a less coherent policy process (Moynihan 1969). Likewise, it seems unrealistic to expect participatory designs to erase systemic inequalities or to unilaterally empower people who are disadvantaged in a variety of ways.

These limitations, however, should not overshadow the importance of meaningful collective decision making for individuals who are often denied effective control over their own lives (Handler 1996). The findings presented here suggest that a more participatory program design encourages more positive orientations toward political involvement. Head Start provides clients with evidence that participation can be effective and fulfilling. From the perspective of participatory theory, it is not surprising that these experiences have spillover effects. "The taste for participation is whetted by participation. . . . [A] little experience with self-government and political action inspire[s] a desire for a great deal more" (Barber 1984, 265–66).

Internal Efficacy: Beliefs about One's Political Abilities

I have argued that participation experiences in AFDC undermine feelings of external efficacy. In this section, I address the additional possibility that AFDC clients retreat from broader modes of political action because they lack internal efficacy, or confidence in their political abilities.

According to the passivity explanation, welfare provision leads recipients to become dependent and hence politically passive. As noted earlier, this claim founders on evidence that SSDI recipients participate at the same rate as other citizens. For two other reasons, however, internal efficacy may still help account for the political quiescence of AFDC recipients. First, some observers argue that passivity and self-doubt explain why a subset of poor people apply to AFDC in the first place (see Gilder 1981). This argument suggests that even before they enter the program, AFDC recipients may feel less efficacious than other people with similar backgrounds. Second, people who see repeated evidence that important outcomes are beyond their control sometimes develop doubts about their personal efficacy. This insight provides the foundation for expectancy theories of learned helplessness (Gurin and Gurin 1970). From this perspective, a welfare program designed to be directive rather than open to client choices may foster a sense of personal incapacity (Kane 1987, 416).

The evidence does not support either of these propositions. With only a few exceptions, AFDC recipients do not doubt their political capacities. To see how this may be possible, it is necessary to be precise about how internal political efficacy relates to two other concepts. First, internal political efficacy should not be confused with a global evaluation of the self. It is a specific dimension of self-categorization that exists among the many that contribute to an individual's self-concept (Turner et al. 1987). Thus, a recipient who classifies herself as a failure in relation to employment may nevertheless place herself among the highly competent when it comes to rearing children or negotiating the maze of bureaucracy at the welfare agency.

Second, a single experience can have very different implications for feelings of internal and external political efficacy. For example, if I manage to get what I need from an agency that appears intransigent or even hostile, I may become increasingly impressed with my own abilities precisely because I am getting responses from an unresponsive institution. As each interaction with the agency leads me to a more pessimistic view of its responsiveness (external efficacy), I may experience a corresponding rise in my perception that I am capable of accomplishing a difficult task (internal efficacy).

Thus, while AFDC clients frequently complain of low self-esteem related to welfare receipt, neither this sentiment nor their low levels of external political efficacy should be seen as requiring a correspondingly low level of internal political efficacy. AFDC recipients tended to doubt that the government would respond to "people like them" because of their poverty, client status, and/ or race and because "that's just the way government is." But while recipients gave many reasons to be pessimistic about political action, these reasons typically did not include a low estimation of their own political abilities. Lashell, for example, said that public officials would not listen to her "because I don't have any money and because I'm black." When asked if a lack of political knowledge or skills might make it harder for her to gain a response, she smiled at the suggestion and confidently replied, "Oh, I can talk all day long." Cheryl echoed these sentiments: "I could speak up as much as anybody because I know I'm just as good as anybody else."

These recipients' faith in their own political abilities can be traced to their experiences in AFDC. Clients perceive themselves as successfully meeting the challenges of a government institution and almost always emphasize that AFDC participation is a particularly demanding relationship with government. To maintain this relationship, a client must pay diligent attention to fluctuating requirements, keep up with necessary documents, and anticipate the expectations of the caseworker. Celina was one of many who pointed out that AFDC participation requires planning and organization: "I have everything in a folder, so when they ask you for birth certificates, Social Security numbers, whatever . . . you have to be able to pull that stuff out on demand." The general consensus was that if a client does not know what she is doing, she and her children will quickly find themselves in desperate circumstances. Alissa said, "I'm maybe a little more educated than some. . . . If someone doesn't have the means and know-how, they're just railroaded through."

Because they deal with the system regularly, clients tend to have considerable faith in their understanding of how it works. In fact, they expressed far more doubts about my ability to understand it, as a nonparticipant, than about their own. Sarat (1990, 350–51) recorded similar comments asserting clients' superior "insider knowledge" when he interviewed welfare recipients seeking legal services. Young's more recent study of legal-service usage (1995) offers additional evidence that welfare participation leads to a sense of institutional competence and that this perception gets generalized to government as a whole. Young asked whether clients valued lawyers as "spokespersons" who could express their views in appropriate language, as "legal experts" who knew existing laws, or as "system insiders" who were familiar with government officials and procedures. She found that other poor people valued lawyers in all three roles, but welfare clients were far less likely to see insider knowledge as something they needed from a lawyer. One client said, "I just know how they are, because I've been dealing with them so long, you know" (18). Young concludes,

> In contrast with wealthier informants, the welfare poor rarely suggested that insider knowledge was an important advantage gained from legal representation. . . . The welfare poor often described how experience with "the system" increased their ability to handle their own public benefit issues. (11)

Regardless of whether recipients' high estimates of their own understanding are correct, the interviews conducted by Young and Sarat as well as those from this study suggest that, all else being equal, AFDC participation may lead individuals to develop higher evaluations of their ability to deal with government. This claim can be tested by returning to the NES data and constructing a multivariate model of internal political efficacy. Table 3 shows an OLS regression analysis that predicts placement on a scale created by adding together four items that researchers have found to be the clearest and most satisfactory measures of internal political efficacy (on the four-item scale, see Niemi, Craig, and Mattei 1991).

The results of this analysis indicate a significantly higher level of internal political efficacy among men, people with a higher level of education, stronger partisans, those who live in more urban areas, and (although the estimate does not quite reach conventional levels of significance) possibly African Americans. After controlling for these factors as well as for age, income, and region, it appears that SSDI clients' beliefs in their own political capacities are indistinguishable from the rest of the population. By contrast, the estimated coefficient for AFDC participation offers support for the hypothesis suggested by the interviews. Relative to people who resemble them on other characteristics included in the model, AFDC recipients express significantly higher evaluations of their own political capacities ($b = 3.19, p < .001$).

In addition, tests for interactions with other variables in the model suggest that the effects of AFDC participation vary for two groups. First, the significant negative coefficient for the interaction with education suggests that AFDC makes a smaller marginal contribution to internal efficacy among those who have a higher level of education, a finding that makes considerable sense given the high level of efficacy already associated with this group. Second, the coefficient for the interaction of AFDC and urban suggests that AFDC participation may boost the internal political efficacy of central city welfare recipients to a degree that is even greater than the effects found among other AFDC recipients.

These regression results corroborate the statements made in the interviews and urge the conclusion that, on average, program participation makes a positive contribution to AFDC recipients' belief that they have the specific skills and knowledge needed to deal with government. Thus, for evaluating the political consequences of welfare participation, the distinction between internal and external efficacy turns out to be crucial. In their program experiences, AFDC clients see evidence that government institutions are hostile places and that officials do not understand, care about, or respond to "people like them."

TABLE 3.   Internal Political Efficacy by Program Participation and Control Variables (OLS regression)

Independent Variables	Coefficient	Standard Error	Probability Level
Program Participation			
SSDI	.241	.359	.503
AFDC	3.190	1.023	.001
Demographics and Partisanship			
Woman	−1.685	.171	.001
Black	.477	.252	.059
South	.135	.180	.452
Education	.666	.054	.001
Age	.002	.005	.697
Income	.012	.015	.422
Urban	.548	.190	.004
Partisanship	.370	.081	.001
Interactions			
AFDC × Education	−.762	.313	.008
AFDC × Urban	1.395	.859	.052
Constant	9.122	.392	.001
Overall model	$F = 33.91$; $p < .001$ $R^2 = .17$ $N = 1976$ $N_{AFDC} = 85$ $N_{SSDI} = 110$		

Note: Coefficients are from the OLS regression procedure in SPSS; one-tailed test for AFDC and interactions, two-tailed tests otherwise. Data are from the 1992 NES (Miller, Kinder, and Rosenstone 1993).

Yet the same experiences also lead clients to infer that they have developed the knowledge and skills needed to deal with government. Women in AFDC tend to believe that they are capable of participating in politics; they simply do not think that anyone in a position of power will listen to them.

Conclusion

Few concerns are more fundamental to students of politics than the relationship between public policy and democracy. In most liberal traditions of political theory, citizen participation is cast as a creative force that precedes and determines public policies. This view lies at the heart of systems theories that identify public demands as "inputs" and distinguish government policies as "outputs" (Easton 1965, 1971). In varying degrees of formality, this view can also be found at the core of economic theories of democracy (Downs 1957), pluralist models of politics (Dahl 1967), and traditional behavioral analyses of political participation (Milbrath and Goel 1982; Verba and Nie 1972; Verba, Schlozman, and Brady 1995). In these accounts, public policies are the ultimate results of the political process.

From another perspective, however, the vigor of democracy itself appears to be an uncertain outcome that depends on public policies. Various scholars have argued that public policies engender characteristic forms of politics depending on their goals (Lowi 1964), the ways they distribute costs and benefits (J. Wilson 1980), the symbolic cues they express to the citizenry (Edelman 1964), and the ways in which they structure political interaction (Pierson 1993). These theories all serve as reminders that citizen involvement is fragile and malleable and that public policy can either support or discourage an engaged citizenry (Schneider and Ingram 1997). As Smith and Ingram (1993, 15) point out, "it is usually believed that in a democracy citizens shape policies. It is less commonly realized that the far-reaching policies of modern governments shape citizens and may do so in directions harmful to democracy."

In the case of welfare policy, both images of this relationship have considerable merit. As the most recent round of reforms has underscored, program designs are outcomes shaped by the fears, hopes, and discontents of policymakers and citizens. Indeed, the responsiveness of public policy to shifting sentiments might be considered a major source of volatility in welfare provision (Heclo 1994). At the same time, however, welfare policy designs are more than just government outputs, and citizens' encounters with them are more than just "apolitical outtakes" (Milbrath and Goel 1982, 9). The evidence presented in this chapter suggests that welfare policy designs are political forces that have important effects on the beliefs and actions of citizens. From this perspective, the most significant political outcomes of any round of welfare reform may not be new program requirements or initiatives per se. The more decisive outcomes may be found in the way these design elements affect democracy itself.

A number of observers have recently called on scholars and practitioners to "envision a democracy in which policy plays a new role: to empower, enlighten, and engage citizens in the process of self-government" (Smith and Ingram 1993, 1). To the extent that one values democratic participation, the findings presented here suggest that this value is relevant for measuring the success or failure of welfare policies. Political debates over how welfare programs affect incorporation in the market (i.e., employment) should be joined by discussions of how they affect incorporation in the polity.

This chapter offers an empirical starting point for such a discussion by illuminating how welfare policy designs affect political learning. The heart of the matter is that welfare programs provide many people with their most direct exposure to a government institution. When clients think about government, their program experiences provide the handiest and most reliable points of reference. When they think about whether their own political demands can be effective, civics-book images of democracy pale next to vivid impressions of how welfare agencies respond to clients. Program designs not only communicate information about client status and agency decision making but also teach lessons about citizenship status and government.

Beyond the single case of welfare policy, the findings presented in this chapter suggest the potential for a political learning perspective that links the study of policy design and implementation to the study of political thought and action in mass publics. In a society in which the policy-making process is so often relegated to the status of a distant spectacle (Edelman 1964), public bureaucracies provide relatively immediate experiences with government. Legislatures may host more dramatic political activities, but the police station, the motor vehicle office, and the Internal Revenue Service are more likely to supply citizens with lessons about government that ring with the truth of firsthand experience. As participatory democratic theory suggests, such firsthand experiences engaging government will tend to shape the political beliefs and actions of the citizenry (Pateman 1970; Schneider and Ingram 1997). From mundane encounters at the post office to the more total experience of prison life, public bureaucracies should be studied as sites of political learning.

In the specific case of the U.S. welfare system, the findings presented here support theories of social control and dual social citizenship (Gordon 1994; Piven and Cloward 1993). The two tiers of the U.S. welfare system differ markedly in their designs, and these differences shape clients' status and assertiveness, not only in welfare programs but also in the broader polity. Relative to SSDI, the AFDC program constructs a decidedly inferior form of social citizenship for its recipients, and it does so in a way that has far-reaching political implications.

Policy designs provide citizens with scripts that indicate how government can be expected to act. In AFDC, clients receive little opportunity to make consequential choices about their own lives, they deal with the agency when they are summoned, and they must respond to their caseworkers' detailed questions and directives. What image of government does this convey to a group that already tends to be disadvantaged in political life? The answer seems clear from the evidence presented here. It also seems clear that nothing essential to welfare provision requires these particular lessons. Very different scripts are written for participants in SSDI. In that program, clients are allowed greater privacy and initiative, and it appears that officials have both authority over clients and obligations to respond to their requests. Experiences in both AFDC and SSDI shape clients' views of government. The process of political learning is constant across programs, but the lessons taught differ sharply.

Head Start provides a third model of how welfare policy design may affect democracy. In that program, poor parents are brought together with one another to deliberate and make policy. Policy councils formalize the expectation that participants will speak out. They demonstrate that the agency serves the clients, not the other way around. Each month, the parents on the councils see their decisions recorded and (at least some of the time) implemented. The evidence suggests that these experiences matter for democracy. Despite sharing similar backgrounds and program experiences with other AFDC clients and despite their lower level of education, women in Head Start had dramatically different views of government and whether it is worthwhile to become politically involved.

In his cross-national study, *Three Worlds of Welfare Capitalism,* Esping-Andersen (1990, 23) writes, "The welfare state is not just a mechanism that intervenes in, and possibly corrects, the structure of inequality; it is, in its own right, a system of stratification. It is an active force in the ordering of social relations." This comment and the title of the book refer to variation in welfare provision across different political economies. Yet they also can be appropriated as a fitting end to this analysis. Through their different designs, AFDC, SSDI, and Head Start construct three worlds of welfare participation. Welfare programs not only respond to needs created by a stratified society but also constitute an active force in the ordering of political relations. The same political process that assembles welfare programs is, in turn, reshaped by its own products.

CHAPTER 8

Conclusion

For poor people in capitalist democracies, the extent and form of welfare provision are critical factors shaping the quality of political life. Depending on their designs, welfare systems can draw the poor into a more inclusive and active polity or treat them in ways that reinforce their marginality. This book has presented a political analysis of the U.S. welfare system—not as an object of contention for political elites or voters but rather as a site of politics for the people who make up its applicants and clients. For these individuals, the welfare system provides a major channel for demands on public resources and an institutional setting for a direct relationship with government. My goal in the preceding chapters has been to illuminate the welfare system as a site of political action and, hence, political learning. This final chapter draws together these different strands of analysis to suggest a more general set of conclusions about the political dimensions of welfare claiming and participation.

As a mode of political action, welfare claiming is distinguished by the fact that it allows citizens to gain a direct and personalized response from government.[1] Welfare bureaucracies are more accessible than most government institutions and offer citizens more immediate, targeted, and tangible remedies. Forms of political action such as voting, grassroots organizing, or protesting may hold the potential to exert broader influence on the legislative process, but these efforts require greater amounts of time and resources, and their potential for success (especially for the poor) is far less certain. For a single mother who cannot meet her family's basic needs, for example, a campaign to change policies regarding wages, health care, or child care may be appealing, but a claim on an existing welfare policy offers a faster and more effective way to mobilize government.

This signature feature of welfare claiming—its capacity to provide individuals with direct access to public resources—is frequently invoked to suggest that welfare provision may undermine more collective or broadly effective forms of political action. Individuals who can get what they need through a particularistic claim are, in this view, less likely to recognize and press collective grievances. To be sure, students of politics should attend to the potential for collective demand-making to be undermined by extensions of public relief (Piven and Cloward 1993). But the dampening of a particular mode of political action, if it occurs, should not be misconstrued as a negation of political activity as a whole. Diverting political action into bureaucratic settings is not the same as subverting the practice of politics. Through welfare claims, citizens enter new political institutions, take on new political statuses, and engage in different forms of political action (Piven and Cloward 1993; Wolin 1989).[2] This book has sought to follow this trail—that is, to investigate the quality of political life constructed for citizens in the welfare system and to seek out the political functions, origins, and consequences of individuals' welfare participation.

To grasp the functions of welfare participation for individual citizens, it is necessary to begin with the social and political effects of poverty. In this regard, clients' accounts underscore two critical points. First, as social citizenship theory suggests, extreme poverty is debilitating and isolating. By preventing individuals from fulfilling expectations that they and others deem important, poverty threatens the self-respect and social dignity needed to enjoy full and equal citizenship. In addition, the persistent needs created by poverty tend to strip individuals of the ability and time needed to follow or participate in political affairs. Second, as social control theory suggests, poverty is more than just debilitating, it is coercive. It pushes individuals and families toward a precarious state of dependency on others that can strip individuals of the autonomy needed for self-government.

By lessening the debilitating and coercive effects of poverty, welfare claims offer individuals a means to achieve and protect the basic preconditions of full community membership. To see this, one need only consider Darryl wandering the streets alone, homeless, hungry, scared of being attacked or sent to jail, and dependent on the whims of strangers. Or one might consider Hope and the other women in this study who were trapped by poverty in abusive relationships that subjected them to daily terror and prohibited all but the most minimal attachments to the broader community. Or one could consider Nancy, who worked herself to exhaustion trying to raise two kids in an abandoned house with no utilities, supporting them by holding down the minimum-wage graveyard shift at a convenience store, where she was robbed on numerous occasions. By easing these life conditions and others like them, welfare claims protect the minimal prerequisites of full citizenship: autonomy, self-respect, social dignity, the ability to fulfill duties to others, and the capacity to exercise civil and political rights.

Many of the clients in this study sought and received assistance from friends, family, or local organizations before claiming welfare. Such assistance can play an essential role in clients' efforts to make ends meet each month (Edin and Lein 1997). Taken alone, however, these informal sources of support are generally incapable of lifting and keeping families out of poverty. Perhaps more important from a political standpoint, dependence on these sources of aid frequently forces individuals to endure their benefactors' efforts to control their lives. Here, one encounters a major reason why social networks and local organizations cannot offer citizens an equivalent replacement for the welfare state. Whatever its failings, the impersonal bureaucracy of the welfare system is unique in its potential to ameliorate the political effects of poverty without positioning recipients as vulnerable supplicants within the social relations that make up their everyday lives.

To the functions of welfare claiming for the individual, one must add the functions of welfare claiming for the community. Although applying for welfare is to some degree an individual act, it is a mistake to assume that those who seek benefits act alone, do so for individualistic reasons, or alter only their own circumstances. On the contrary, the evidence from this study supports what participatory democratic theory suggests: formal demands on government grow out of and reshape informal social and political relations in communities.

Welfare demands emerge out of community members' collective daily struggles to fulfill needs, pursue aspirations, meet obligations, and in the end, survive. By making welfare-based claims on government, individuals gain resources (food, clothing, cash, time, and so forth) that they can contribute to broader social networks. Doing so allows them to fulfill the expectations of others while obligating others to offer assistance in return (Stack 1974). As resources circulate through social networks, the personal welfare check is transformed into something akin to a community good. Thus, while the formal applicant for welfare benefits may be an individual, the claim itself may articulate and serve the needs of a broader social group. In these cases, the act of welfare claiming appears to be only an isolated personal act but functions as an instrument of community-based survival politics (Hardy-Fanta 1993). Stepping back from the individual level, rates of welfare participation may be seen as an important determinant of economic, social, and political resources in poor communities.

A broader community-based perspective is also important for understanding how welfare claims are advanced on government. Welfare demands typically emerge through an interpersonal process of mobilization. The probability that an individual will recognize her eligibility and convert it into a successful claim on government is likely to depend on the amount of information and assistance she can derive from social networks and local organizations. Later, in the context of welfare participation, this informal political context serves to shape patterns of client assertiveness. Ties to local organizations can bolster clients' ability and willingness to advocate on their own behalf. In general, clients are more likely to be assertive when their fellow community members inform them of their rights and impute legitimacy to their claims. As a result, the citizen's ability to be an effective political actor in relation to the welfare state, both as an applicant and as a client, depends on informal political processes that are likely to vary across time and locale.

Because it is a site of political action, the welfare system is equally a site of political learning. As participatory democratic theory suggests, the experience of participation has educative effects that transform citizens' political orientations (Mansbridge 1999; Pateman 1970). Previous empirical research has tended to offer only mixed evidence of such effects, in large part because citizens' "experiences of political participation are too weak to produce great effects" (Mansbridge 1999, 317). Welfare participation, however, is more direct, intense, and prolonged than many forms of political action. Through this experience, clients learn program-specific lessons about their own status and the nature of government institutions. Beginning from the first moments of the application encounter, clients draw inferences about how they are expected to behave and what kinds of treatment they can expect to receive. Within the context of the welfare relationship, these lessons shape clients' beliefs about whether it is wise or effective to speak up on their own behalf. Consequently, political learning through welfare participation functions as an important influence on patterns of client assertiveness.

The political significance of these educative effects, however, does not end at the agency doorway. Instead, lessons learned through welfare participation spill over to affect citizens' broader political orientations. The welfare agency provides many clients with their most salient and direct experience of government. As a result, perceptions of the agency shape beliefs about the nature of government; expectations regarding client demand-making influence beliefs about the efficacy of other forms of political action; and individuals' perceptions of their status as clients spill over to affect their perceptions of their status as citizens. In all of these ways, the political learning that takes place in welfare programs can help to explain broader patterns of political thought and action.

Thus, the politics of welfare participation has a reciprocal relationship to the formal and informal dimensions of political life that surround it. At one level, the welfare system may be thought of as an arena of politics. It is a channel for demands on government and its allocation of public resources, a site for making discretionary decisions regarding public policy, and a point of contact at which the state and the individual negotiate the practical rights and duties of citizenship. In addition to being an arena of politics, the welfare system is also an active force that shapes the ways individuals and groups relate to one another and to government in the broader polity. Welfare systems mediate the relationship between economic hardship and political marginality. They condition individuals' abilities to exercise the rights and fulfill the duties of citizenship. They construct categories of social and political status and alter patterns of dependence and vulnerability. Through the benefits they supply and the cues they convey, welfare systems exert a significant influence on political thought and action in the citizenry.

Social Citizenship and Social Control
in the U.S. Welfare System

The simple fact of welfare provision (the existence of public welfare institutions) offers citizens a site for political action and political learning, but the form of welfare provision determines how these activities proceed. The U.S. welfare system offers citizens a variety of different settings for welfare claiming and participation. Historical and institutional scholarship has done a great deal to identify disparities across the two channels of this system and to locate the roots of these disparities in systems of class (Piven and Cloward 1993), gender (Abramovitz 1988; Gordon 1994; Nelson 1984, 1990), and race (Brown 1999; Lieberman 1998). Employing the concept of social rights as an ideal-typical standard of evaluation (Barbalet 1988, 67), a number of observers have argued that the inequalities of the U.S. welfare system may be understood as a hierarchy of social citizenship (Fraser 1987, 1989; Fraser and Gordon 1993; Gordon 1994). In the preceding chapters, I have sought to make two contributions to this thesis.

First, this book has presented a microlevel analysis of individual participation in the welfare system that complements macrolevel research on dual social citizenship. In-depth interviews with clients offer a standpoint for investigation that differs considerably from what is provided by historical and institutional research. This bottom-up perspective makes it possible to assess how, if at all, institutional differences affect citizens' lives. This viewpoint augments political histories of welfare provision by supplying a political phenomenology of welfare participation—that is, an analysis of citizenship experiences constructed for clients in the two tiers of the welfare system.

Second, this book offers an explicitly political analysis of participation in the two-tier welfare system. Previous work has illuminated the political forces that shape the welfare system and has suggested that welfare participation can be viewed as a political activity (Gordon 1994; Nelson 1984; Piven and Cloward 1993). This book, however, has made welfare participation itself the target of political analysis and has asked whether the two-tier welfare system entails not only social inequalities but also political inequalities. Put slightly differently, this book has sought to illuminate how, if at all, the U.S. welfare system might constitute a hierarchy of political citizenship.

The evidence suggests that differences in welfare policy design have major consequences for patterns of political status, capacity, belief, and action. As suggested by participatory theory, patterns of political action and political learning are shaped by the institutions in which they occur. And consistent with theories of social control and dual social citizenship, policy designs in the U.S. welfare system tend to place public assistance recipients at a severe disadvantage. Relative to social insurance programs, the means-tested program designed to serve poor families with children in the U.S. (AFDC during the period of this study, now Temporary Assistance for Needy Families [TANF]) constructs a decidedly inferior form of social citizenship for its recipients. Unlike SSDI, the AFDC program was designed in a manner that, in important respects, reinforced the political marginality of its clients. And although the current TANF program differs from AFDC in significant respects, it has retained many of these key design features.[3]

Inequalities across the welfare system are politically significant in part because they are tied so closely to existing group-based hierarchies. The policy designs that citizens encounter in the welfare system have been shaped by gender and the family wage system (Gordon 1994), class and capitalist markets (Piven and Cloward 1993), and various dimensions of racial exclusion, subordination, and conflict (Brown 1999; Gilens 1999). The type of program that serves as the site of participation for a given individual is also likely to depend on factors tied to gender, race, and class. Citizens channeled into public assistance programs are disproportionately likely to be female, people of color, and people who have lived in poverty and worked at the low end of the labor market (U.S. House of Representatives 1998). Thus, to investigate the political dimensions of inequality across the welfare system is, in effect, to illuminate disparities in the political status occupied by different social groups. The major features of this political inequality, as clients experience it, can be summarized as follows.

First, people who make demands on public assistance programs gain access to fewer resources than their counterparts in social insurance programs. AFDC benefits have always been set lower than those provided in social insurance programs, and the real-dollar value of AFDC benefits has declined steadily over the past twenty-five years (Albelda and Tilly 1997). As a result, recipient families are rarely able to escape poverty (Danziger and Weinberg 1994, 40–44) and hence only partially free themselves from dependence on aid supplied by family, friends, and local organizations (Edin and Lein 1997). Thus, demands on the AFDC program do a less adequate job of serving the political functions of welfare claiming. Relative to SSDI clients, people who claim AFDC benefits remain more vulnerable to coercion in their everyday lives and less able to achieve the self-respect and social dignity that comes from fulfilling obligations to others. AFDC clients also gain less relief from the urgent needs of poverty that strip them of the time and energy required to engage public affairs.

Second, the AFDC program is designed to be more supervisory, disciplinary, and discretionary, a setup that has a number of important political ramifications. First, it can deter welfare claiming. Eligible people who suspect that welfare agencies will adopt a hostile and punitive orientation toward clients are likely to see good reasons not to act on their entitlements. Such fears tend to be exacerbated by the inferior conditions AFDC claimants find in the application encounter, conditions that lead many applicants to infer that their claims are unwanted and that clients endure mistreatment. As clients, AFDC recipients occupy an institutional position that is, politically speaking, inferior to the one constructed for SSDI recipients. Participation experiences supply AFDC and SSDI clients with very different lessons about their own vulnerability and the welfare agency's responsiveness. AFDC clients become less likely than SSDI clients to believe in the wisdom and efficacy of speaking up on their own behalf. As a result, AFDC participants become less willing to raise legitimate grievances and tend to retreat from discretionary decision-making processes that are critical to their well-being.

Third, people who claim AFDC benefits suffer a far more degraded social and political status than do SSDI clients. Because the U.S. welfare system segregates public assistance clients from more "deserving" social insurance clients, the system isolates recipients of public assistance as targets of social stigma. Clients' feelings of degradation reflect a broad atmosphere of public hostility (Gilens 1999) as well as more direct experiences within the AFDC program itself. As potential claimants, people eligible for AFDC benefits are more likely than those who qualify for SSDI to feel dissuaded by the pressure to avoid being stigmatized. Later, as clients, AFDC recipients are more likely to feel that they occupy a degraded status in the eyes of agency workers, public officials, and their fellow citizens. Relative to SSDI participation, AFDC participation poses a greater threat to the social dignity needed for full political membership and tends to produce an insecurity of status that leads clients to surmise that elected officials will not listen to or care about "people like them." In the eyes of government officials, whether agency workers or elected representatives, AFDC clients tend to suspect that they are, "and can be, no more than 'just a welfare recipient'" (Sarat 1990, 352).

Fourth, clients in AFDC and SSDI learn very different lessons about the nature of government and the efficacy of political action. SSDI clients tend to find the SSA reasonably responsive and rarely find themselves on the receiving end of a summons or threat. Based on these experiences, they tend to draw moderately positive inferences about government. Their levels of political efficacy and participation are virtually indistinguishable from those of the rest of the population. In contrast, clients who participate in the AFDC program are far more likely to develop perceptions of the welfare agency that emphasize a lack of responsiveness and even a degree of hostility. Relative to SSDI clients and to others who share their demographic characteristics, AFDC clients become significantly less likely to believe that government is responsive and to engage in most traditional forms of political action.

In sum, the evidence of political inequality across the tiers of the welfare system lies on multiple dimensions and is quite striking. Citizens from advantaged social groups are disproportionately likely to enter welfare programs in which they enjoy political advantages. These political advantages include superior material security and autonomy, social dignity and political status, institutional treatment and position, and patterns of belief that support political action.

To what extent, then, is it reasonable to describe the U.S. welfare state as a bifurcated system in which social insurance recipients enjoy a full measure of social citizenship that supports political engagement while public assistance recipients are positioned as objects of a politically enervating form of social control? The inequalities in the system are profound, but I think this characterization overstates and oversimplifies the case in a number of politically important ways. The U.S. welfare system constructs forms of social control and social citizenship that are incomplete and contradictory. Clients' experiences with the SSDI and AFDC programs are too complex to support such a sweeping and one-sided description of each program.

Consider, first, the quality of welfare provision offered by U.S. social insurance programs. Full social rights, as Marshall (1964) understood them, would provide a common share to all citizens based on membership in a political community and would do so in a manner designed to "express the solidarity of a national community" (Heclo 1995, 671). By contrast, SSDI and other social insurance programs delineate specific categories of citizens and offer them benefits on the basis of a quasi-contractual obligation established through wage-based contributions.[4] Rather than a shared set of social rights grounded in full membership, one finds here a particularistic application of the civil right to contract (Fraser and Gordon 1993). On one side, this "contract" allows many clients to feel that their claims have a legitimacy that distinguishes them from the undeserving poor. On the other side, however, the particularistic nature of their claim to benefits distinguishes them as a special class of citizens who bear some resemblance to those who receive public assistance.

Thus, the stigma associated with public assistance "handouts" has a tendency to spill over, in a categorical system of provision, to taint participation in social insurance programs. The degree to which this is the case may vary across social insurance programs. For example, because they are more likely to be viewed as ineligible for work, those who receive benefits based on old age may be more insulated from this association than those who receive compensation for unemployment. Nevertheless, it is telling that many people with disabilities in this study felt high levels of ambivalence and anxiety as they applied for SSDI benefits. These applicants had a strong sense that, as Phil put it, "social welfare programs were kind of like a taboo." Social insurance programs in the United States do not unite citizens as coparticipants in a common share. They create specific categories of exemption and remuneration that may be more benign than what is found in the inferior tier of the system but still set clients apart from their fellow community members.

In addition, while social insurance clients enjoy more autonomy than do public assistance clients, it would be a mistake to infer from this relative comparison that social insurance programs do not include elements of social control. Relative to AFDC, the SSDI program has fewer directive and supervisory components and does not place clients under the direct authority of a caseworker. These differences allow clients to develop a stronger sense of initiative and control and in fact make SSDI a less paternalistic program. Still, institutional structures and program rules remain effective elements of social control in both tiers of the welfare system. As Gordon (1994, 162) explains, social control in the welfare system can take on different forms: "The social insurance orientation . . . broke away from the personal, caretaking dimension of social work [found in public assistance programs] and moved toward a structural relation of social control . . . that was distant, not individually supervisory."

Finally, the participation experience constructed for clients in the SSDI program must also be judged by more than just a comparison to AFDC. Unlike Head Start, for example, the SSDI program does not engage clients as active decision makers or bring them together in a collective setting. And on balance, the evidence presented here does not suggest that SSDI participation has an appreciable positive effect on clients' political orientations. In the final analysis, the political merits of the SSDI design appear to lie primarily in its minimalism. It is, in important respects, a liberal design in which the welfare state adopts a responsive stance toward citizens, offering them protection from poverty with a degree of autonomy and anonymity. Clients are not invited to become active coparticipants in self-government, but they typically feel safe from state surveillance, arbitrary decision making, and retribution. They are allowed to accumulate and retain feelings of security, control, and entitlement.

In the public assistance tier of the welfare system, one finds a more direct form of social control that has a variety of negative political consequences for clients. Like the form of social citizenship offered by the SSDI program, however, social control in the AFDC program is also incomplete. The social control thesis, as formulated by Piven and Cloward (1993), identifies the welfare system as a contradictory site of political action, not as a unilateral mechanism of discipline. Two features of the argument are critical in this regard. First, Piven and Cloward identify the poor as significant political agents whose actions matter for policy outcomes. In this view, poor people's demands play a key role in establishing welfare provision and in shaping the distribution of welfare resources. Second, Piven and Cloward point to social control in a variety of relationships and pay particular attention to the coercive force of market discipline. For the poor, the alternative to involvement with the welfare state is not freedom from social control but compliance with terms set by those who exercise power and control resources through the market (such as employers or sole breadwinners).

Unfortunately, these elements of the social control thesis are frequently ignored. The social control exercised by the state is taken out of context and presented as an unmitigated fact. Consequently, historical research has tended to cast the welfare state's political impact as primarily one of social control and to present clients as passive objects of management (van Krieken 1991). As a number of critics have pointed out, such a one-sided account seriously distorts the social control thesis as well as the actual social and political conditions of clients' lives (Gordon 1990; Piven 1990).[5] Evidence discussed in the preceding chapters serves to underscore this point and to suggest that the political consequences of AFDC participation are complex and contradictory.

Despite the fact that participation in the AFDC program is rarely adequate to lift families out of poverty, such participation allows clients to lessen their dependence and vulnerability in a variety of social relationships. While it may stigmatize clients as failures in relation to the work ethic, it also permits them to fulfill duties to others that are prerequisites for social dignity and self-respect. The experience of AFDC participation may encourage clients to conclude that government is unresponsive, but it also tends to leave them convinced that they have important knowledge and skills needed to deal with government. And although AFDC participation may create doubts about the efficacy of conventional political action aimed at government, it also serves as an important support for informal modes of survival politics (and potentially more confrontational politics) in poor communities.

Thus, a close look at clients' lives and their experiences of welfare participation casts doubt on one-sided political descriptions of the welfare state. For clients in this study, AFDC participation was both a means of empowerment and an encounter with social control. An adequate understanding of the politics of welfare participation must maintain an emphasis on the agency of individuals within an environment that includes multiple social relationships and intersecting forces of social control. Moreover, none of these features of welfare participation are immutable. The political characteristics and consequences of welfare participation are likely to vary over time depending on both the nature of policy designs and the extent to which a broader political context encourages clients to believe that they can be effective political actors.

Policy Design, Democracy, and Citizen Participation

A central claim of this book is that welfare policy designs alter citizens' political status and orientations in ways that can have major implications for a democratic polity. By conditioning access and determining benefit levels, these designs shape the extent to which citizens can use welfare claiming as a means to secure a measure of autonomy and security in their communities. By establishing the terms of welfare relationships, these designs structure the political interactions between state and citizen that take place in the welfare system. And by conveying lessons about the citizen's status and the nature of government, policy designs influence broad patterns of political belief and action. In this final section, I turn to the question of what one can infer from these findings about how policy designs might be used to bolster welfare recipients' citizenship and political engagement. If we value an active citizenry that participates in the process of self-government, what kinds of welfare institutions might best put this value into practice?

On this question, it is possible to contrast two contemporary schools of thought, each of which draws on a long tradition of ideas regarding poverty, welfare provision, and democratic citizenship. The first is the "new paternalism" exemplified by the work of Lawrence Mead (1985, 1992, 1997a, 1997b). Mead and others argue that welfare policy should be used more self-consciously and vigorously as an instrument of social control, as a means to cultivate the personal responsibility and competence poor people need to become equal citizens (see Besharov and Gardiner 1996; Paden 1992; Rector and Lauber 1995). A second approach is offered by the "design for democracy" thesis exemplified by the work of Anne Schneider and Helen Ingram (1993, 1997; Smith and Ingram 1993). Drawing on theories of participatory democracy and symbolic politics, this thesis argues for policy designs that engage citizens in self-government and convey to citizens that they are equal and effective participants sharing common institutions.

The two viewpoints share some distinctive claims that align them with the approach taken in this book. Each contends that welfare provision has political dimensions that make it more than just a social dilemma, technical problem, financial transaction, or administrative matter. Each suggests that welfare policy designs are causal forces that should bolster but can undermine the quality of citizenship and amount of participation found among the poor. Each argues that the experience of welfare participation can be instructive and that the lessons citizens learn will depend on policy designs. And finally, each asserts that these lessons have significant implications for the overall health of a democratic polity. Beyond this point, however, the two perspectives diverge in their assumptions and, hence, in their claims about what kinds of policy designs would improve citizenship and encourage political engagement. I believe the empirical results from this study point to deficiencies in the new paternalism thesis and lend support to the design for democracy thesis.

New paternalists focus attention on the question of individual competence and make two basic claims. First, because of a culture of poverty that has allegedly grown more intense, poor people now lack the personal responsibility and organization needed to participate as full and equal citizens. Second, directive and supervisory welfare policies offer an effective therapeutic tool for rehabilitating the poor and, hence, reinvigorating democracy. Poor people, in this view, have become unfit for citizenship, first because they are too dysfunctional to fulfill its obligations, and second because their incompetence leads others to properly view them as less than "regular" citizens. Mead (1997a, 229) argues, for example, that the poor no longer "show enough self-command to merit the esteem of others [or make] a community of equal citizens imaginable." As a result, they now lack "moral standing" in relation to government and the community (Mead 1992, 13).

Based on this assessment, new paternalists argue that political integration of the poor can only be achieved through policies that bring authority and structure to poor people's lives. Paternalist policies are designed to teach responsibility and competence by requiring, supervising, and enforcing particular patterns of behavior (especially work-related behavior). In addition to "restoring some coherence to the lives of the poor" (Mead 1997a, 230), such policies are expected to allow the welfare state to function as a moral tutor: clients will learn to accept and act on widely held values and citizenship obligations (Mead 1985, 1997b; Paden 1992). The expectations of this learning process are that the poor will be moved steadily toward higher levels of self-respect and community standing as well as higher levels of civic and political engagement.

Despite its name, the new paternalism carries forward a very old tradition suggesting that poor people need moral uplift and behavior modification and that these goals can be achieved through carefully designed social-welfare interventions (Gordon 1994; Handler and Hasenfeld 1991; M. Katz 1986, 1989, 1995; Piven and Cloward 1993). U.S. welfare history has included a steady stream of voices charging that poor people's behaviors are dysfunctional, that they are a major cause of poverty, and that they pose a barrier to community membership. Such claims have often been tied to arguments that particular groups (especially groups other than white, male property owners) lacked the independence and competence needed to function as full citizens (Fraser and Gordon 1994; Smiley 1989, 1999). And in response, welfare reformers have frequently implemented directive and supervisory approaches to "improving poor people" (M. Katz 1995). Recognizing these precursors is important not because they suggest that the new paternalism is less than novel but because the historical record offers so little evidence that "old paternalist" policy designs bolstered the poor's social standing or made them more engaged citizens (Handler and Hasenfeld 1991; M. Katz 1986, 1995).

Despite the lack of historical support for new paternalist claims, the thesis and its call for policy designs that emphasize direction and supervision have become extremely influential among policymakers. The new paternalism played a key role in motivating and justifying the Personal Responsibility and Work Opportunity Reconciliation Act of 1996, which replaced the AFDC program with a more discretionary system of block grants to the states. Under this new

TANF system, states have adopted a wide variety of policy tools designed to enforce work and modify behavior through a combination of incentives, monitoring procedures, and disciplinary measures (Albelda and Tilly 1997; L. Wilson, Stoker, and McGrath 1999). Thus, there are important and immediate reasons to ask whether directive and supervisory policy designs should be expected to teach welfare recipients lessons that bolster their citizenship and political engagement.[6]

The expectation that paternalist policies will have positive effects is premised on a very strong and rarely questioned model of social learning. Bypassing developmental dimensions of political learning (T. Cook 1985; Sapiro 1994), new paternalists presume a model that is, in two senses, analogous to the one applied in early studies of childhood political socialization (Easton and Dennis 1969; Hyman 1959). First, like socialization processes that instill values in children, welfare relationships are presumed to be "pre-political" (Sapiro 1994)—that is, new paternalists suggest that the welfare relationship should be evaluated not as a political relationship experienced by citizens in a democracy but rather as a training ground for future citizens who must be shaped to fulfill their eventual democratic role. Second, the socialization process that takes place in welfare programs is presumed to involve an active and potent agent on one side and a passive and receptive target on the other. Thus, little attention is given to the possibility that clients may actively interpret their program experiences and do so in ways that deviate from the lessons intended by policymakers.

The analysis presented in this book should raise troubling questions about each of these assumptions. First, however much paternalist policy designs may convey value lessons, such designs must also be recognized as structures for direct political relationships between individuals and the state. These structures have important consequences for citizens' abilities to exercise due process rights, articulate needs and interests, protect themselves against invidious uses of discretion, and influence decisions that have direct effects on their well-being. To position clients as objects of agency paternalism is to position citizens as objects of a paternalistic government and to value their compliance more than their engagement. The comparison of AFDC and SSDI presented in chapters 5 and 6 makes it clear that more directive and supervisory policy designs can leave citizens feeling that they occupy a degraded status in relation to government and can have a chilling effect on client assertiveness.

Under the TANF system, poor people now encounter policy designs that are far more paternalistic than what clients experienced in AFDC during the period of this study. Although states vary in their specific program characteristics, there has been a dramatic increase in the use of paternalist tools: stronger work enforcement, stiffer sanctions, time limits, caps on reproduction, regulations regarding parenting behavior, requirements to cooperate with child support enforcement, the use of finger-imaging and tracking procedures, drug testing, and so on (Albelda and Tilly 1997; Schram and Soss 1998). These policy changes, especially sanctions, have contributed to large declines in caseloads (Rector and Youssef 1999), but how are they affecting citizenship and political engagement within the welfare system?

Early reports point to significant threats to clients' due process rights as well as their access to remaining entitlements such as food stamps and Medicaid (Houppert 1999). In addition, emerging evidence suggests that new paternalist policies are not teaching clients citizenship values but are having the sort of negative political effects that one would predict based on what I found in the earlier AFDC program. Laura A. Wilson, Robert P. Stoker, and Dennis McGrath, for example, find that instead of cultivating new values or greater knowledge among clients, a new paternalist program in Maryland only taught clients to comply with a tougher regime of government rules regulating their behavior. The researchers conclude,

> The results of our study cast doubt on the logic of paternalist reform. If paternalism is supposed to teach clients to behave responsibly, our analysis of PPI [Primary Prevention Initiative] indicated that most clients did not learn the intended lessons. But welfare agencies in Maryland did tutor their clients. Clients were taught to obtain the required verification information and cooperate with welfare caseworkers to maintain their eligibility. In the end, the paternalist reform seems to be a lesson about power, not responsibility. (1999, 485)

This finding, that paternalist policy taught clients political lessons about power rather than moral lessons about responsibility, points to the second flawed assumption in the new paternalist argument. The evidence presented in this book suggests that welfare clients are anything but passive learners who can be counted on to internalize only the messages intended by paternalist reformers. Instead, clients tend to be motivated learners who actively try to understand how the welfare agency works, how they are expected to act, and how they are likely to be treated if they assert themselves. As a result, clients draw a variety of inferences from policy designs, and many of these inferences focus on the nature of government and their relation to it.

New program requirements backed up by threats of case termination are likely to be capable of directly altering client behavior. It is even possible (though by no means obvious) that such measures might change individual values. But if these objectives are achieved, they will represent only a portion of the political consequences associated with directive and supervisory policy designs. The evidence presented in this book strongly suggests that coercive welfare policies do not cultivate better citizens, if by "better" one means more efficacious and engaged. Repeated encounters with intensive information gathering and directives backed up by threats of termination tend to leave clients feeling degraded, vulnerable, and pessimistic about government. Regardless of what else they may accomplish, such policy designs appear to deter client assertiveness, depress beliefs in government responsiveness, and dampen levels of political participation among the poor.

Thus, whether one looks inside welfare institutions or to the broader polity, there are good reasons to doubt that paternalist policy designs will enhance citizenship and political engagement among the poor. By contrast, the findings presented in this book offer support for two claims associated with the design for democracy thesis (Schneider and Ingram 1997). First, as policy designs achieve their instrumental purposes, they simultaneously express cues to the citizenry that influence patterns of political belief and action (Edelman 1964, 1971).[7] Second, policy designs construct institutional settings that shape citizens' firsthand experiences of participation; these experiences, in turn, influence the ways citizens' perceive their status and orient themselves toward their community and government. Schneider and Ingram explain,

> The elements of policy design impart messages to target populations that inform them of their status as citizens and how they and people like themselves are likely to be treated by government. Such information becomes internalized into a conception of the meaning of citizenship that influences their orientations toward government and their participation. . . . Citizens encounter and internalize [these] messages not only through observation of politics and media coverage, but also through their direct, personal experiences with public policy. (1997, 140–41)

To promote democratic citizenship and political engagement, policymakers must attend to how policy designs position citizens in relation to government and to the cues these designs are likely to convey to citizens about their status and the nature of government. Democratic citizenship, in this view, is not a set of individual traits that can be instilled through a paternalistic process of socialization. Rather, it is a political characteristic of relationships that depends on the ways institutions portray and position members of the community. Welfare policies built around the premise that clients are incompetent, dependent, and deviant are unlikely to reduce the political marginality of the poor or enhance their esteem in the eyes of others. Policies that position clients as objects of paternalism—as targets of coercion, surveillance, and discipline—are unlikely to leave participants feeling that government is responsive or that action aimed at government can be effective. For welfare policy designs to foster democracy, they must reflect democratic values. If the goal is to create a politically equal and engaged citizenry, then we must construct government institutions that position citizens as equals and convey that their engagement can be effective.

This conclusion, of course, only returns us to a key theme in Marshall's (1964) account of social citizenship: the idea that social rights must be embodied in both the fact and the form of welfare provision. In Marshall's view, the goals of political democracy are best served by welfare institutions that are designed to express "liberal themes of rights and equal respect; communitarian norms of solidarity and shared responsibility; and republican ideals of participation in public life" (Fraser and Gordon 1993, 45–46). Social welfare institutions, in this view, are most likely to promote democratic practice if they allow citizens to experience themselves as equal and effective participants in relation to a common share. How might welfare policy in the United States do a better job of realizing this inclusive political goal? This question deserves a far longer treatment than it can receive here, but the analysis presented in this book suggests four points.

First, welfare benefits should be provided at a level high enough to supply a meaningful degree of security, autonomy, and dignity in recipients' everyday lives. Welfare policy can support an engaged citizenry only to the extent that it lifts recipients out of poverty and relieves them of its debilitating effects. The meager benefits doled out in AFDC and now TANF offer clients only an incomplete reprieve from food shortages, homelessness, the draining struggle to meet daily needs, the inability to fulfill obligations to others, and vulnerability to coercion. Social insurance benefits in the United States may be lower than the benefits offered in many European countries, but they tend to be reasonably successful in fulfilling this most basic political function. To support democracy, the welfare system must overcome two weaknesses of the AFDC program: leaving large numbers of eligible citizens unassisted and failing to lift recipients above the poverty line.

Second, welfare benefits should be provided in a fashion that cuts across social cleavages and offers roughly equivalent institutions to all citizens (see Schneider and Ingram 1997, 203). Only through this form of provision can pity for distant others and the punishment of deviants be displaced by a politics of shared status, interests, rights, and obligations. Scholars have proposed a variety of approaches worth consideration: a negative income tax (Block and Manza 1997), a guaranteed annual income (Funicello 1993), employment assurance or active labor-market policies (Weir 1992), a child support assurance system (Garfinkel 1996), federal child care and benefit provisions (Bergmann 1996), universal health insurance (Marmor, Mashaw, and Harvey 1990), or a combination of programs based on "targeting within universalism" (Skocpol 1992b). All these proposals share political features that could promote democratic practice—that is, they could link citizens to one another under a common set of institutions, they could position citizens similarly in relation to government, and by constructing comparable participation experiences, they could encourage clients to learn similar lessons about government, citizenship, and political action.

Third, welfare institutions should be structured and benefits administered in a manner that protects recipients' status as rights-bearing participants in relation to the state. This study underscores the potential for formal rights in welfare programs to be undermined by policy designs that leave clients feeling that their actions cannot be effective and that they are vulnerable to retribution. Clients are unlikely to speak up for themselves or pursue their formal due process rights if they are afraid of losing benefits that provide them with the necessities of survival. Social insurance programs in the U.S. welfare system, or at least SSDI in this study, demonstrate that welfare benefits can be provided in ways that leave clients feeling confident of their abilities to raise questions and grievances. Such a design not only makes clients better advocates on their own behalf but also provides agencies with a more engaged clientele and, hence, superior information about performance and responsiveness. Likewise, this sort of design combats the belief that government is an autonomous and/or hostile actor that citizens cannot influence.

Fourth, welfare policies should be designed to promote clients' individual and collective participation in decision-making processes. In practice, this means increasing the number of points at which clients are presented with choices and fostering conditions that support clients' abilities to make effective use of these choices. In addition to encouraging clients to develop a sense that they control their own fate (Kane 1987), repeated opportunities to exercise choice would also convey a more responsive image of government. Client effectiveness in relation to these opportunities for choice can be bolstered in several ways. First, as Handler (1992, 1996) outlines, policy designs must make creative use of street-level discretion, providing clients with the information, institutional leverage, and sense of security they need to join agency workers as participants in decision-making processes. Second, policy designs should follow the example of Head Start programs by providing arenas for collective participation that combat individual isolation and support the client's effectiveness as a political agent. Finally, policy designs should strive to cultivate and involve local civic and political organizations that bolster the effectiveness and standing of clients (Handler 1996; Schneider and Ingram 1997).

All of these proposals are feasible in economic and administrative terms, and all would improve the civic and political status of the poor. But of course, welfare policy design is not a technical activity settled according to the best ideas. It is a political process shaped by power, ideology, values, and interests. As Piven and Cloward (1997b, 526) have noted, advocates in the United States have rarely lacked universalist and humane policy blueprints to offer as an alternative to paternalism: "what we have lacked is political muscle." Compared to European polities, the United States has a number of structural features that make it an "unusually inhospitable environment" for expanding social provision in ways that would promote the political incorporation of the poor (Esping-Andersen 1990; Noble 1997; Piven and Cloward 1993; Skocpol 1992a). And although public opinion in the U.S. continues to support the necessity and desirability of government welfare provision, public sentiment is also laced with a considerable amount of hostility toward welfare recipients, who are often presumed to be lazy, undeserving, and African American (see Gilens 1999).

The U.S. welfare system can be remade in ways that would realize the inclusive ideals of social citizenship and draw the poor into a more vibrant democracy. But these sorts of policy reforms are unlikely to be achieved in the absence of political leadership from above and more vigorous political activism from below (Albelda and Tilly 1997, 165–81). To make this point is not to offer the technocrat's lament that politics is an unfortunate barrier to good policy designs. On the contrary, it is to underscore that welfare institutions are inherently an element of political practice. Welfare institutions are outcomes constructed through political conflict and compromise; they are political forces that influence patterns of status, belief, and action; and they are, in their own right, critical sites of political activity in modern democratic polities. Welfare systems and citizens' activities in relation to them pose critical challenges both for students of politics and for friends of democracy.

Description of the Interview Sample

Name	Age	Race/Ethnicity[a]	Education
		AFDC	
Lynn	29	White	College diploma
Debber	31	Latina	High school diploma
Elizabeth	35	African American	Some college
Nona Mae	26	African American	Some college
Josephine	21	African American	Some high school
Mary	34	White	No high school
Nancy	37	Native American	Some college
Tina	20	White	Some high school
Kisha	22	African American	Some high school
Karla	37	African American	Some high school
Renee	20	African American	High school diploma
Lisa	22	African American	Some high school
Sandra	31	Latina	Some high school
Celina	19	—	High school diploma
Cheryl	30	White	Some high school
Anna	26	Latina	Some high school
Sarah	27	African American	High school diploma
Julie	30	White	High school diploma
Alicia	18	African American	Some high school
Alissa	21	African American	High school diploma
Shelly	48	White	Some college
Penny	23	African American	High school diploma
Vanessa	20	African American	High school diploma
Lashell	20	African American	Some high school
Hope	27	White	Some high school
		SSDI	
Marie	29	White	Some college
Phil	38	White	Some college
Bridget	61	White	College diploma
Kitty	51	White	College diploma
Dizzy	44	White	High school diploma
Molly	38	White	High school diploma
Sarah	39	White	College diploma

(Continued)

Appendix A—*Continued*

Name	Age	Race/Ethnicity[a]	Education
Lee-Ann	34	White	High school diploma
Starr	30	White	Some college
Katrina	45	White	College diploma
Emerald	47	White	College diploma
Donna	51	White	College diploma
J	33	White	College diploma
Holly	37	White	High school diploma
Patty	53	White	College diploma
Mark	36	Native American	Some high school
Darryl	44	African American	Some college
Frank	43	White	High school diploma
Francis	35	White	College diploma
Michael	43	African American	High school diploma
Joe	65	White	Some high school
Mike	50	White	High school diploma
Joy	53	African American	High school diploma
Betty	55	White	College diploma
Merton	53	White	College diploma

[a]All informants named their own preferred label for race or ethnicity. These are summary categories. Celina preferred to have no listing or to be listed as "other." In her words, "My mother is half Jewish Russian and half Puerto Rican. My father is half African American and half Cherokee Indian. You can say that if you want."

Variable Constructions and Descriptions

Note: Variable names in square brackets refer to variable numbers in Miller, Kinder, and Rosenstone 1993.

Electoral Participation (0, 1) indicates a yes (1) or no (0) response: "In talking to people about the elections, we often find that a lot of people were not able to vote because they weren't registered, they were sick, or they just didn't have time. How about you—did you vote in the election this November?" [v5601]

Internal Political Efficacy (1 to 20) is a scale constructed from the following items: I feel that I have a pretty good understanding of the important political issues facing our country" [v6105], "I consider myself well qualified to participate in politics" [v6106], "I feel that I could do as good a job in public office as most other people" [v6107], and "I think that I am better informed about politics and government than most people" [v6108]. Higher values indicate higher internal efficacy.

External Political Efficacy (1 to 10) is a scale constructed from the following items: "People like me don't have any say about what the government does" [v6102], "I don't think public officials care much what people like me think" [v6103]. The scale is flipped so that higher values indicate higher external efficacy.

Woman (0, 1) indicates whether the respondent is male (0) or female (1) [v4201].

Black (0,1) indicates whether the respondent identifies herself or himself as African American (1) or did not identify herself or himself as an African American (0) [v4202].

Strength of Partisanship (1 to 4) indicates self-placement on a dimension marked at the low end (1) by "independent" and at the high end (4) by either "strong Republican" or "strong Democrat" [v3634].

South (0,1) indicates whether the respondent is from one of the ten "solid South" states (1) or from somewhere else in the United States (0). [v3017]

Income (1 to 24) indicates the respondent's family income before taxes in 1991. It ranges from a low of "none or less than $2,999" (1) to a high of "$105,000 and over" (24). [v4104].

Education (1 to 7) indicates the highest level of formal education reported by the respondent. It ranges from "eighth grade or less" (1) to "advanced degree" (7). [v3908]

Age (17 to 91) indicates the age of the respondent. [v3903]

AFDC (0, 1) indicates that the respondent received benefits from Aid to Families with Dependent Children (1) or did not receive such benefits (0). The data set includes ninety-four AFDC recipients. [v3445]

SSDI (0, 1) indicates that the respondent received benefits from Social Security Disability Insurance (1) or did not receive such benefits (0). The data set includes 129 SSDI recipients. [v3448]

Interview Schedule

The following questions provided a baseline schedule for client interviews. The format for each interview was semi-structured. Depending on the flow of a given client's account and other circumstances of the interview, I routinely altered, omitted, or added questions. The sequence of issues tended to follow a consistent pattern across the fifty interviews, but I made no effort to impose a rigid question order.

Welfare Claiming

1. Could you start by telling me a little bit about what was going on for you at the time you applied for [AFDC/SSDI]? What led up to your decision to apply?
2. How did you know about the [AFDC/SSDI] program at the time you applied? Do you recall how you first heard about the program?
   a) At the time you applied, had you known any people who had been in the [AFDC/SSDI] program? Who?
3. Before you decided to apply for [AFDC/SSDI], did you consider any other options? Did you feel like you had any other options open to you at the time?
4. Did you know ahead of time that you were eligible for the program, or did you just contact the agency to find out what kinds of help might be available?
5. Were there ever any times in the past when you thought you were probably eligible for benefits but did not apply?
   a) Could you tell me about that time?
6. At the time you decided to apply, did you have any major fears or concerns about going into the program or what it might mean for you?
7. At the time you decided to apply, were there any things you were hoping the program might help you accomplish, or was it more that you just needed the money?
8. During the time when you decided to apply, did you talk about your deci-

sion with anyone close to you, or did you make the decision basically on your own?
   a) Who did you talk it over with?
   b) Did they encourage you to apply, or did they think it was a bad idea?
9. How did the people you were close to react when they found out you were applying to the program (or that you had applied)?

The Application Encounter

1. Could you tell me a little about what it was like to go down and apply? What happened that day?
   a) Do you recall having any reactions to [that particular aspect of your first experience]?
   b) Did [that particular aspect of your first experience] leave you with any particular impressions of what it would be like to be an [AFDC/SSDI] client?
2. When you went to the agency, did you have to wait at all before you could actually file an application?
   a) About how long do you think you waited?
   b) Did you feel like that was an acceptable amount of time to have to wait, or was it too long?
3. When you dealt with the agency that first time, did you feel like the people who worked there had any particular reaction to the fact that you were applying? Were they supportive in any way? Did you feel at all like they looked down on you?
4. Do you remember anything about what kinds of questions they asked you when you applied?
   a) Did you feel like the questions they asked you were appropriate under the circumstances? Did any of them strike you as overly personal?
   b) Did you have trouble answering any of the questions they asked? Why?
   c) Were there any particular questions that bothered you more than the others? Why?
   d) Overall, how did you feel about the questions that they asked you when you applied to [AFDC/SSDI]?
5. When you first applied, did you feel like you were able to describe your situation the way you saw it? Did you feel like you were given a chance to explain why you were there and what you needed from the program? How did all of that work?
6. Thinking back to when you applied, how would you evaluate the agency workers you dealt with? How well do you think they did their jobs? How did they treat you? What was it like to deal with them that first day?

7. Thinking back to when you went through that process of applying to the program, did that first experience leave you with any image of what it would be like for you in the program? Did you come away with any thoughts about how you would be expected to act in the program or how you would be treated in the future?

8. Did you feel basically the same about entering the [AFDC/SSDI] program before and after you applied? Or did the actual experience of applying change the way you felt about it?

9. Looking back on it now, do you think the experiences you had when you applied were similar to what most people go through? Or were they different in some way?

Welfare Participation

1. Let's talk a little bit now about actually being in the program. Is being in the program different from applying to the program? How?

   a) Could you tell me in general what the experience of being in the program has been like for you?

   b) Have your feelings about the being in the program changed at all over time? How?

2. When you think back on your time in the program, are there any particular experiences that stick out to you as a good example of what being in [AFDC/SSDI] is like?

3. Would you say that your reasons for being in [AFDC/SSDI] are typical or not typical of the reasons why most other people are in the program? In what ways?

4. Do you think other people view you differently if they know you're in [AFDC/SSDI]? Is there a stigma associated with receiving benefits from [AFDC/SSDI]?

   a) How do you think most people view people in the [AFDC/SSDI] program?

5. [For AFDC] Since I've never actually been in the AFDC program, could you tell me what happens on a typical day when you go to the agency to see your caseworker? Just basically what happens from beginning to end. Or if it's easier, could you just pick a particular day, and tell me about it?

6. [For AFDC] When you go to see your caseworker, what sorts of things do you usually talk about?

   a) Who usually asks most of the questions? Do you both usually spend some time talking and some time listening?

7. Have you ever raised a complaint or grievance in your dealings with the agency?

    a) What was the complaint about?

    b) How did [your caseworker / the worker you dealt with at the agency] react?

8. If you ever had a grievance or a complaint in dealing with the agency, do you think you would feel comfortable bringing it up?

    a) Would it matter if it was an especially important problem?

    b) If you had a complaint you wanted to bring up, would you worry at all about what [your caseworker / the agency worker] might do in response?

9. Has there ever been a time when you had a complaint that you didn't say anything about or didn't feel you could bring up?

    a) At the time, did you feel like you had a legitimate complaint?

    b) Do you still feel the same way about it now?

10. Speaking in general, if someone in the program were to challenge a worker's decision, how do you think it would turn out?

    a) Does challenging a worker ever have a positive effect on getting clients the things they need or deserve?

    b) In general, then, would you say that challenging them is a good thing to do or a bad thing to do?

11. Do you feel like you have much influence or power in dealing with [your caseworker / workers at the agency]? Do you feel like you have much say-so over what happens to your case?

12. How much power do you think individual workers at the agency have? Most of the time, can they do what they want, or are they pretty limited?

13. Based on your experiences in the program, do you have any thoughts about what agency workers care most about in their relationships with clients?

    a) Overall, how would you evaluate [your caseworker / workers at the agency]?

    b) Do you feel like you're usually treated fairly?

    c) Do you feel like you're usually treated with respect?

    d) Do you feel like they generally listen to your concerns?

    e) Do you feel like they usually respond to your questions or problems?

14. If you could change anything you wanted about the [AFDC/SSDI] program, what would be the main things you would change?

Broader Politics

1. What sorts of things would you say are important in determining the kinds of policies we get from government? In your opinion, are there any particular factors that really explain why political outcomes turn out the way they do?

2. In general, would you say that government does what the citizens want?
3. Do people in this country have a fairly equal amount of influence on what government does, or do some people have more political influence than others?
   a) In your opinion, is there any particular group that has an especially large amount of political influence? Is there any group that is especially likely to get what they want from government?
4. Do you feel like public officials care much what people like you think? Do you feel like government officials listen to people like you?
5. In general, would you say that your own individual actions can affect government decisions?
   a) Do you say that because of something about government, because of something about your own abilities, or both?
6. Overall, would you say that you have a pretty good understanding of how government works? Compared to most people out there, would you say that you know a lot or only a little about politics and government?
7. If a group of [AFDC/SSDI] recipients got together and formed a collective movement, do you think it could actually influence the kinds of policies we get from government? Why?
8. Would you say that you and other people in [AFDC/SSDI] share anything in common in terms of what you might want government to do? Do you share any political interests as a group?
9. If a group of [AFDC/SSDI] recipients created an activist organization to press for changes in government policies, would you want to join it?

Notes

Chapter 1

1. In 1996, 42 percent of all families in the United States lived in households that received income from Social Security, supplemental security income, public assistance, veterans payments, unemployment compensation or workers' compensation (U.S. Census Bureau 1998). In contrast, turnout at midterm elections did not exceed 40 percent of adults in any year from 1974 through 1998 (CSAE 1999).

2. Students of public administration, for example, study government bureaucracies as major targets for the political demands of interest groups (Aberbach, Putnam, and Rockman 1981; Chubb 1983; Kaufman 1981; Seidman 1986), elected officials (Derthick 1990; Wood and Waterman 1994), and corporations (Schlozman and Tierney 1986, 330–57).

3. The NWRO's efforts in the 1960s provide a classic example. Closed off from direct influence on the policy-making decisions of elected officials in the legislative and executive branches, the demands of the poor flowed into the government's more accessible institutions of policy implementation, the welfare bureaucracy and the courts (Davis 1993; Piven and Cloward 1977, chap. 5).

4. In fact, Sidney Verba made these and other consistent points more than two decades ago. He concludes, "The more government takes a role in such matters as welfare . . . the more likely the average citizen is to find himself or herself in a position where day-to-day welfare depends on the government. From this perspective, the distinction among the parochial, the subject, and the participant requires some revision. . . . Though [the parochial applicant's] concern is narrow, he may be aware of the government's impact on those narrow concerns; he may expect the government to be of assistance in connection with such concerns, and he may be active in trying to obtain that assistance. In the latter sense, a parochial can also be a participant. . . . Is parochial [welfare] participation also *political* participation? Yes, if one means by political participation activities by which the individual tries to influence some allocational decision on the part of government" (1978, 4–5).

5. In Abrahams's definition, "resources include, but are not limited to, money, time, space, prestige, and deference. . . . [V]alues are the sets of expectations and beliefs that inform our behavior, emotions, and thoughts by telling us how we are supposed to think, feel, and behave" (1992, 331).

6. Hardy-Fanta (1993) and Singerman (1995) have made similar arguments. As these authors point out, the conventional government-centered definition of political action not only obscures important dimensions of political life for the poor but also produces a distorted view of political action along lines defined by race, ethnicity, and gender.

215

7. As a contrasting example, Marshall cites the 1834 Poor Law, through which the poor "ceased to be citizens in any true sense of the word. For paupers forfeited in practice the civil right of personal liberty, by internment in the workhouse, and they forfeited by law any political rights they might possess" (1964, 80).

8. Just as social-control theory suggests that political pacification is achieved through both the material and symbolic dimensions of policy action, it also suggests that both of these dimensions are essential for the maintenance of economic coercion. At the material level, the terms and benefits of poor relief are maintained according to the old "doctrine of less eligibility" so that welfare remains less attractive than the worst forms of employment in the local economy. Symbolically, the low benefits and degrading terms of welfare benefits constitute a dramaturgy of work that celebrates any form of employment as better than public assistance.

9. This pattern can be traced back to the Social Security Act of 1935, which excluded from social-insurance coverage people who did not have regular paid employment and people who worked in agricultural, domestic, and nonprofit settings. These gaps in coverage made it particularly difficult for women and people of color to make social-insurance claims (Brown 1999; Gordon 1994; Quadagno 1994). Similar patterns across the tiers of the system persist today largely because of the types of work counted by social-insurance programs and because women and people of color are disproportionately poor (Albelda and Tilly 1997; Mink 1998).

Chapter 2

1. This strategy follows what Yin calls "theoretical replication logic," the selection of cases so that they can be expected to produce similar or contrary results for predictable reasons (1989, 53–55). My discussion here refers primarily to the analyses presented in chapters 5, 6, and 7. The analyses of welfare claiming presented in chapters 3 and 4 place less emphasis on causal inference. Instead, these chapters employ a sample of successful claimants as a basis for an interpretive analysis of the processes that link program eligibility to claims on government (for discussion of this strategy, see Lin 1998).

2. In more formal terms, demographic differences between the program groups serve as a source of antecedent variable explanations. For example, if women are more likely than men to be in AFDC and are less likely to believe that government is responsive to citizens, gender differences may produce a spurious relationship between program participation and beliefs about governmental responsiveness. This problem of inference can be resolved, however, if the link between program participation and feelings of efficacy remains after controlling for gender by removing men from the analysis.

3. In other words, the cases have been selected to serve as a basis for what Yin calls "analytic generalization." Although the cases may not be representative of the complete universe of social welfare programs, they do provide the characteristics needed to generalize to broader theories of participation and the two-tier welfare system (see Yin 1989, chap. 2).

4. To avoid undermining my fieldwork at the shelter, I did not conduct any formal interviews with residents. In some cases, however, residents who had already left the shelter provided referrals to friends. No overlap occurred between the formal interview sample and the group of residents at the shelter.

5. All informants named their own preferred label for race or ethnicity. These are summary categories. The percentages do not add up to 100 because one woman did not prefer a single category (see appendix A).

6. I informed the director of the shelter and the facilitators of the disability support groups in advance about my status as a researcher. My research became common knowledge both at the shelter and in the support groups.

Chapter 3

1. This conceptualization of welfare benefits as ends rather than means leads predictably to a focus on how these benefits might serve as a goal or perhaps an ulterior motive for poor people's behaviors. This assumption underlies most research on welfare programs' incentive effects and supports a number of potent myths surrounding welfare—for example, that the poor have children or move across state lines in a strategic effort to enhance their welfare benefits (Albelda and Tilly 1997; Moffitt 1992; Schram and Soss 1999).

2. For example, "I think it was my only choice" (Mary, AFDC); "It seemed like that was the only option for me. It didn't seem like there was anything else in the world to do" (Alissa, AFDC); "It was the only thing to do. I had no choice. What were the options?" (Merton, SSDI); "I didn't feel like I had an option" (Patty, SSDI).

3. Following participatory-democratic theorists, the term *autonomy* in this chapter is not intended to signify an absolute state of unencumbered self-rule (see Gaffaney 1999). Instead, I use this term in a relational sense, to identify "the range of *control* that participants in a particular social situation have with respect to each other over their own private action and over the exercise of their respective processes of decision making, valuing, and willing. Autonomy is thus a relational notion because the actual range of a participant's social autonomy is mostly a function of his [or her] *role* relatedness to the other participants" (Rosenbaum 1986, 107).

4. For example, when I asked Dizzy about people who believe it is wrong to be dependent on welfare, he shouted, "I feel like those idiots don't know what they're talking about. I feel like they should walk in my shoes for one day. Then they would know. If I didn't have [SSDI], I'd be another crack in the street like I was when I applied. I felt like I had fallen through the cracks of society."

5. This proportion seems especially high given the reticence of many women to discuss abuse experiences, the fact that I did not ask questions about domestic violence, and the fact that I am a man. However, it is consistent with other researchers' estimates (Bassuk, Browne, and Buckner 1996; Raphael 1995, 1996).

6. The $10,000 to which Hope refers came from a court settlement she received after she and her sister were raped by three men when she was six.

7. This emphasis on maternal obligation has been found consistently in earlier interview research with AFDC clients (see Seccombe 1999). Edin reports, for example, that the AFDC recipients she interviewed "convincingly stressed they had one simple but overriding drive—to provide for their children. This explains why they had turned to welfare in the first place" (1995, 8).

8. As Spalter-Roth and Hartmann note of the AFDC clients in their study, "Even if

they worked full-time, year-round at the jobs they held, these women would generally not have been able to bring their families above the poverty level through their employment earnings alone" (1994, 198).

9. Here again, my findings closely follow those reported by Edin (1995, 7): "The mothers we interviewed displayed a striking degree of confidence in the education system as a way to better their economic positions. But they also believed that combining child rearing, full-time work, and full-time schooling was nearly impossible. They could, however, combine welfare with schooling much more easily without sacrificing their children's welfare."

Chapter 5

1. In what follows, I use the terms *application encounter* and *first encounter* as synonyms. Each may be seen as a variation on the broader terms *bureaucratic encounter* and *public encounter* used in research on bureaucracies (Goodsell 1981; D. Katz et al. 1975).

2. Clients typically responded with long accounts that included their interpretations of events (such as, "I remember thinking to myself . . ."). When clients did not offer interpretations on their own, I asked them how they viewed the experiences they had described.

3. Lisa underscored this interpretation as she described the more inviting atmosphere at Head Start centers: "With Head Start, they'll say, 'Just bring [your kids] to the meeting, and let them play off to the side.' And then I can still get my business taken care of, even with my kids. That's how you know they want you there."

4. This symbolic connection may be even stronger for clients in states that have responded to reports of welfare migration and fraud by "fingerprinting prospective recipients to prevent persons from receiving duplicate benefits" (Vobejda and Havemann 1996, A4; Schram and Soss 1998).

5. SSA administrators received a dramatic lesson on this point when they took over the means-tested SSI program from state governments in the 1970s. For an excellent discussion of this case and of how information gathering differs for means-tested programs, see Derthick 1990, esp. 23–24.

6. The rules allow applicants to seek good-cause exemptions in some cases; but in every state, these requests tend to be made and granted in extremely small numbers (Keiser and Soss 1998; Mannix, Freedman, and Best 1987). Only one woman in this study reported being informed of this option at the time she applied.

7. Indeed, child support may be more likely to enable an individual to avoid welfare participation in SSDI than in AFDC. Because the fathers of AFDC clients' children generally make low wages, the maximum child support available from fathers usually would not obviate the need for public assistance (Edin and Lein 1997).

8. This description is accurate for the AFDC program during the time period of these interviews. The Personal Responsibility and Work Opportunity Reconciliation Act passed in 1996, however, gave states the freedom to eliminate entirely the fifty-dollar pass-through.

9. Josephson 1997 reports that, in some locales, this information automatically becomes part of the public record through court hearings.

10. Prottas (1979, 29) notes the same dynamic in his observation study of welfare agencies: "When the applicant objects to the paucity of the grant, the delay in its arrival, or to any of the procedural requirements, the worker commiserates, generally expresses agreement, but denies responsibility. The injustices are a function of the rules to which the worker is no less subject than the applicant."

11. The specific wording of the item is "Remarks (You may use this space for any explanation. If you need more space, attach a separate sheet.)."

12. For example, Phil recalled, "Even though I was going through kidney failure, and that was probably my top priority at the time (my blindness was secondary to my kidney failure), the kidney failure was not a certified disability. The blindness was. So you had to phrase what you were talking about in a way that would fit their guidelines. . . . You had to prioritize your disability to their liking instead of what was actually going on with you."

13. Clients' beliefs about specific workers' judgments probably varied in accuracy. Observation research, however, suggests that workers do make these sorts of moral judgments and that they affect bureaucratic outcomes (see Hasenfeld and Steinmetz 1981, 86; Prottas 1979, 39). Regardless of whether workers actually judged applicants in this way, clients' emphasis on this point underscores their feelings of dependence in the process.

Chapter 6

1. All probability levels reported in this chapter are based on Fisher's exact tests.

2. This response may play an important role in the practice of "churning," in which families are cut off the rolls on technical grounds and then reappear within the next couple of months (see Casey and Mannix 1986; Funiciello 1993, chap. 6). AFDC clients who are churned may consider fighting a termination notice less effective than waiting to reapply at the soonest possible date. Filing for a fair hearing is an unknown gamble; by contrast, clients have already succeeded in the claiming process at least once before.

3. In most cases, the penalty for not showing up is termination of benefits. In one case, a woman reported that she was (inappropriately) told that she would go to jail if she did not bring her baby to a child support hearing. However, other clients in this study did not report this sort of threat.

4. A ninth client provides an ambiguous case. Mary answered "Yeah" when I asked her if she would feel comfortable bringing up a problem with her worker. But three pieces of evidence seem to point in the opposite direction: (1) She did not elaborate on this answer at all and never said anything else in the interview that indicated that she would be willing to speak out. (2) She was expecting to receive a notice of termination because she had found mandatory schooling too difficult to maintain. When I asked her what she was going to do about the problem, she told me that instead of seeking a good-cause exemption, "I'm going to let them cut me off." (3) She also made the following comments during the interview: "Whenever they want, they send a notice, and I read it. And if that's what they say, that's what goes. . . . You don't really talk about anything [during a review]. They're going to do what they want to do regardless of what you've got to say. . . . It's always been smooth because I've never raised anything." In the end, I decided to include Mary with the majority who were reluctant to raise grievances.

5. Like the entire AFDC sample, these clients are all women. They represent 43 percent of white clients, 31 percent of black clients, and 33 percent of Latinas. Excluding one outlier (a forty-eight-year-old client), this subgroup has a mean age, 27.7 years old, that is comparable to the 25.4-year-old average in the majority. Clients with college experience were more likely to be in the vocal group (three of five), but below the college level, there was no clear association with formal education. While clients with at least a high school diploma made up a slight majority of the overall AFDC sample (thirteen of twenty-five), they made up a minority of the more assertive group (three of eight).

6. Mary, the woman I classified with the reticent majority, was neither an activist nor a Head Start client. If I had decided to settle the ambiguity in the other direction, there would have been one member of the minority group whose willingness to speak up could not be explained by a spillover effect. This change, however, would not have altered the statistical significance of the difference of proportions reported here.

7. Case reviews in the SSDI program are extremely limited. Each year, the SSA conducts continuing disability investigations on a very small number of cases that are expected to show improvement. However, SSDI participation does not entail mandatory case reviews at regular intervals.

8. I base this comparison on informal conversations with residents at the shelter. I did not ask informants about this issue in in-depth interviews.

9. The Social Security Disability Amendments of 1980.

Chapter 7

1. Verba, Schlozman, and Brady (1995, 220) make this point explicit: "Our point is not . . . to argue that receipt of means-tested benefits causes low levels of activity, but rather to demonstrate that a group that is dependent on the government is, by virtue of its lack of education or any other factors, less active in expressing its concerns, and therefore, less visible to public officials."

2. Interpretation of these results is complicated by overreporting of turnout in the NES surveys. Validation studies suggest that false reports of voting are especially common among nonvoters who are African American or who have higher levels of education (Abramson and Claggett 1992; Silver, Anderson, and Abramson 1986). Thus, the positive relationship with education reported here may be artificially inflated, and a real relationship between race and electoral participation may be obscured by overreporting among black respondents. After including these variables in the model, however, the key estimates for AFDC and SSDI should be unbiased.

3. McMiller (1995) presents consistent results using a different national sample and a different set of control variables. McMiller concludes that "means-tested welfare dependency significantly reduces participation" in both traditional and nontraditional forms of political activity (19).

4. On this point, my findings are again consistent with those of Sarat (1990, 352): "Unable to transcend the welfare bureaucracy by going to legal services, [the client] is unable to transcend or leave behind the self constituted by being on welfare. Whether talking to a caseworker or a lawyer he is caught yet again, only this time he is, and can be, no more than 'just a welfare recipient.' "

5. The four activists in the AFDC are somewhat less helpful for addressing this question because with a cross-sectional design one cannot know whether their feelings of efficacy or their activism came first. As a result, evidence of a relationship could only point toward a trivial conclusion: people who are politically involved are more likely to believe involvement worthwhile.

6. Probability levels in this and the next paragraph are based on Fisher's exact tests.

Chapter 8

1. Although this characteristic sets welfare claiming apart from most conventional forms of political participation, personalized responses are also generally a property of political "contacting" activities (see Verba and Nie 1972).

2. Piven and Cloward (1993) are frequently cited to suggest that welfare provision can function to pacify the poor. This point, however, is only one part of the more complex analysis found in their work. Consistent with the argument made here, Piven and Cloward suggest that welfare institutions serve, in their own right, as important and effective sites of politics for the poor. While the historical period of my analysis leads me to treat welfare participation as an element of survival politics, Piven and Cloward point to its additional potential to serve as an element of confrontational politics: "A great rise in applications for welfare can express defiance, although this is not always the case. . . . Mass defiance need not be organized or led, or even widely noticed, except in the form of official statistics reporting sharp rises in application rates . . . If there is anything distinctive about our work, it is that we assign political meaning to forms of lower-class action that are typically viewed as inchoate" (464–65).

3. For consistency of presentation, and because of this study's time period, I continue to refer to this program as AFDC. Changes in policy design under the newer TANF program receive more attention in the final section of this chapter.

4. As many observers have noted, the terms *insurance* and *contract* in this context are largely metaphorical. The image of insurance earned through contributions and protected by a contractual agreement has served as a (mainly successful) political fiction designed to protect social-insurance provision in the United States (see Cates 1983; Fraser and Gordon 1994, 322; Gordon 1994, 295; Hasenfeld, Rafferty, and Zald 1987, 400).

5. Piven (1990, 250, 254) writes that an overemphasis on the state as an agent of social control is "based on a series of misleading and simplistic alternatives. On the one hand, there is the possibility of power and autonomy; on the other, dependence on a controlling state. But these polarities are unreal: All social relationships involve elements of social control, and yet there is no possibility for power except in social relationships. . . . The availability of benefits and services reduces the dependence of younger women with children on male breadwinners, as it reduces the dependence of older women on adult children. The same holds in the relations of working women with employers." Similarly, Gordon (1990, 195) argues that "an accurate view of the meanings of [the welfare state's] outside intervention into the family must maintain in its analysis, as the women clients did in their strategic decisions, awareness of a tension between various forms of social control and the variety of factors that might contribute to improvements in personal life."

6. Because of the nature of my evidence, I focus here on the policy-design recommendations of the new paternalism, leaving aside its claim that the poor are too incompetent to function as full citizens. There are, however, important reasons why this premise, on its face, should raise concerns. As Smiley (1999) points out, the label of incompetence can be applied in a manner that is consistent with democratic values, but in this case, the use of this label merits close scrutiny. A judgment of incompetence is being applied to an entire social category of people. The criteria that determine who qualifies as a competent citizen are poorly specified. Little attention is given to the question of who has the authority to set such criteria. And finally, little systematic evidence is offered to confirm that individuals in the group fail to meet the criteria. Thus, the broad attributions of incompetence that serve as the starting point for the new paternalism require far more normative and empirical justification than has been produced to date. Purely as a matter of personal judgment, I find it hard to square such sweeping generalizations with the remarkable amount of heterogeneity I found among the AFDC recipients I met at the shelter and interviewed for this project.

7. This insight is equally emphasized in theories of social control. Piven and Cloward (1993) argue that the political importance of welfare policy lies not only in its manifest content but also in its dramaturgical properties. Welfare policies convey important messages about status to welfare recipients and their fellow citizens.

Bibliography

Aberbach, Joel, Robert Putnam, and Bert A. Rockman. 1981. *Bureaucrats and Politicians in Western Democracies.* Cambridge: Harvard University Press.

Abrahams, Naomi. 1992. "Towards Reconceptualizing Political Action." *Sociological Inquiry* 62 (3): 327–47.

Abramovitz, Mimi. 1988. *Regulating the Lives of Women: Social Welfare Policy from Colonial Times to the Present.* Boston: South End Press.

Abramson, Paul R. 1983. *Political Attitudes in America: Formation and Change.* San Francisco: W. H. Freeman.

Abramson, Paul R., and William Claggett. 1992. "The Quality of Record Keeping and Racial Differences in Validated Turnout." *Journal of Politics* 54 (3): 871–80.

Adler, Patricia A., and Peter Adler. 1987. *Membership Roles in Field Research.* Newbury Park, CA: Sage.

Albelda, Randy, and Chris Tilly. 1997. *Glass Ceilings and Bottomless Pits: Women's Work, Women's Poverty.* Boston: South End Press.

Albrecht, Gary L. 1992. *The Disability Business: Rehabilitation in America.* Newbury Park, CA: Sage.

Albrecht, S. L., and K. E. Carpenter. 1976. "Attitudes as Predictors of Behavior versus Behavioral Intention: A Convergence of Research Traditions." *Sociometry* 39: 1–10.

Alcabes, Abraham, and James A. Jones. 1985. "Structural Determinants of 'Clienthood.'" *Social Work* 30 (1): 49–53.

Aldrich, John H., and Forrest D. Nelson. 1986. *Linear Probability, Logit, and Probit Models.* Beverly Hills, CA: Sage.

Almond, Gabriel A., and Harold D. Lasswell. 1934. "Aggressive Behavior by Clients toward Public Relief Administrators: A Configurative Analysis." *American Political Science Review* 28:643–55.

Almond, Gabriel A., and Sidney Verba. 1963. *The Civic Culture.* Princeton: Princeton University Press.

Amott, Theresa L. 1990. "Black Women and AFDC: Making Entitlement Out of Necessity." In *Women, the State, and Welfare,* ed. Linda Gordon, 280–300. Madison: University of Wisconsin Press.

Anechiarico, Frank. 1998. "Administrative Culture and Civil Society: A Comparative Perspective." *Administration and Society* 30 (1): 13–34.

Bachrach, Peter. 1967. *The Theory of Democratic Elitism.* Boston: Little, Brown.

Bachrach, Peter, and Morton S. Baratz. 1962. "The Two Faces of Power." *American Political Science Review* 56:947–52.

223

Bane, Mary Jo, and David T. Ellwood. 1994. *Welfare Realities: From Rhetoric to Reform.* Cambridge: Harvard University Press.

Banfield, Edward C. 1974. *The Unheavenly City Revisited.* Boston: Little, Brown.

Barbalet, J. M. 1988. *Citizenship: Rights, Struggle, and Class Inequality.* Minneapolis: University of Minnesota Press.

Barber, Benjamin. 1984. *Strong Democracy: Participatory Politics for a New Age.* Berkeley: University of California Press.

Barnes, Samuel, and Max Kaase. 1979. *Political Action: Mass Participation in Five Western Democracies.* Beverly Hills, CA: Sage.

Basow, Susan. 1992. *Gender: Stereotypes and Roles.* New York: Brooks/Cole.

Bassuk, Ellen, Angela Browne, and John C. Buckner. 1996. "Single Mothers and Welfare." *Scientific American* 275:60–67.

Becker, Howard S. 1998. *Tricks of the Trade: How to Think about Your Research while You're Doing It.* Chicago: University of Chicago Press.

Beeghley, Leonard. 1989. *The Structure of Social Stratification in the United States.* Boston: Allyn and Bacon.

Behrman, Jere R., and Paul Taubman. 1990. "The Intergenerational Correlation between Children's Adult Earnings and Their Parents' Income: Results from the Michigan Panel Study of Income Dynamics." *Review of Income and Wealth* 36:115–27.

Benello, C. George, and Dimitros Roussopoulos. 1971. *The Case for Participatory Democracy: Some Prospects for a Radical Society.* New York: Viking.

Benhabib, Seyla. 1987. "The Generalized and the Concrete Other: The Kohlberg-Gilligan Controversy and Feminist Theory." In *Feminism as Critique: On the Politics of Gender,* ed. Seyla Benhabib and Drucilla Cornell, 77–95. Minneapolis: University of Minnesota Press.

Bennett, Susan D. 1995. "'No Relief but upon the Terms of Coming into the House': Controlled Spaces, Invisible Disentitlements, and Homelessness in an Urban Shelter System." *Yale Law Journal* 104 (8): 2157–2212.

Berg, Bruce. 1998. *Qualitative Research Methods for the Social Sciences.* Boston: Allyn and Bacon.

Berger, Peter L., and Thomas Luckman. 1967. *The Social Construction of Reality: A Treatise in the Sociology of Knowledge* Garden City, NY: Anchor.

Bergmann, Barbara R. 1996. *Saving Our Children from Poverty: What the U.S. Can Learn from France.* New York: Sage.

Berry, Jeffrey M., Kent E. Portnoy, and Ken Thomson. 1991. "The Political Behavior of Poor People." In *The Urban Underclass,* ed. Christopher Jencks and Paul E. Peterson, 357–73. Washington, DC: Brookings Institution.

Berry, Jeffrey M., Kent E. Portnoy, and Ken Thomson. 1993. *The Rebirth of Urban Democracy.* Washington, DC: Brookings Institution.

Besharov, Douglas, and Karen Gardiner. 1996. "Paternalism and Welfare Reform." *Public Interest* 122:70–84.

Blank, Rebecca M. 1997. *It Takes a Nation: A New Agenda for Fighting Poverty.* Princeton: Princeton University Press.

Blank, Rebecca M., and Patricia Ruggles. 1993. *When Do Women Use AFDC and Food Stamps? The Dynamics of Eligibility and Participation.* NBER Working Paper Series 4429. Cambridge, MA: National Bureau of Economic Research.

Block, Fred, and Jeff Manza. 1997. "Could We End Poverty in a Postindustrial Society? The Case for a Progressive Negative Income Tax." *Politics and Society* 25 (4): 473–511.

Blumer, Herbert. 1966. "Sociological Implications of the Thought of George Herbert Mead." *American Journal of Sociology* 71:535–44.

Blumer, Herbert. 1969. *Symbolic Interactionism: Perspective and Method.* Berkeley: University of California Press.

Brodkin, Evelyn Z. 1992. "The Organization of Disputes: The Bureaucratic Construction of Welfare Rights and Wrongs." *Studies in Law, Politics, and Society* 12:53–76.

Brown, Michael K. 1999. *Race, Money, and the American Welfare State.* Ithaca: Cornell University Press.

Cain, Bruce, John Ferejohn, and Morris P. Fiorina. 1987. *The Personal Vote: Constituency Service and Electoral Independence.* Cambridge: Harvard University Press.

Calvert, Randall L. 1985. "The Value of Biased Information: A Rational Choice Model of Political Advice." *Journal of Politics* 47:530–55.

Campbell, Angus, Philip Converse, Warren Miller, and Donald Stokes. 1960. *The American Voter.* New York: Wiley.

Campbell, Angus, Gerald Gurin, and Warren Miller. 1954. *The Voter Decides.* Evanston, IL: Row, Peterson.

Carmines, Edward G., and James H. Kuklinski. 1990. "Incentives, Opportunities, and the Logic of Public Opinion in American Political Representation." In *Information and Democratic Processes,* ed. J. A. Ferejohn and J. H. Kuklinski, 240–68. Urbana: University of Illinois Press.

Casey, Timothy, and Mary Mannix. 1986. *Quality Control and the "Churning Crisis."* New York: Center on Social Welfare Policy and Law.

Cates, Jerry R. 1983. *Insuring Inequality: Administrative Leadership in Social Security, 1935–1954.* Ann Arbor: University of Michigan Press.

Chong, Dennis. 1993. "How People Think, Reason, and Feel about Rights and Liberties." *Journal of Politics* 37 (3): 867–99.

Chubb, John. 1983. *Interest Groups and the Bureaucracy.* Stanford: Stanford University Press.

Conway, M. Margaret. 1985. *Political Participation in the United States.* Washington, DC: CQ Press.

Conway, M. Margaret. 1991. "The Study of Political Participation: Past, Present, and Future." In *Political Science: Looking to the Future,* ed. William Crotty, 31–50. Evanston, IL: Northwestern University Press.

Cook, Terrence E., and Patrick M. Morgan. 1971. *Participatory Democracy.* San Francisco: Canfield.

Cook, Timothy E. 1985. "The Bear Market in Political Socialization and the Costs of Misunderstood Psychological Theories." *American Political Science Review* 79: 1079–93.

Cornelius, Wayne A. 1978. "Urbanization and Political Demand-Making: Political Participation among the Migrant Poor in Latin American Cities." In *The Citizen and Politics: A Comparative Perspective,* ed. Sidney Verba and Lucien Pye, 29–63. New York: Greylock.

CSAE. 1999. "Final Post Election Report." Washington, DC: Committee for the Study of the American Electorate.

Culpitt, Ian. 1992. *Welfare and Citizenship: Beyond the Crisis of the Welfare State.* Newbury Park, CA: Sage.

Dahl, Robert A. 1967. *Pluralist Democracy in the United States: Conflict and Consent.* Chicago: Rand McNally.

Dahl, Robert A. 1985. *A Preface to Economic Democracy.* Berkeley: University of California Press.

Danziger, Sheldon H., and Daniel H. Weinberg. 1994. "The Historical Record: Trends in Family Income, Inequality, and Poverty." In *Confronting Poverty: Prescriptions for Change*, ed. Sheldon Danziger, Gary Sandefur, and Daniel Weinberg, 18–50. Cambridge: Harvard University Press.

Davis, Martha F. 1993. *Brutal Need: Lawyers and the Welfare Rights Movement, 1960–1973.* New Haven: Yale University Press.

Delli Carpini, Michael, and Scott Keeter. 1996. *What Americans Know about Politics and Why It Matters.* New Haven: Yale University Press.

Derthick, Martha. 1990. *Agency under Stress: The Social Security Administration in American Government.* Washington, DC: Brookings Institution.

Dietz, Mary G. 1984. "Context Is All: Feminism and Theories of Citizenship." *Daedalus* 116 (4): 1–24.

Downs, Anthony. 1957. *An Economic Theory of Democracy.* New York: Harper and Row.

Eagly, Alice H., and Shelly Chaiken. 1993. *The Psychology of Attitudes.* New York: Harcourt Brace Jovanovich.

Easton, David. 1965. *A Framework for Political Analysis.* Englewood Cliffs, NJ: Prentice-Hall.

Easton, David. 1971. *The Political System.* New York: Knopf.

Easton, David, and Jack Dennis. 1969. *Children in the Political System.* New York: McGraw-Hill.

Edelman, Murray. 1964. *The Symbolic Uses of Politics.* Urbana: University of Illinois Press.

Edelman, Murray. 1971. *Politics as Symbolic Action: Mass Arousal and Quiescence.* New York: Academic Press.

Edelman, Murray. 1977. *Political Language: Words That Succeed and Policies That Fail.* New York: Academic Press.

Edin, Kathryn J. 1995. "The Myths of Dependence and Self-Sufficiency: Women, Welfare, and Low-Wage Work." *Focus* 17 (2): 1–9.

Edin, Kathryn J., and Laura Lein. 1997. *Making Ends Meet: How Single Mothers Survive Welfare and Low-Wage Work.* New York: Sage.

Edwards, Bob, and Michael W. Foley. 1998. "Civil Society and Social Capital beyond Putnam." *American Behavioral Scientist* 42 (1): 124–39.

Ehrenreich, Barbara. 1995. "Battered Welfare Syndrome." *Time,* April 3, 82.

Ellwood, David T. 1988. *Poor Support: Poverty in the American Family.* New York: Basic Books.

England, Paula. 1993. "The Separative Self: Androcentric Bias in Neoclassical Assumptions." In *Beyond Economic Man: Feminist Theory and Economics,* ed. Marianne A. Ferber and Julie A. Nelson, 37–53. Chicago: University of Chicago Press.

Esping-Andersen, Gøsta. 1990. *Three Worlds of Welfare Capitalism.* Princeton: Princeton University Press.

Eulau, Heinz. 1986. *Politics, Self, and Society: A Theme and Variations.* Cambridge: Harvard University Press.

Feagin, Joe R. 1972. "America's Welfare Stereotypes." *Social Science Quarterly* 52:921–33.

Felstiner, William L. F., Richard L. Abel, and Austin Sarat. 1981. "The Emergence and Transformation of Disputes: Naming, Blaming, and Claiming . . ." *Law and Society Review* 15:631–54.

Fenno, Richard F. 1978. *Home Style: House Members in Their Districts.* Boston: Little, Brown.

Ferejohn, John A., and Morris P. Fiorina. 1974. "The Paradox of Not Voting: A Decision Theoretic Analysis." *American Political Science Review* 67:525–36.

Ferejohn, John A., and James H. Kuklinski. 1990. *Information and Democratic Processes.* Urbana: University of Illinois Press.

Fetterman, David M. 1989. *Ethnography: Step by Step.* Newbury Park, CA: Sage.

Finkel, Steven E. 1985. "Reciprocal Effects of Participation and Political Efficacy: A Panel Analysis." *American Journal of Political Science* 29:891–913.

Finkel, Steven E. 1987. "The Effects of Political Participation on Political Efficacy and Political Support." *Journal of Politics* 49:441–64.

Fiorina, Morris P. 1977. *Congress: Keystone of the Washington Establishment.* New Haven: Yale University Press.

Fishbein, Martin, and Icek Ajzen. 1975. *Belief, Attitude, Intention, and Behavior.* Reading, MA: Addison-Wesley.

Fox, Susan Anne. 1996. "'Let the Wheelchair Through!': An Intergroup Approach to Interability Communication." In *Social Groups & Identities,* ed. W. P. Robinson, 215–48. Oxford: Butterworth-Heinemann.

Fraser, Nancy. 1987. "Women, Welfare, and The Politics of Need Interpretation." *Hypatia* 2 (1): 103–21.

Fraser, Nancy. 1989. "Talking about Needs: Interpretive Contests as Political Conflicts in Welfare-State Societies." *Ethics* 99:291–313.

Fraser, Nancy, and Linda Gordon. 1993. "Contract versus Charity: Why Is There No Social Citizenship in the United States?" *Socialist Review* 22 (3): 45–67.

Fraser, Nancy, and Linda Gordon. 1994. "A Genealogy of Dependency: Tracing a Keyword of the U.S. Welfare State." *Signs: Journal of Women in Culture and Society* 19 (2): 309–36.

Freedberg, S. 1989. "Self-Determination: Historical Perspectives and Effects on Current Practice." *Social Work* 34 (1): 33–38.

Fukayama, Francis. 1995. *Trust: The Social Virtues and the Creation of Prosperity.* New York: Free Press.

Fullinwider, Robert K. 1988. "Citizenship and Welfare." In *Democracy and the Welfare State,* ed. Amy Gutmann, 261–78. Princeton: Princeton University Press.

Funiciello, Theresa. 1993. *Tyranny of Kindness: Dismantling the Welfare System to End Poverty in America.* New York: Atlantic Monthly Press.

Gaffaney, Timothy J. 1999. "A Democratic Approach to the Problem of Poverty." Paper presented at the annual meeting of the Western Political Science Association, March 25–27, Seattle.

Gamson, William A. 1992. *Talking Politics.* Cambridge: Cambridge University Press.

Garfinkel, Irwin. 1996. "Economic Security for Children: From Means Testing and Bifurcation to Universality." In *Social Policies for Children,* ed. I. Garfinkel, J. L. Hochschild, and S. S. McLanahan, 33–82. Washington, DC: Brookings Institution.

Geddes, Barbara. 1990. "How the Cases You Choose Affect the Answers You Get: Selection Bias in Comparative Politics." *Political Analysis* 2:131–50.

Gilder, George. 1981. *Wealth and Poverty.* New York: Basic Books.

Gilens, Martin. 1996. "'Race Coding' and White Opposition to Welfare." *American Political Science Review* 90 (3): 593–604.

Gilens, Martin. 1999. *Why Americans Hate Welfare: Race, Media, and the Politics of Antipoverty Policy.* Chicago: University of Chicago Press.

Gilligan, Carol. 1982. *In a Different Voice: Psychological Theory and Women's Development.* Cambridge: Harvard University Press.

Goffman, Erving. 1959. *The Presentation of Self in Everyday Life.* New York: Anchor Press.

Goffman, Erving. 1961. *Asylums: Essays on the Social Situation of Mental Patients and Other Inmates.* Chicago: Aldine.

Goffman, Erving. 1971. *Relations in Public.* New York: Basic Books.

Goffman, Erving. 1974. *Frame Analysis: An Essay on the Organization of Experience.* Boston: Northeastern University Press.

Goodban, Nancy. 1985. "The Psychological Impact of Being on Welfare." *Social Service Review* 59:403–22.

Goodsell, Charles T. 1977. "Bureaucratic Manipulation of Physical Symbols: An Empirical Study." *American Journal of Political Science* 21 (1): 79–91.

Goodsell, Charles T. 1980. "Client Evaluations of Three Welfare Programs: A Comparison of Three Welfare Programs." *Administration and Society* 12:123–36.

Goodsell, Charles T. 1981. "The Public Encounter and Its Study." In *The Public Encounter: Where State and Citizen Meet,* ed. Charles T. Goodsell, 3–20. Bloomington: Indiana University Press.

Goodsell, Charles T. 1984. "Welfare Waiting Rooms." *Urban Life* 12 (4): 467–77.

Goodsell, Charles T. 1985. *The Case for Bureaucracy: A Public Administration Polemic.* 2d ed. Chatham, NJ: Chatham House.

Gordon, Linda. 1988. "What Does Welfare Regulate?" *Social Research* 55 (4): 609–30.

Gordon, Linda. 1990. "Family Violence, Feminism, and Social Control." In *Women, the State, and Welfare,* ed. Linda Gordon, 178–98. Madison: University of Wisconsin Press.

Gordon, Linda. 1994. *Pitied but Not Entitled: Single Mothers and the History of Welfare.* New York: Free Press.

Gottschalk, Peter, Sara McLanahan, and Gary Sandefur. 1994. "The Dynamics and Intergenerational Transmission of Poverty and Welfare Participation." In *Confronting Poverty: Prescriptions for Change,* ed. Sheldon Danziger, Gary Sandefur, and Daniel Weinberg, 85–108. Cambridge: Harvard University Press.

Gould, Carol C. 1988. *Rethinking Democracy: Freedom and Social Cooperation in Politics, Economy, and Society.* Cambridge: Cambridge University Press.

Gould, Roger. 1993. "Collective Action and Network Structure." *American Sociological Review* 58:182–96.

Gouldner, Alvin. 1952. "Red Tape as a Social Problem." In *Reader in Bureaucracy,* ed. Robert K. Merton, Alisa P. Gray, Barbara Hockey, and Hanan C. Selvin, 410–18. New York: Free Press.

Granovetter, Mark. 1985. "Economic Action and Social Structure: The Problem of Embeddedness." *American Journal of Sociology* 91 (3): 481–510.

Green, David. 1993. *Reinventing Civil Society: The Rediscovery of Welfare without Politics.* London: Institute for Economic Affairs.

Greenberg, Edward S. 1986. *Workplace Democracy: The Political Effects of Participation.* Ithaca: Cornell University Press.

Gurin, Gerald, and Patricia Gurin. 1970. "Expectancy Theory in the Study of Poverty." *Journal of Social Issues* 26:83–104.

Gutek, Barbara. 1992. "Disputes and Dispute-Processing in Organizations." *Studies in Law, Politics, and Society* 12:31–52.

Hamilton, Dona Cooper, and Charles V. Hamilton. 1997. *The Dual Agenda: The African American Struggle for Civil and Economic Equality.* New York: Columbia University Press.

Handler, Joel F. 1986. *The Conditions of Discretion: Autonomy, Community, Bureaucracy.* New York: Sage.

Handler, Joel F. 1992. "Discretion: Power, Quiescence, and Trust." In *The Uses of Discretion,* ed. Keith Hawkins, 331–60. Oxford: Clarendon Press.

Handler, Joel F. 1995. *The Poverty of Welfare Reform.* New Haven: Yale University Press.

Handler, Joel F. 1996. *Down from Bureaucracy: The Ambiguity of Privatization and Empowerment.* Princeton: Princeton University Press.

Handler, Joel F., and Yeheskel Hasenfeld. 1991. *The Moral Construction of Poverty: Welfare Reform in America.* Newbury Park, CA: Sage.

Handler, Joel F., and Yeheskel Hasenfeld. 1997. *We the POOR People: Work, Poverty, and Welfare.* New Haven: Yale University Press.

Handler, Joel F., and Jane Hollingsworth. 1971. *The "Deserving Poor": A Study of Welfare Administration.* Chicago: Markham.

Hardy-Fanta, Carol. 1993. *Latina Politics, Latino Politics.* Philadelphia: Temple University Press.

Harris, Deborah. 1988. "Child Support for Welfare Families: Family Policy Trapped in Its Own Rhetoric." *Review of Law and Social Change* 16 (4): 619–57.

Hartman, Ann. 1993. "The Professional Is Political." *Social Work* 38 (4): 365–66.

Hasenfeld, Yeheskel. 1985. "Citizens' Encounters with Welfare State Bureaucracies." *Social Service Review* 59 (December): 622–35.

Hasenfeld, Yeheskel. 1987. "Power in Social Work Practice." *Social Service Review* 61 (September): 469–83.

Hasenfeld, Yeheskel, Jane Rafferty, and Mayer Zald. 1987. "The Welfare State, Citizenship, and Bureaucratic Encounters." *Annual Review of Sociology* 13:387–414.

Hasenfeld, Yeheskel, and Daniel Steinmetz. 1981. "Client-Official Encounters in Social Service Agencies." In *The Public Encounter: Where State and Citizen Meet,* ed. Charles T. Goodsell, 83–101. Bloomington: Indiana University Press.

Head Start Bureau. 1992. *Head Start Program Performance Standards.* Washington, DC: U.S. Department of Health and Human Services.

Heclo, Hugh. 1994. "Poverty Politics." In *Confronting Poverty: Prescriptions for*

Change, ed. Sheldon Danziger, Gary Sandefur, and Daniel Weinberg, 396–437. Cambridge: Harvard University Press.

Heclo, Hugh. 1995. "The Social Question." In *Poverty, Inequality, and the Future of Social Policy,* ed. Katherine McFate, Roger Lawson, and William Julius Wilson, 665–91. New York: Sage.

Held, Virginia. 1990. "Mothering versus Contract." In *Beyond Self-Interest,* ed. Jane Mansbridge, 287–304. Chicago: University of Chicago Press.

Hibbing, John R., and Elizabeth Theiss-Morse. 1995. *Congress as Public Enemy: Public Attitudes toward American Political Institutions.* Cambridge: Cambridge University Press.

Hirsch, Amy E. 1988. "Income Deeming in the AFDC Program: Using Dual Track Family Law to Make Poor Women Poorer." *Review of Law and Social Change* 16 (4): 713–40.

Hochschild, Jennifer L. 1981. *What's Fair? American Beliefs about Distributive Justice.* Cambridge: Harvard University Press.

Hochschild, Jennifer L. 1993. "Disjunction and Ambivalence in Citizens' Political Outlooks." In *Reconsidering the Democratic Public,* ed. George Marcus and Russell Hanson, 187–210. University Park: Pennsylvania State University Press.

Hochschild, Jennifer L. 1995. *Facing Up to the American Dream.* Princeton: Princeton University Press.

Houppert, Karen. 1999. "You're Not Entitled!" *The Nation* 269 (13): 11–18.

Howards, Irving, Henry P. Brehm, and Saad Z. Nagi. 1980. *Disability: From Social Problem to Federal Program.* New York: Praeger.

Huckfeldt, Robert, Paul Allen Beck, Russell J. Dalton, and Jeffrey Levine. 1995. "Political Environments, Cohesive Social Groups, and the Communication of Public Opinion." *American Journal of Political Science* 39 (4): 1025–54.

Huckfeldt, Robert, and John Sprague. 1993. "Citizens, Contexts, and Politics." In *Political Science: The State of the Discipline II,* ed. Ada Finifter, 281–303. Washington, DC: American Political Science Association.

Huckfeldt, Robert, and John Sprague. 1995. *Citizens, Politics, and Social Communication: Information and Influence in an Election Campaign.* New York: Cambridge University Press.

Hummel, Ralph. 1977. *The Bureaucratic Experience.* New York: St. Martin's.

Hutchens, Robert. 1981. "Entry and Exit Transitions in a Government Transfer Program: The Case of Aid to Families with Dependent Children." *Journal of Human Resources* 16 (2): 217–37.

Hyman, Herbert. 1959. *Political Socialization.* Glencoe, IL: Free Press.

Ingram, Helen, and Steven Rathgeb Smith. 1993. *Public Policy for Democracy.* Washington, DC: Brookings Institution.

Jackman, Robert W. 1993. "Rationality and Political Participation." *American Journal of Political Science* 37 (1): 279–90.

Jackson, John E., ed. 1990. *Institutions in American Society: Essays on Market, Political, and Social Organizations.* Ann Arbor: University of Michigan Press.

Jargowsky, Paul A. 1997. *Poverty and Place: Ghettos, Barrios, and the American City.* New York: Sage.

Jencks, Christopher, and Susan E. Mayer. 1990. "The Social Consequences of Growing

Up in a Poor Neighborhood." In *Inner-City Poverty in the United States,* ed. Lawrence E. Lynn Jr. and Michael G. H. McGeary, 48–72. Washington, DC: National Academy Press.

Jencks, Christopher, and Paul E. Peterson, eds. 1991. *The Urban Underclass.* Washington, DC: Brookings Institution.

Johannes, John R. 1984. "Congress, the Bureaucracy, and Casework." *Administration and Society* 16 (1): 41–69.

Jones, Kathleen B. 1988. "Towards the Revision of Politics." In *The Political Interests of Gender: Developing Theory and Research with a Feminist Face,* ed. Kathleen B. Jones and Anna G. Jónasdóttir, 11–32. London: Sage.

Jones, Kathleen B. 1990. "Citizenship in a Woman-Friendly Polity." *Signs: Journal of Women in Culture and Society* 15 (4): 781–812.

Jorgensen, Danny. 1989. *Participant Observation.* Newbury Park, CA: Sage.

Josephson, Jyl. 1997. "Public Policy as if Women Mattered: Improving the Child Support System for Women in AFDC." *Women and Politics* 17 (1): 1–26.

Kane, Thomas J. 1987. "Giving Back Control: Long-Term Poverty and Motivation." *Social Service Review* 61:405–18.

Kaplan, Abraham. 1964. *The Conduct of Inquiry: Methodology for Behavioral Science.* San Francisco: Chandler.

Katz, Daniel, Barbara A. Gutek, Robert L. Kahn, and Eugenia Barton. 1975. *Bureaucratic Encounters.* Ann Arbor: University of Michigan Press.

Katz, Michael B. 1986. *In the Shadow of the Poorhouse.* New York: Basic Books.

Katz, Michael B. 1989. *The Undeserving Poor: From the War on Poverty to the War on Welfare.* New York: Pantheon.

Katz, Michael B. 1995. *Improving Poor People.* Princeton: Princeton University Press.

Kaufman, Herbert. 1981. *The Administrative Behavior of Federal Bureau Chiefs.* Washington, DC: Brookings Institution.

Keiser, Lael R. 1996. "Bureaucracy, Politics, and Public Policy: The Case of Child Support." Ph.D. diss., University of Wisconsin-Milwaukee.

Keiser, Lael R., and Joe Soss. 1998. "With Good Cause: Bureaucratic Discretion and Child Support Enforcement." *American Journal of Political Science* 42 (4): 1133–57.

Kerr, S. 1982. "Deciding about Supplementary Pensions: A Provisional Model." *Journal of Social Policy* 11:505–17.

Kerr, S. 1983. *Making Ends Meet: An Investigation into the Non-Claiming of Supplementary Pensions.* London: Bedford Square Press.

Kerwin, Cornelius M. 1994. *Rulemaking: How Government Agencies Write Law and Make Policy.* Washington, DC: CQ Press.

Kinder, Donald, and Lynn Sanders. 1996. *Divided by Color: Racial Politics and Democratic Ideals.* Chicago: University of Chicago Press.

King, Desmond S., and Jeremy Waldron. 1988. "Citizenship, Social Citizenship, and the Defence of Welfare Provision." *British Journal of Political Science* 18:415–43.

King, Gary, Robert O. Keohane, and Sidney Verba. 1994. *Designing Social Inquiry: Scientific Inference in Qualitative Research.* Princeton: Princeton University Press.

Kirk, Jerome, and Marc Miller. 1986. *Reliability and Validity in Qualitative Research.* Newbury Park, CA: Sage.

Kluegel, James R., and Eliot R. Smith. 1986. *Beliefs about Inequality: Americans' Views of What Is and What Ought to Be.* New York: Aldine de Gruyter.

Knoke, David. 1990. "Networks of Political Action: Toward Theory Construction." *Social Forces* 68 (4): 1041–63.

Kritzer, Herbert. 1996. "The First Thing We Do, Let's "Replace" All the Lawyers: Lawyers and Non-Lawyers as Advocates." Unpublished ms.

Kronebusch, Karl, and Laura Tiehen. 1996. "Measuring the Implementation of AFDC and SSI: Fair to Minorities? Fair to the Poor?" Paper presented at the annual meeting of the American Political Science Association, August 28–September 1, San Francisco.

Krueger, Richard. 1994. *Focus Groups: A Practical Guide for Applied Research.* Thousand Oaks, CA: Sage.

Kuklinski, James H. 1990. "Information and the Study of Politics." In *Information and Democratic Processes,* ed. John A. Ferejohn and James H. Kuklinski, 391–95. Urbana: University of Illinois Press.

Lane, Robert E. 1959. *Political Life: Why People Get Involved in Politics.* Glencoe, IL: Free Press.

Lane, Robert E. 1962. *Political Ideology: Why the American Common Man Believes What He Does.* New York: Free Press.

Lasswell, Harold D. 1936. *Politics: Who Gets What, When, How?* New York: McGraw-Hill.

Lasswell, Harold D. 1979. *The Signature of Power: Buildings, Communication, and Policy.* New Brunswick, NJ: Transaction Books.

Lawson, Stephen F. 1976. *Black Ballots: Voting Rights in the South, 1944–1969.* New York: Columbia University Press.

Leacock, Eleanor Burke. 1971. *The Culture of Poverty: A Critique.* New York: Simon and Schuster.

Leighley, Jan. 1991. "Participation as a Stimulus of Political Conceptualization." *Journal of Politics* 53 (1): 198–211.

Lewis, Oscar. 1966. *La Vida: A Puerto Rican Family in the Culture of Poverty—San Juan and New York.* New York: Random House.

Lieberman, Robert. 1995. "Comment." *American Political Science Review* 89 (2): 437–41.

Lieberman, Robert. 1998. *Shifting the Color Line: Race and the American Welfare State.* Cambridge: Harvard University Press.

Liebow, Elliot. 1967. *Tally's Corner: The Lives of Negro Streetcorner Men.* Boston: Little, Brown.

Liebow, Elliot. 1993. *Tell Them Who I Am: The Lives of Homeless Women.* New York: Free Press.

Lin, Ann Chih. 1998. "Bridging Positivist and Interpretivist Approaches to Qualitative Methods." *Policy Studies Journal* 26 (1): 162–80.

Lineberry, Robert L. 1977. *American Public Policy.* New York: Harper and Row.

Lipsky, Michael. 1980. *Street-Level Bureaucracy: Dilemmas of the Individual in Public Services.* New York: Sage.

Lipsky, Michael. 1984. "Bureaucratic Disentitlement in Social Welfare Programs." *Social Science Review* 58 (March): 3–27.

Livneh, Hanoch. 1988. "A Dimensional Perspective on the Origin of Negative Attitudes Toward Persons with Disabilities." In *Attitudes Toward Persons with Disabilities*, ed. H. Yuker, 35–46. New York: Springer Publishing.

Lofland, John, and Lyn H. Lofland. 1995. *Analyzing Social Settings: A Guide to Qualitative Observation and Analysis*. Belmont, CA: Wadsworth.

Loseke, Donileen R. 1987. "Lived Realities and the Construction of Social Problems." *Symbolic Interaction* 10 (2): 229–43.

Lowi, Theodore J. 1964. "American Business, Public Policy, Case Studies, and Political Theory." *World Politics* 16:677–715.

Lubiano, Wahneema. 1992. "Black Ladies, Welfare Queens, and State Minstrels: Ideological War by Narrative Means." In *Race-ing Justice, En-gendering Power: Essays on Anita Hill, Clarence Thomas, and the Construction of Social Reality*, ed. Toni Morrison, 323–63. New York: Pantheon.

Luker, Kristin. 1996. *Dubious Conceptions: The Politics of Teenage Pregnancy*. Cambridge: Harvard University Press.

Luttbeg, Norman R. 1991. "Political Attitudes: A Historical Artifact or a Concept of Continuing Importance in Political Science?" In *Political Science: Looking to the Future*, ed. William Crotty, 13–30. Evanston, IL: Northwestern University Press.

Mannix, Mary R., Henry A. Freedman, and Natarlin R. Best. 1987. "The Good Cause Exception to the AFDC Child Support Requirement." *Clearinghouse Review* 21 (4): 339–46.

Mansbridge. Jane. 1980. *Beyond Adversarial Democracy*. Chicago: University of Chicago Press.

Mansbridge, Jane. 1999. "On the Idea that Participation Makes Better Citizens." In *Citizen Competence and Democratic Institutions*, ed. S. L. Elkin and K. E. Soltan, 291–325. University Park: Pennsylvania State University Press.

Marmor, Theodore R., Jerry L. Mashaw, and Philip L. Harvey. 1990. *America's Misunderstood Welfare State: Persistent Myths, Enduring Realities*. New York: Basic Books.

Marshall, T. H. 1964 [1949]. "Citizenship and Social Class." In *Class, Citizenship, and Social Development: Essays by T. H. Marshall*, ed. Seymour Martin Lipset, 65–122. Chicago: University of Chicago Press.

Marshall, T. H. 1972. "Value Problems of Welfare Capitalism." *Journal of Social Policy* 1 (1): 15–32.

Marston, Sallie A. 1993. "Citizen Action Programs and Participatory Politics in Tucson." In *Public Policy for Democracy*, ed. Helen Ingram and Steven Rathgeb Smith, 119–62. Washington, DC: Brookings Institution.

Martin, Elaine. 1986. "Consumer Evaluation of Human Services." *Social Policy and Administration* 20 (3): 185–200.

Marziali, Elsa. 1988. "The First Session: An Interpersonal Encounter." *Social Casework: The Journal of Contemporary Social Work* 69:23–27.

Massey, Douglas S., and Nancy A. Denton. 1993. *American Apartheid: Segregation and the Making of the Underclass*. Cambridge: Harvard University Press.

Mayhew, David R. 1974. *Congress: The Electoral Connection*. New Haven: Yale University Press.

McAdam, Doug. 1982. *Political Process and the Development of Black Insurgency, 1930–1970*. Chicago: University of Chicago Press.

McAdam, Doug, and Ronnelle Paulsen. 1993. "Specifying the Relationship between Social Ties and Activism." *American Journal of Sociology* 98:640–67.

McLanahan, Sara S. 1988. "Family Structure and Dependency: Early Transitions to Female Household Headships." *Demography* 25:1–16.

McMiller, Darryl. 1995. "The Effects of Economic Circumstances and Attitudes on Blacks' Political Attitudes and Participation." Paper presented at the annual meeting of the Midwest Political Science Association, April 6–8, Chicago.

Mead, Lawrence M. 1985. *Beyond Entitlement: The Social Obligations of Citizenship.* New York: Free Press.

Mead, Lawrence M. 1992. *The New Politics of Poverty: The Nonworking Poor in America.* New York: Basic Books.

Mead, Lawrence M. 1995. "An Administrative Approach to Welfare Reform." In *Welfare Reform: An Analysis of the Issues,* ed. Isabel V. Sawhill, 21–24. Washington, DC: Urban Institute.

Mead, Lawrence M. 1997a. "Citizenship and Social Policy: T. H. Marshall and Poverty." *Social Philosophy and Policy* 14 (2): 197–230.

Mead, Lawrence M., ed. 1997b. *The New Paternalism: Supervisory Approaches to Poverty.* Washington, DC: Brookings Institution.

Meier, Kenneth J. 1993. *Politics and the Bureaucracy: Policymaking in the Fourth Branch of Government.* Monterey, CA: Brooks/Cole.

Merelman, Richard. 1986. "Revitalizing Political Socialization." In *Political Psychology,* ed. Margaret Hermann, 279–319. San Francisco: Jossey-Bass.

Milbrath, Lester, and M. L. Goel. 1982. *Political Participation.* 2d ed. Washington, DC: University Press of America.

Miles, Matthew, and A. Michael Huberman. 1984. *Qualitative Data Analysis: A Sourcebook of New Methods.* Newbury Park, CA: Sage.

Miller, Warren E., Donald R. Kinder, and Steven J. Rosenstone. 1993. *American National Elections Study, 1992: Pre- and Post-Election Survey.* Ann Arbor, MI: Inter-University Consortium for Political and Social Research.

Mills, C. Wright. 1959. *The Sociological Imagination.* New York: Oxford University Press.

Mincy, Ronald B. 1994. "The Underclass: Concept, Controversy, and Evidence." In *Confronting Poverty: Prescriptions for Change,* ed. Sheldon Danziger, Gary Sandefur, and Daniel Weinberg, 109–46. Cambridge: Harvard University Press.

Mink, Gwendolyn. 1998. *Welfare's End.* Ithaca: Cornell University Press.

Moffitt, Robert. 1983. "An Economic Model of Welfare Stigma." *American Economic Review* 73 (5): 1023–35.

Moffitt, Robert. 1992. "Incentive Effects of the U.S. Welfare System: A Review." *Journal of Economic Literature* 30:1–61.

Mondak, Jeffrey. 1990. "Determinants of Coattail Voting." *Political Behavior* 12:265–88.

Monroe, Kristen Renwick. 1994. "'But What Else Could I Do?' Choice, Identity, and a Cognitive-Perceptual Theory of Ethical Political Behavior." *Political Psychology* 15 (2): 201–26.

Moon, David, George Serra, and Jonathan P. West. 1993. "Citizens' Contacts with Bureaucratic and Legislative Officials." *Political Research Quarterly* 46:931–41.

Morgan, David. 1997. *Focus Groups as Qualitative Research.* 2d ed. Newbury Park, CA: Sage.

Morgen, Sandra, and Ann Bookman. 1988. "Rethinking Women and Politics: An Introductory Essay." In *Women and the Politics of Empowerment,* ed. Ann Bookman and Sandra Morgen, 3–29. Philadelphia: Temple University Press.

Moynihan, Daniel P. 1969. *Maximum Feasible Misunderstanding: Community Action in the War on Poverty.* New York: Free Press.

Murray, Charles. 1984. *Losing Ground: American Social Policy.* New York: Basic Books.

Nelson, Barbara J. 1980. "Help-Seeking from Public Authorities: Who Arrives at the Agency Door?" *Policy Sciences* 12:175–92.

Nelson, Barbara J. 1981. "Client Evaluations of Social Programs." In *The Public Encounter: Where State and Citizen Meet,* ed. Charles T. Goodsell, 23–42. Bloomington: Indiana University Press.

Nelson, Barbara J. 1984. "Women's Poverty and Women's Citizenship: Some Political Consequences of Economic Marginality." *Signs: Journal of Women's Culture and Society* 10 (2): 209–31.

Nelson, Barbara J. 1990. "The Origins of the Two-Channel Welfare State: Workmen's Compensation and Mothers' Aid." In *Women, the State, and Welfare,* ed. Linda Gordon, 123–51. Madison: University of Wisconsin Press.

Newman, Katherine S. 1999. *No Shame in My Game: The Working Poor in the Inner City.* New York: Knopf.

Niemi, Richard, Stephen Craig, and Franco Mattei. 1991. "Measuring Internal Political Efficacy in the 1988 National Election Study." *American Political Science Review* 85 (4): 1407–13.

Noble, Charles. 1997. *Welfare as We Knew It: A Political History of the American Welfare State.* Oxford: Oxford University Press.

Olasky, Marvin. 1992. *The Tragedy of American Compassion.* Washington, DC: Regnery.

Oliker, Susan J. 1996. "The Proximate Contexts of Workfare and Work: A Framework for Studying Poor Women's Economic Choices." *Sociological Quarterly* 36 (2): 251–72.

Olson, Mancur. 1965. *The Logic of Collective Action.* Cambridge: Harvard University Press.

Osterman, Paul. 1991. "Welfare Participation in a Full Employment Economy: The Impact of Neighborhood." *Social Problems* 38 (4): 475–91.

Paden, Roger. 1992. "Welfare Policy and the Moral Depravity of the Poor." *Public Affairs Quarterly* 6:289–304.

Page, Benjamin I., and Robert Y. Shapiro. 1992. *The Rational Public: Fifty Years of Trends in Americans' Policy Preferences.* Chicago: University of Chicago Press.

Pateman, Carole. 1970. *Participation and Democratic Theory.* Cambridge: Cambridge University Press.

Patterson, James T. 1986. *America's Struggle against Poverty, 1900–1985.* Cambridge: Harvard University Press.

Pearce, Diana M. 1990. "Welfare Is Not *for* Women: Why the War on Poverty Cannot Conquer the Feminization of Poverty." In *Women, the State, and Welfare,* ed. Linda Gordon, 265–79. Madison: University of Wisconsin Press.

Peterson, Paul E. 1995. *The Price of Federalism.* Washington, DC: Brookings Institution.

Pierson, Paul. 1993. "When Effect Becomes Cause: Policy Feedback and Political Change." *World Politics* 45:595–628.

Pitkin, Hanna Fenichel. 1981. "Justice: On Relating Public and Private." *Political Theory* 9 (3): 327–52.

Pitkin, Hanna Fenichel, and Sara M. Shumer. 1982. "On Participation." *Democracy* 2 (4): 43–54.

Piven, Frances Fox. 1990. "Ideology and the State: Women, Power, and the Welfare State." In *Women, the State, and Welfare,* ed. Linda Gordon, 250–64. Madison: University of Wisconsin Press.

Piven, Frances Fox. 1995. Foreword to *Words of Welfare: The Poverty of Social Science and the Social Science of Poverty,* by Sanford F. Schram, ix–xv. Minneapolis: University of Minnesota Press.

Piven, Frances Fox, and Richard A. Cloward. 1975. *The Politics of Turmoil.* New York: Vintage.

Piven, Frances Fox, and Richard A. Cloward. 1977. *Poor People's Movements.* New York: Vintage.

Piven, Frances Fox, and Richard A. Cloward. 1988. "Welfare Doesn't Shore Up Traditional Family Roles: A Reply to Linda Gordon." *Social Research* 55 (4): 631–47.

Piven, Frances Fox, and Richard A. Cloward. 1989. *Why Americans Don't Vote.* New York: Pantheon.

Piven, Frances Fox, and Richard A. Cloward. 1993 [1971]. *Regulating the Poor: The Functions of Public Welfare.* New York: Vintage.

Piven, Frances Fox, and Richard Cloward. 1997a. *The Breaking of the American Social Compact.* New York: New Press.

Piven, Frances Fox, and Richard Cloward. 1997b. "We Should Have Made a Plan!" *Politics and Society* 25 (4): 525–32.

Prottas, Jeffrey M. 1979. *People-Processing: The Street-Level Bureaucrat in Public Service Bureaucracies.* Lexington, MA: Lexington Books.

Putnam, Robert D. 1995. "Bowling Alone: America's Declining Social Capital." *Journal of Democracy* 6 (1): 65–78.

Putnam, Robert D., with Robert Leonardi and Raffaella Y. Nanetti. 1993. *Making Democracy Work: Civic Traditions in Modern Italy.* Princeton: Princeton University Press.

Quadagno, Jill S. 1994. *The Color of Welfare: How Racism Undermined the War on Poverty.* New York: Oxford University Press.

Ragin, Charles C. 1987. *The Comparative Method: Moving beyond Qualitative and Quantitative Strategies.* Berkeley: University of California Press.

Rainwater, Lee, and William L. Yancey. 1967. *The Moynihan Report and the Politics of Controversy.* Cambridge: MIT Press.

Rank, Mark R. 1994. *Living on the Edge: The Realities of Welfare in America.* New York: Columbia University Press.

Raphael, Jody. 1995. *Domestic Violence: Telling the Untold Welfare-to-Work Story.* Chicago: Taylor Institute.

Raphael, Jody. 1996. "Prisoners of Abuse: Policy Implementation of the Relationship between Domestic Violence and Welfare Receipt." *Clearinghouse Review* 1:186–94.

Rector, Robert, and William Lauber. 1995. *America's Failed $5.4 Trillion War on Poverty.* Washington, DC: Heritage Foundation.

Rector, Robert, and Sarah E. Youssef. 1999. *The Impact of Welfare Reform: The Trend in State Caseloads, 1985–1998.* Washington, DC: Heritage Foundation.

Rees, Stuart, and Alison Wallace. 1982. *Verdicts on Social Work.* London: E. Arnold.

Reich, Charles. 1964. "The New Property." *Yale Law Journal* 73 (5): 733–87.

Riker, William H., and Peter C. Ordeshook. 1968. "A Theory of the Calculus of Voting." *American Political Science Review* 62:25–42.

Roberts, Paula. 1991. *Turning Promises into Realities: A Guide to Implementing the Child Support Provisions of the Family Support Act of 1988.* 2nd ed. Washington, D.C.: Center for Law and Social Policy.

Rosenbaum, Alan S. 1986. *Coercion and Autonomy: Philosophical Foundations, Issues, and Practices.* New York: Greenwood.

Rosenberg, Morris. 1990. "The Self-Concept: Social Product and Social Force." In *Social Psychology: Sociological Perspectives,* ed. M. Rosenberg and R. Turner, 593–624. New Brunswick, NJ: Transaction Books.

Rosenblatt, Rand E. 1982. "Legal Entitlement and Welfare Benefits." In *The Politics of Law: A Progressive Critique,* ed. David Kairys, 262–78. New York: Pantheon.

Rosenbloom, David H., and Rosemary O'Leary. 1997. *Public Administration and Law.* 2d ed. New York: Marcel Dekker.

Rosenstone, Steven J., and John Mark Hansen. 1993. *Mobilization, Participation, and Democracy in America.* New York: Macmillan.

Sapiro, Virginia. 1990. "The Gender Basis of American Social Policy." In *Women, the State, and Welfare,* ed. Linda Gordon, 36–54. Madison: University of Wisconsin Press.

Sapiro, Virginia. 1993. "'Private' Coercion and Democratic Theory: The Case of Gender-Based Violence." In *Reconsidering the Democratic Public,* ed. George Marcus and Russell Hanson, 427–50. University Park: Pennsylvania State University Press.

Sapiro, Virginia. 1994. "Political Socialization during Adulthood: Clarifying the Political Time of Our Lives." *Research in Micropolitics* 4:197–223.

Sarat, Austin. 1990. "'The Law Is All Over': Power, Resistance and the Legal Consciousness of the Welfare Poor." *Yale Journal of Law and the Humanities* 2:343–79.

Scheff, Thomas J. 1968. "Negotiating Reality: Notes on Power in the Assessment of Responsibility." *Social Problems* 16 (1): 3–17.

Schlozman, Kay Lehman, and John T. Tierney. 1986. *Organized Interests and American Democracy.* New York: Harper & Row.

Schlozman, Kay Lehman, and Sidney Verba. 1979. *Injury to Insult: Unemployment, Class, and Political Response.* Cambridge: Harvard University Press.

Schneider, Anne, and Helen Ingram. 1993. "Social Construction of Target Populations." *American Political Science Review* 87 (2): 334–47.

Schneider, Anne, and Helen Ingram. 1995. "Response." *American Political Science Review* 89 (2): 441–46.

Schneider, Anne, and Helen Ingram. 1997. *Policy Design for Democracy.* Lawrence: University of Kansas Press.

Schram, Sanford F. 1995. *Words of Welfare: The Poverty of Social Science and the Social Science of Poverty.* Minneapolis: University of Minnesota Press.

Schram, Sanford F., and Joe Soss. 1998. "Making Something Out of Nothing: Welfare Reform and a New Race to the Bottom." *Publius* 28 (3): 67–88.

Schram, Sanford F., and Joe Soss. 1999. "The Real Value of Welfare: Why There Is No Welfare Migration." *Politics & Society* 27 (1): 39–66.

Schwartz, Barry. 1975. *Queuing and Waiting: Studies in the Social Organization of Access and Delay.* Chicago: University of Chicago Press.

Schwarz, John E. 1997. *Illusions of Opportunity: The American Dream in Question.* New York: Norton.

Scott, James C. 1985. *Weapons of the Weak: Everyday Forms of Peasant Resistance.* New Haven: Yale University Press.

Scott, James. 1990. *Domination and the Arts of Resistance.* New Haven: Yale University Press.

Seccombe, Karen. 1999. *So You Think I Drive a Cadillac? Welfare Recipients' Perspectives on the System and Its Reform.* Boston: Allyn and Bacon.

Seidman, Harold. 1986. *Politics, Position, and Power.* New York: New York University Press.

Shapiro, Robert, and John Young. 1989. "Public Opinion and the Welfare State: The United States in Comparative Perspective." *Political Science Quarterly* 104:59–89.

Sheingold, Carl A. 1973: "Social Networks and Voting: The Resurrection of a Research Agenda." *American Sociological Review* 38:712–20.

Silver, Brian D., Barbara Anderson, and Paul R. Abramson. 1986. "Who Overreports Voting?" *American Political Science Review* 80 (2): 613–24.

Simon, Herbert. 1985. "Human Nature in Politics: The Dialogue of Psychology with Political Science." *American Political Science Review* 79:293–304.

Singerman, Diane. 1995. *Avenues of Participation: Family, Politics, and Networks in Urban Quarters of Cairo.* Princeton: Princeton University Press.

Skocpol, Theda. 1992a. *Protecting Soldiers and Mothers: The Political Origins of Social Policy in the United States.* Cambridge: Harvard University Press.

Skocpol, Theda. 1992b. *Social Policy in the United States: Future Possibilities in Historical Perspective.* Princeton: Princeton University Press.

Smiley, Marion. 1989. "Paternalism and Democracy." *Journal of Value Inquiry* 23:299–318.

Smiley, Marion. 1999. "Democratic Citizenship: A Question of Competence?" In *Citizen Competence and Democratic Institutions,* ed. S. L. Elkin and K. E. Soltan, 371–83. University Park: Pennsylvania State University Press.

Smith, Steven Rathgeb, and Helen Ingram. 1993. "Public Policy and Democracy." In *Public Policy for Democracy,* ed. Helen Ingram and Steven Rathgeb Smith, 1–18. Washington, DC: Brookings Institution.

Snow, David A., and Robert Benford. 1992. "Master Frames and Cycles of Protest." In *Frontiers of Social Movement Theory,* ed. Carol Mueller and Aldon Morris, 133–55. New Haven: Yale University Press.

Snow, David A., Burke Rochford, Steven Worden, and Robert Benford. 1986. "Frame Alignment Processes, Micromobilizations, and Movement Participation." *American Sociological Review* 51:464–81.

Solomon, Barbara. 1976. *Black Empowerment: Social Work in Oppressed Communities.* New York: Columbia University Press.

Solon, Gary. 1992. "Intergenerational Income Mobility in the United States." *American Economic Review* 82 (3): 393–408.

Solow, Robert M. 1998. *Work and Welfare*. Princeton, NJ: Princeton University Press.

Soss, Joe, and Lael Keiser. 1999. "Challenged Bureaucracies: The Politics of Disability Applications and Appeals." Paper presented at the annual meeting of the Midwest Political Science Association, April 15–17, Chicago.

Spalter-Roth, Roberta M., and Heidi I. Hartmann. 1994. "AFDC Recipients as Care-Givers and Workers: A Feminist Approach to Income Security Policy for American Women." *Social Politics* 1 (2): 190–210.

Sparer, Edward. 1970. "The Right to Welfare." In *The Rights of Americans: What They Are—What They Should Be,* ed. Norman Dorsen, 65–93. New York: Pantheon.

Spencer, Herbert. 1880. *Social Statics*. New York: D. Appleton.

Spradley, James P. 1979. *The Ethnographic Interview*. Fort Worth: Holt, Rinehart, and Winston.

Stack, Carol B. 1974. *All Our Kin: Strategies for Survival in a Black Community*. New York: Harper and Row.

Stack, Carol B. 1987. "A Critique of Method in the Assessment of Policy Impact." *Research in Social Problems and Public Policy* 4:137–47.

Stone, Deborah A. 1984. *The Disabled State*. Philadelphia: Temple University Press.

Strauss, Anselm. 1987. *Qualitative Analysis for Social Scientists*. Cambridge: Cambridge University Press.

Trattner, Walter. 1989. *From Poor Law to Welfare State: A History of Social Welfare in America*. New York: Free Press.

Turner, John C., Michael A. Hogg, Penelope J. Oakes, S. D. Reicher, and Margaret S. Wetherell. 1987. *Rediscovering the Social Group*. New York: Basil Blackwell.

Tussing, A. Dale. 1974. "The Dual Welfare System." *Society* 11:50–57.

Tussing, A. Dale. 1975. *Poverty in a Dual Economy*. New York: St. Martin's.

U.S. Census Bureau. 1998. *Statistical Abstract of the United States*. Washington, DC: U.S. Government Printing Office.

U.S. House of Representatives. Committee on Ways and Means. 1998. *The Green Book*. Washington, DC: U.S. Government Printing Office.

van Krieken, Robert. 1991. "The Poverty of Social Control: Explaining Power in Historical Sociology of the Welfare State." *Sociological Review* 1:1–25.

van Oorschot, Wim. 1991. "Non-Take-Up of Social Security Benefits in Europe." *Journal of European Social Policy* 1 (1): 15–30.

Verba, Sidney. 1978. "The Parochial and the Polity." In *The Citizen and Politics: A Comparative Perspective,* ed. Sidney Verba and Lucien Pye, 3–28. New York: Greylock.

Verba, Sidney, and Norman Nie. 1972. *Participation in America*. New York: Harper and Row.

Verba, Sidney, Kay Lehman Schlozman, and Henry E. Brady. 1995. *Voice and Equality: Civic Voluntarism in American Politics*. Cambridge: Harvard University Press.

Verba, Sidney, Kay Lehman Schlozman, Henry Brady, and Norman H. Nie. 1993. "Citizen Activity: Who Participates? What Do They Say?" *American Political Science Review* 87 (2): 303–18.

Vobejda, Barbara, and Judith Havemann. 1996. "States Take Variety of Paths to Welfare Reform." *Washington Post,* October 6, A4.

Weatherford, Bernadyne. 1984. "The Disability Insurance Program: An Administrative

Attack on the Welfare State." In *The Attack on the Welfare State,* ed. Anthony Champagne and Edward J. Harpham, 37–60. Prospect Heights, IL: Waveland Press.

Weber, Max. 1946. "Bureaucracy." In *From Max Weber: Essays in Sociology,* ed. H. H. Gerth and C. Wright Mills, 196–266. New York: Oxford University Press.

Weir, Margaret. 1992. *Politics and Jobs: The Boundaries of Employment Policy in the United States.* Princeton: Princeton University Press.

West, Guida. 1981. *The National Welfare Rights Movement: The Social Protest of Poor Women.* New York: Praeger.

White, Lucie E. 1990. "Subordination, Rhetorical Survival Skills, and Sunday Shoes: Notes on the Hearing of Mrs. G." *Buffalo Law Review* 38 (1): 1–58.

Wilson, James Q. 1980. "The Politics of Regulation." In *The Politics of Regulation,* ed. James Q. Wilson, 357–94. New York: Basic Books.

Wilson, Laura A., Robert P. Stoker, and Dennis McGrath. 1999. "Welfare Bureaus as Moral Tutors: What Do Clients Learn from Paternalistic Welfare Reforms?" *Social Science Quarterly* 80 (3): 473–86.

Wilson, William Julius. 1987. *The Truly Disadvantaged.* Chicago: University of Chicago Press.

Witte, John F. 1980. *Democracy, Authority, and Alienation in Workers' Participation in an American Corporation.* Chicago: University of Chicago Press.

Wolin, Sheldon. 1989. *The Presence of the Past: Essays on the State and the Constitution.* Baltimore: Johns Hopkins University Press.

Wood, B. Dan, and Richard W. Waterman. 1994. *Bureaucratic Dynamics: The Role of Bureaucracy in a Demcracy.* Boulder: Westview Press.

Yin, Robert K. 1989. *Case Study Research: Design and Methods.* Newbury Park, CA: Sage.

Young, Rosalie. 1995. "Subsidized Legal Service Applicants: Perceptions of Legal and Political Issues." Paper presented at the annual meeting of the Law and Society Association, June 1, Toronto.

Yuker, Harold, ed. 1988. *Attitudes Toward Persons with Disabilities.* New York: Springer Publishing.

Zemans, Frances Kahn. 1983. "Legal Mobilization: The Neglected Role of the Law in the Political System." *American Political Science Review* 77:690–703.

Index

activists, 5, 61, 71, 139
advocates, 1, 16
African Americans, 21, 22, 181, 203; discrimination against, 5–6; as single mothers, 39; voting and, 161, 214n. 2
Aid to Families with Dependent Children (AFDC), 4, 5, 69, 87, 157, 201; abolition of, 18; application encounter and, 91–123; applications for, rejected, 70; casework relationships and, 30; client autonomy and, 31; client political activity and, 159–77, 184–85; clients' internal political efficacy and, 179–83; community organizations and, 78; comparative study and, 16, 17–19, 149–53, 191–95, 198; dependence and, 33–34, 36; economic security and, 47–52, 54–57; education level, of recipients, and, 205, 214n. 5; eligibility for, 60, 67, 73–74; government personnel and, 84; grievances and, 127–29; Head Start and, 177–79, 185; homeless families and, 20; identity and, 38–42; interviews, with clients of, 23; means testing and, 31, 47, 103, 133; obligation and, 43–44; participation in, lessons of, 129–37; personnel of, waiting for access to, 94–95, 96–100; service professionals and, 81–82; social citizenship and, 58; as topic of conversation, in poor communities, 75–77; welfare claiming and, 27; women, as clients of, 21, 183, 210n. 2, 214n. 5
alcohol, 23, 41, 114
American Dream, 56

Americans with Disabilities Act, 98
anonymity, sense of, 146–47, 149, 154, 194
antipoverty measures, 26
application encounter, 3–4, 90–91, 119–23, 189; clients' circumstances defined during, 107–12; clients' responses to, 91–94; group differences and, 116–19; information gathering during, 100–106; personal interaction during, 112–16; personnel, waiting for access to, and, 94–100. *See also* welfare claiming
Arendt, Hannah, 11
attitudes, behaviors and, 176–77
authoritarianism, 29
autonomy, 59, 154, 187, 194; community and, 88; confrontational politics and, 89; defined, 211n. 3; welfare system, two-tiered, and, 58

behaviors, attitudes and, 176–77
benefits, termination of: appointments, missed, and, 213n. 3; client challenges to, 138; Reagan administration and, 152; threats of, 129–30, 131, 145, 199
block grants, 18, 197
bureaucracy, 2, 5, 8, 26; application encounter and, 90; claims process and, 70; client satisfaction with, 92, 93, 94; clients' privacy and, 133; funding cuts and, 94; political demands and, 7; poverty, amelioration of, and, 188; power of, 31; self-presentation and, 156

bureaucrats, 84, 112; caseworkers, absence of, and, 147, 151, 155; clients' disputes with, 127–29, 129–30, 136–43; clients' personal interaction with, 112–16; clients' satisfaction with, 121–23; helpfulness of, 111, 114, 118–19, 147; power of, 29–30, 92, 100–101, 129, 130–31, 134

capitalism, 11, 120, 170
case reviews, 131, 144, 150, 152
case studies, multiple, 17–19
caseworkers. *See* bureaucrats
casework relationships, 17, 30, 130, 133–37
child care, 69, 95, 142, 186, 201
Child Protective Services (CPS), 85, 129, 167
children, 34, 43–44, 46, 73, 180; economic security and, 48–49; health care and, 51; nutrition and, 81; sexual abuse of, 35, 85; socialization of, 198; welfare agency waiting rooms and, 98–99; well-being of, 66. *See also* families
child support, 17, 44, 47, 131; Aid to Families with Dependent Children (AFDC) and, 101, 104–5; clients' grievances and, 138; Supplemental Security Income Program (SSI) and, 150; Temporary Assistance to Needy Families (TANF) and, 198–99; welfare, eligibility for, and, 212n. 7
churning, 213n. 2
citizens, 8, 10, 16; autonomy and, 36; democracy and, 183; marginalization of, 11; participation of, in political action, 27, 157, 195–203; privacy of, 100, 101–2; "public issues" and, 7; self-government and, 8; welfare claiming, political action, and, 187
citizenship, 3, 12, 184, 200; poor people and, 196, 197; quality of, 124, 196; representative democracy and, 6
civil rights, 6, 12, 193
civil society, 3, 14, 77, 78

class, 14, 119, 170, 190
clients (SSDI), grievances of, 150
clients (welfare recipients), 1, 65–66, 68–69, 107–12; age of, 18, 21, 117, 119, 128, 161; anonymity and, 146–47; application encounter, evaluation of, and, 90–94; choices of, 48–49; "client role" and, 90, 113, 114, 115, 124; decision making and, 124–25; degradation of, 92–93, 98, 105, 122; dilemmas of action and, 125–29, 137, 156; education level of, 21, 161, 175, 177–78, 182; fear, of caseworkers, and, 134; grievances of, 25, 126, 127, 129, 135, 137–43, 164; information gathering by, 66–68; institutional designs and, 18; interviews with, 2, 4–5, 20, 21, 22, 24, 34–36, 82–83, 141–43, 146, 164–65, 181; marginalization of, 156; as passive objects of management, 195; as political actors, 2, 159–77; public opinion against, 203; self-presentation of, 114–15, 120; socioeconomic status of, 117–18
clothing, 18
Cloward, Richard A., 6, 11, 158, 194
coercion, 200, 201
community, 32, 37, 88; defining problems and, 66; friends and neighbors as, 75–77; organizations in, 77–81; political groups as, 193; survival politics and, 61, 188; welfare claiming and, 187, 188
confrontational politics, 62, 71, 88–89, 195; health care and, 162–63; welfare applications and, 215n. 2
conservatives, 28, 77, 158
courts, 166, 167
crime/criminal behavior, 41, 187

data analysis, 24–25
day care centers, 22
decision making, 126, 127, 133, 142; clients' exclusion from, 124–25, 139, 165–66; institutional and individual, 130, 144

degradation rituals, 92–93, 105, 106, 120, 122

democracy, 1, 3, 6, 78, 158; design for, 15–16, 200; participatory theory and, 8–9, 10, 195–203; public policy and, 183–85

dependence, 2, 24, 29–37, 54, 77, 187; of claimants, resistance to, 68; cycle of, 110–11; escape from, 59; political involvement and, 158

determinism, 28

disability, 18, 46, 61, 84; associations with, 78; community and, 76–77; discrimination and, 51; employment options and, 49–50, 66; long-term, 42, 53; official definition of, 101; political activism and, 162–63; poverty and, 32; proof of status and, 41; social networks and, 71; as stigma, 38; support groups and, 18, 19, 23, 28, 113, 152; welfare, decision to apply for, and, 68

disadvantaged groups, 11, 12–13

discipline, 31, 37, 58, 200

discrimination, 51–52, 89

doctors, 69, 70, 79, 81–82, 84, 102

domestic abuse/violence, 3, 33–36, 42, 85; community advice and, 66; economic security and, 48; welfare claiming and, 51

drugs, 23, 34, 41, 114

economic security, 29, 46–57, 155, 195

Edin, Kathryn, 55–56

education, 22, 56, 110, 128, 142; access to, 58; capitalist market and, 12; clients' level of, 21, 161, 175, 177–78, 182; government, views of, and, 175; Head Start and, 177–78; socioeconomic status and, 71, 117; voting and, 214n. 2; welfare applicants' level of, 116–17

elected officials, 85–86, 159, 167

elections, 1, 161, 165, 209n. 1

eligibility: information gathering and, 105–6; maintaining benefits and, 132–33

embarrassment, 100

employment, 1–2, 12, 47; as option, 49–52, 57; unreported wages and, 54; worst forms of, 13

entitlement, sense of, 154, 194

ethnicity, 14, 205–6

European countries, social welfare in, 201, 203

factoring, data analysis and, 24

false consciousness, 121

families, 3, 14, 63; claiming process and, 72–75; dependence on, 36; homelessness and, 76, 78, 127; poverty and, 50, 187, 191; privacy and, 103–4. *See also* children; significant others

fear, feelings of, 61

feminism, 6, 8, 10, 33

fieldwork, 20, 21, 23, 76, 162, 210n. 4

food, 47, 65, 163, 188; inability to pay for, 66; shortages of, 201

food stamps, 38, 47, 114; access to, 199; eligibility for, 60, 75, 135

Fraser, Nancy, 7

friends/neighbors, claim process and, 75–77

gender, 14, 22, 52, 117, 119, 191

gifts, 47

government, 4, 25, 124–25, 153; citizens' demands on, 1, 2, 57, 120; civil society and, 78; clients' views of, 169–77; democracy and, 183; direct relationship with, 30, 90, 186; elements, administrative and political, of, 166; personnel within, 84–87; responsiveness of, 132, 164, 168, 192, 200, 210n. 2

grievances, 4, 9, 126, 127, 164; collective, 186; sense of futility and, 129, 135; willingness to voice, 25, 192

guilt, feelings of, 43

hardship, 65, 66, 107

Hardy-Fanta, Carol, 61, 70

Head Start, 21, 55, 139, 194; Aid to Families with Dependent Children (AFDC) and, 177–79, 185; decision making and, 140–42, 143, 150, 154; policy designs modeled on, 202

health care, 12, 18, 47, 162, 186; costs of, 32; jobs without, 49–50; significant others and, 52; universal health insurance and, 201

holding pattern strategy, 53–54

homelessness, 3, 42, 69, 168, 201; families and, 76, 78, 127; mental health and, 32; shelters and, 78, 127

housing, 12, 165

humiliation, 38, 43, 90, 102, 105, 120

identity, 24, 37–46

incarceration, 168

income bundling strategy, 53, 54, 55

income deeming, 103

individual agency, 27–28, 59, 62–63, 187

information gathering, 100–106, 150

institutionalization, 3, 42

interest groups, 174

Internal Revenue Service (IRS), 184

job training, 142

Johnson administration, 140, 177

judgmental sampling, 21

justice, 9, 12

Keiser, Lael, 87

knowledge, 71, 74, 75, 84

Latinas/Latinos, 21, 70, 138

lawyers, 69, 70, 82, 83, 181

liberals, 29

marketplace, 14

Marshall, T. H., 11, 12–13, 201

McGrath, Dennis, 199

Mead, Lawrence, 196

means testing: clients' education level and, 158; Aid to Families with Dependent Children (AFDC) and, 17, 31, 47, 103, 133; information gathering and,

103, 133; Supplemental Security Income Program (SSI) and, 150

media, 152, 200

Medicaid, 199

medical bills, 32, 52

Medicare, 167

men, 40–41, 44, 105, 117, 181

mental health, 32, 80, 108

minimum wage, 48, 49, 50; poverty and, 187; unwillingness to accept, 56; welfare benefits, loss of, and, 96

Moffitt, Robert, 27

Monroe, Kristen Renwick, 42

motherhood, 43, 103

motor vehicle office, 184

National Association for the Advancement of Colored People (NAACP), 5

National Elections Study (NES), 5, 19, 175

National Multiple Sclerosis Society, 79–80, 113

National Urban League, 5

National Welfare Rights Organization (NWRO), 5, 78, 209n. 2; confrontational politics and, 88–89, 139; crisis strategy of, 6, 61–62; lawyers and, 84

Native Americans, 21, 22, 168

Nelson, Barbara, 6, 64, 65

networks, social, 3, 21, 45, 61; claiming process and, 71; as replacements for welfare state, 188; as sources of information, 67

New Deal, 5, 139

nonprofit organizations, 87

nursing homes, 33

nutrition, 81

obligation, identity and, 24, 37–46

parenting, 43–44, 51, 56, 198

participatory theory, 8–10, 154, 188, 190; political action, educative effects of, and, 189; welfare system, two-tiered, and, 16

part-time jobs, 47, 53, 55, 56

passivity, 158, 179
paternalism, 144, 194, 198–200, 216n. 6;
   alternatives to, 202; as deliberate policy, 158, 196; welfare critics and, 29
paternity, 105, 131
pattern matching, 24–25
people of color, 18, 117, 161, 191,
   210n. 9
personal resonsibility, 196
Personal Responsibility and Work Opportunity Reconciliation Act (1996),
   197, 212
Pitkin, Hanna, 9
Piven, Frances Fox, 6, 11, 158, 194
Planned Parenthood, 81–82
policy design, 158
political action, 7, 19, 62, 64; citizens' attitudes toward, 139; clients' views of,
   169–77; as educative experience, 10;
   government-centered definition of,
   209n. 6; patterns of, 160–64; policy
   implementation and, 7–8; research on,
   6–7; welfare politics, broader politics,
   and, 165–69. *See also* confrontational
   politics; survival politics
Poor Law (1834), 210n. 7
poor people, 1, 5, 30, 158; citizenship
   and, 216n. 6; confrontational politics
   and, 89; demands, on government,
   and, 78, 194; "deserving" and "undeserving," 13–14, 15, 121, 192; as labor
   source, 13; marginalization of, 14,
   186, 200; paternalism, of welfare policy, and, 196–97; political participation of, 177, 200; politics, disengage-
   ment from, and, 11; powerlessness of,
   170; public opinion and, 38; welfare
   provision, quality of life, and, 186
poverty, 1, 6, 31, 47, 61, 84, 164; autonomy and, 37; coercion and, 14, 187;
   culture-of-poverty thesis and, 72, 87,
   196; debilitating nature of, 187; education, as way out of, 56; inability to escape from, 191; information gathering
   and, 101; Johnson administration and,
   177; marginalizing effects of, 163;

politics and, 9; poverty line, 201; protection from, 194; social control and,
   11–15; as stigma, 38
power, 24, 29–37, 93
pregnancy, 51, 66, 81–82, 110
Primary Prevention Initiative (PPI), 199
privacy, 30, 58, 150; bureaucrats' information gathering and, 100, 101–2,
   103–6; casework relationships and, 31,
   133–34. *See also* surveillance
promiscuity. *See* sexual behavior
public assistance programs, 4, 37, 124;
   application encounters, first, and, 92;
   clients' political activity and, 163; disability and, 101; effectiveness of, in
   combating poverty, 47; eligibility for,
   27, 29; funding of, 94; humiliation
   and, 120; social control and, 193; social insurance programs compared
   with, 116–19; types of people on, 191;
   "undeserving" poor and, 15
public opinion, 38, 203
public resources, 189
punishment, 146, 155, 191

race, 14, 21–22, 52, 180; application en-
   counter, evaluation of, and, 117, 119;
   discrimination based on, 6; interview
   sample and, 205–6; public opinion,
   about welfare, and, 39
Reagan administration, 152
Regulating the Poor (Piven and
   Cloward), 13
Republican Party, 165, 176
Roosevelt administration, 5

safety net, 151
Sarat, Austin, 166, 181
scholars, 2, 7, 15
self-government, 8–9, 12
self-respect, 38, 40, 43, 46, 58, 88; citizenship, obligations of, and, 197; employment and, 54; internal political
   efficacy and, 180; public assistance
   programs and, 191; undermining of,
   128; welfare administrators' standards

self-respect (*continued*)
    of, 115; welfare claiming, as protec-
    tion of, 187
service professionals, 61, 63, 81–84
sexual assault/harassment, 51
sexual behavior, 30, 103, 105, 110; absti-
    nence from, 114; sexual orientation
    and, 52
shame, feelings of, 43, 61, 78
shelters, 47, 65, 163; for homeless fami-
    lies, 55, 76, 78
significant others, 38, 43, 58; advice
    from, 65–66, 67, 68; informal support
    from, 48, 52, 55. *See also* families
social citizenship, 11, 12, 13; application
    encounter and, 91, 93, 119–20; auton-
    omy and, 29; basic necessities of life
    and, 32; democracy and, 201; dual,
    15–16; hierarchy of, 154, 163; ideal
    of, 14, 203; poverty and, 187; quality
    of, 153; social control and, 190–95;
    welfare system, two-tiered, and, 184–
    85
social control, 3, 14–15, 30, 34, 144,
    184; Aid to Families with Dependent
    Children (AFDC) and, 154; applica-
    tion encounter and, 91, 121; economic
    coercion and, 210; forms of, 194; insti-
    tutional design and, 158, 159; pariahs
    and, 37; political action and, 194;
    poverty and, 187; social citizenship
    and, 190–95; state as agent of, 1, 2,
    195, 215
social insurance programs, 4, 190, 202;
    applications encounters, first, and,
    108; "deserving" poor and, 15; effec-
    tiveness of, in combating poverty, 47;
    eligibility for, 27, 29; political activity,
    of clients, and, 160; public assistance
    programs compared with, 116–19; so-
    cial citizenship and, 193
socialization, 62–63, 72
social movements, 65, 154
Social Security, 167, 172
Social Security Administration (SSA),
    80, 94, 95, 98, 121, 143; administra-
tive style of, 152–53; client disputes
    with, 128–29; clients' descriptions of,
    176; eligibility requirements and,
    151–52; individual cases and, 146; in-
    formation gathering of, 101, 102–3,
    106; institutional features of, 147;
    power relations, with clients, and, 145;
    responsiveness of, 154, 168, 192; rules
    of, 148–49
Social Security Disability Insurance
    (SSDI), 4, 5, 69, 87, 157, 202; applica-
    tion encounter and, 91–123; applica-
    tions, rejected, and, 70; case reviews
    in, 214n. 7; client autonomy and, 30,
    31; client political activity and,
    159–77, 184–85; clients' internal po-
    litical efficacy and, 179–83; commu-
    nity organizations and, 78–81; com-
    parative study and, 16, 17–19, 149–53,
    190–94, 198; demographic break-
    down, of study sample, and, 21–22;
    dependence and, 32–33, 36; disability
    support groups and, 20; economic se-
    curity and, 47, 49–51, 53–55, 57; edu-
    cation level, of recipients, and, 205–6;
    eligibility for, 60, 73–74; government
    personnel and, 84–85; grievances and,
    127–29; identity and, 38–41; knowl-
    edge about, 76–77; lessons of partici-
    pation in, 143–49; means-testing and,
    32; obligation and, 44, 46; personnel
    of, waiting for access to, 94–100; po-
    litical activity and, 159–60; service
    professionals and, 82–83; social citi-
    zenship and, 58
Social Security Old-Age Insurance, 18,
    41
social workers, 81
state: alternatives to, as source of aid, 77;
    child support and, 131; citizenship
    and, 12; disciplinary functions of, 58;
    hierarchy of relationships to, 91; re-
    source distribution and, 2; social con-
    trol and, 1, 2, 195, 215
stepping-stone strategy, 54, 55
stereotypes, 41, 54, 103, 174; application

encounter and, 110, 111; application
encounter, evaluation of, and, 121;
self-presentation and, 114–15
Stoker, Robert P., 199
Stone, Deborah, 152
Supplemental Security Income Program
(SSI), 150–51, 212n. 5
surveillance, 146, 153, 194; paternalism
and, 200; vulnerability to, 31, 133;
welfare dependence and, 37. *See also*
privacy
survival politics, 61, 67, 71, 88, 188, 195

taxes, 94, 201
television addiction, 41
Temporary Assistance to Needy Families
(TANF), 18, 191, 198–99, 201
Three Worlds of Welfare Capitalism
(Esping-Andersen), 185
transportation, 50, 71, 95, 96, 132
triangulation, research methodology and,
19

unemployment, 13, 105
unions, 78, 79, 80
United States: bifurcated politics of, 157;
European countries compared with,
201, 203; social insurance programs
in, 18; welfare participation in, 11;
welfare policy in, 201; welfare provision, growth of, in, 124

Voice and Equality (Verba, Schlozman,
and Brady), 160
voting, 1, 26, 27, 62, 186; African Americans and, 161, 214n. 2; intimidation
and, 90; program participation and,
161–62; rights and, 6

wages, 47, 48, 186
War on Poverty (1960s), 140, 177, 178
welfare: administrators and, 23–24; applications, rejected, and, 85; economic
security and, 46–57; eligibility for, 3,
26–29, 60, 61, 64, 87, 102; fraudulent
claims and, 101; as political action,
1–16; political institutions, legitimacy
of, and, 13; social relations, ordering
of, and, 185; stigma of, 58, 113, 154,
167, 193; two-tiered system of, 15–16,
17, 47, 91, 116, 125, 190
welfare agencies, 5, 24, 25, 69; African
Americans and, 6; application encounter and, 90–91; application forms
and, 57, 76; client humiliation and,
130; clients' demands and, 159;
clients' perceptions of, 122, 189; information gathering of, 100–106, 133; as
part of government, 166, 167, 169;
personnel of, waiting for access to,
94–100; as political institutions, 124;
punitive orientation of, 191; responsiveness of, 4, 70–71, 144; social control and, 30, 34; waiting rooms of,
96–99, 121. *See also specific agencies*
welfare claiming, 26–29, 37, 48, 60–62;
doctors and, 82; economic security
and, 47; as educative activity, 90;
functions and dilemmas of, 57–59;
process of, 63–87; public resources,
access to, and, 186; socialization and,
62–63; as stigma, 38; as symbolic defeat, 39, 58; transportation, access to,
and, 95, 96. *See also* application encounter
welfare reform, 2, 183–84
welfare rights movement (1960s), 26
whites, 21, 22, 39, 117
Wilson, Laura A., 199
women, 6, 117, 161; claim process and,
69; dependence, on male breadwinners, and, 14, 33, 215; grievances
and, 127, 138; political efficacy and,
183; social insurance claims and,
210n. 9
work ethic, 14, 40, 41, 195